King Squealer

A True Story

MAURICE O'MAHONEY
WITH DAN WOODING

Edited by Corinna Downes
Typeset by Jonathan Downes,
Cover and Layout by SPiderKaT for CFZ Communications
Using Microsoft Word 2000, Microsoft Publisher 2000, Adobe Photoshop CS.

This edition published in Great Britain by Gonzo Multimedia

c/o Brooks City,
6th Floor New Baltic House
65 Fenchurch Street,
London EC3M 4BE
Fax: +44 (0)191 5121104
Tel: +44 (0) 191 5849144
International Numbers:
Germany: Freephone 08000 825 699
USA: Freephone 18666 747 289

ISBN: 978-1-908728-35-7

The Publisher would like to thank *The Daily Telegraph* and *The Guardian* for permission to
quote copyright material

CONTENTS

Dan Wooding pictured with Maurice O'Mahoney and Rick Wakeman

FOREWORD

By Rick Wakeman

There have always been certain 'careers' that have fascinated the public, newspapers, and the media in general. Such include musicians, actors, sportsmen, police, and not surprisingly, the people who give the police their employment: The criminal.

For the man in the street, all these careers have one thing in common: they are seemingly beyond both his reach and, in many cases, understanding and as such, his only association can be through the media of newspapers or television.

The police, however, will always require the services of the grass, the squealer, the snitch, (call him what you will), in order to assist in their investigations and arrests; and amazingly, this is the area that seldom gets written about.

A very close and long standing friend of mine, a jolly Birmingham chap, by the name of Dan Wooding, who has since 1982 has lived in Southern California, 'Collared' the King of the Squealers and somehow got him to 'spill the beans'......all of them !

I also met and knew 'the King Squealer' well, but his story remained a secret until Dan Wooding managed to persuade him to 'talk'.

His story covers almost every emotion. Sad, serious and sometimes hysterically funny -- you cannot help but be fascinated by the extraordinary life of Maurice O'Mahoney - the King Squealer.

INTRODUCTION
By Dan Wooding

I first met Maurice 'Mo' O'Mahoney on board a floating restaurant on London's River Thames. It was the mid-1970s and, at the time, I was working as a senior reporter with the *Sunday People*, a British tabloid, and I happened to pick up the phone in the newsroom during a lunch hour and there, on the other end of the line, was someone saying that he was the 'King Squealer' and was willing to sell his life story to our paper 'for the right price'. He suggested that we should meet on board the restaurant to discuss 'business'.

'How will I recognize you?' I asked.

'You won't', he replied. 'I'll recognize you. Just stand by the entrance holding a copy of the *Sunday People* under your arm and I'll know you.'

After clearing this with my news editor, I headed over to the Thames and climbed aboard the rendezvous point, and stood there for a while smiling at anyone arriving who looked remotely like a gangster. I got some strange looks, but then finally this mysterious man arrived with a Flying Squad policeman in tow – who, O'Mahoney said, was protecting him. 'Mo' introduced me to his police minder and said, 'Don't worry about him. He goes "deaf" when I talk business.'

The plain-clothed officer nodded and said, 'Yes, I go deaf when he talks business.' It was a little like a scene from a Monty Python TV show.

To cut a long story short, the paper finally agreed a price with O'Mahoney and I was asked to write it up for him, and then once the dramatic newspaper series had been published, he then 'asked' me to work with him on a book and that experience became even stranger.

He would turn up each Monday at my Surrey home with a bulging .44 Magnum in his pocket to protect himself – the police by now had told him he was now on his own – and proceeded to recite his story for me to type up, which I did. Then when he left, I would turn words into a more readable style, but when the time came for me to read them back the first few chapters to him, his tone changed and he became quite angry.
'I don't remember saying that,' he said sharply as I finished. 'Are you changing my words?'

I tried to explain that this was normal and he said, 'I don't agree. People want to know how us gangsters speak.'

It was a rather scary moment, especially as I glanced down at the bulge in his pocked containing his lethal weapon, but once I read out one of his rather strange comments which said, 'The guy vaulted the fence like a half-starved Biafran looking for a banana,' he smiled broadly and seemed happy that I had at least kept that in the story. He then said, 'I like it,' and I breathed a heavy sigh of relief.

We eventually completed the book together and it was launched on a national BBC TV show with him wearing a ski mask and his voice disguised.

Following that, I took him to a studio at a commercial radio studio in London, so he could further help promote the book. When the interview was about to start the recorder, 'Mo' suddenly asked, 'Can you disguise my voice?' The flustered broadcaster said, 'I'm sorry, but we can't'. 'Why not?' Mo pressed on. "The BBC did that for me, so what can't you?' 'Well, we don't have the resources of the BBC.'

'Mo' then turned to him and said, 'If I go on your show and someone recognises my voice and I get killed, you'll be to blame.'

The poor man looked at me in desperation and threw his arms in the air, not knowing what to do in this strange situation.

Then O'Mahoney had a bright idea. 'Do you have any cotton wool?' The man managed to get some from a first aid cupboard and 'Mo' stuffed it into his mouth, and did the whole interview speaking in a muffled way through a mouthful of cotton wool. It was quite hilarious and a London newspaper, who heard about it, later ran a story called 'Concealing Squealing.'

Although he was happy with the book, it nearly cost me my life. One night, after the book was released, I was in the Stab-in-the-Back pub just off Fleet Street with some of my colleagues, when a Scotsman came in and shouted, 'Who is Dan Wooding?' When I said that I was, he came over and said that he had a large knife in his car and said menacingly, 'If you don't tell me where O'Mahoney is, I will go and get it and slit your throat from ear-to-ear.'

Our crime reporter, who didn't really have much sympathy for my plight, said, "Why don't you go and do it. It's been a really quiet evening so far.'

I did some fast talking and explained that I had no idea where he lived and I finally managed to talk him out of killing me there and then, and he even gave me a ten pound note to 'buy a few drinks', as he realized that I had no idea how to make contact with 'Mo', which was true. He always contacted me.

On another occasion, when I was away on an overseas trip, O'Mahoney had been trying to call our home phone number and finally went to the *Sunday People* office to tell the staff there that he was very concerned as he had heard that that someone was planning to come over and kill my wife Norma. After many tries to get Norma on the line, the deputy news editor sent a telegram to her saying, 'Norma, are you alright. We have been trying to contact you all day. Please call right away.'

She got home later that evening, and a neighbour handed her the telegram and because it was late at night, she waited to call and assured them that she was okay.

'Thank God,' she was told. 'We thought that you might be lying dead in your flat.'

There were also some amusing interviews with him. O'Mahoney loved being around well-known people and would often 'ask' if he could accompany on my interviews and, of course, I couldn't turn him down. On one occasion, I was interviewing the father of a very well-known American crooner, who had just married to a lady many years younger than him.

She smiled at me as she said, 'I've lost a weight lately by going out jogging each day."

Our *Sunday People* photographer, who had a wicked sense of humour, immediately shot back, "I'm not saying that you're fat, but your feet's too big…' -- a quote from the famous Fats Waller song.

Instead of seeing the funny side of the comment, 'Mo' leaned over and said to me, 'Did you hear what he just said? He's insulting the lady. Would you like me to break his legs now – or later?'

I managed to calm him down, and fortunately, he didn't hurt the photographer after all.

O'Mahoney also loved to sing and told me one day that his big dream was to appear on the BBC show, 'Top of the Pops' and sing the Rod Stewart hit, 'We are sailing,' but wearing a balaclava helmet so he wasn't recognized. One day, he called me at the paper and said down the phone line, 'Dan, what do you think of this?' He then began singing, 'We are sailing…'"

One of the reporters who overhead it, afterward said, 'Dan, why not get him to change the lyrics to, 'We are squealing?' Of course, I didn't share that with him, as he might have been tempted to all break this man's legs.

On another occasion, he told me he was working for a very well-known rock star and wondered if I would like to meet him outside a studio in Soho. I said I would and so I drove over there and when the superstar arrived in his limo, 'Mo' went over to him, and said, 'Say hello to my friend Dan Wooding. He's from the *Sunday People*.'

So the rock star looked blankly at me and said simply, 'Hello.'

That didn't satisfy 'Mo' and so he turned to him and said, 'Say more than that.'

So he added, 'Hello, Dan, from the *Sunday People!*'

When I and my family moved to Southern California in June of 1982, O'Mahoney arrived at our home to say goodbye to us all, and we never saw him again.

But his story now lives on with this re-issue of his rather amazing story.

Dan Wooding, Los Angeles, California

1

In the Beginning

My shocking life of crime, which included contracts to kill, more than 20 armed robberies, over 65 burglaries mainly in the stock-broker belts in and around London, protection rackets, hijackings, the framing of police officers and even kidnap plots against Elton John and Elizabeth Taylor, all began innocently enough on Christmas Day, 1958.

I was then an unhappy and very scruffy eleven-year-old with no Christmas party to go to. In fact Christmas Day in our Victorian terraced house in a run-down part of Paddington, in West London, was no different to any other.

There were the usual rows between my Southern Irish parents which at that age I didn't really understand. Mostly I would take my dad's side and then my fair-haired mother would hit me across the back with a lethal-looking poker. I would curl up like a hedgehog and hope she'd stop hitting me. It was a nightmare.

I thought Christmas was supposed to be a time of peace, yet for me it was just as awful as the other 364 days of the year. I never received presents like other children. My father gave me 15 shillings (75p) to buy gifts for myself. He would say: 'Here you are Maurice, go and buy something.' I longed for him to actually take the trouble to get the present rather than just hand over the cash, but he never had any time for me, or my three sisters and one brother. Dad was too involved in his job as a self-employed builder. The last thing he wanted to do was form a happy relationship with us. He seemed to think money would make up for his lack of love, but, of course, that is never the case.

As that fateful Christmas Day ground inevitably on, I longed to be somewhere happy. I wanted to be with friends who actually laughed and showed some Christmas spirit.

Then it came to me, I remembered an invitation that I and my friends had received from Jessie, a middle-aged spinster who lived around the corner from us in a large house. We used to spend hours in her old-fashioned home, sipping her sweet tea, munching her biscuits, and generally feeling part of her cosy world. She loved to be surrounded by scruffy children like us. Her father and brother lived with her and they delighted us with their Second World War recollections. Our eyes would nearly pop out as their real-life dramas unfolded before us in the flower-patterned parlour.

So I crept out of my miserable home and walked the hundred yards or so to her front door. I could hear jolly music belting out from a record player upstairs and so, full of happy anticipation, I pressed the bell, and waited and waited. I thumbed the bell again, for a couple of minutes, but still there was no answer. What should I do? I'd spied, at the side of the door, an open window which led to a front room. My friends had got into Jessie's house this way quite often, so I guessed she would not object to me doing the same. I furtively looked down the street and then heaved my ample frame through the open window and silently dropped on to the floor in the unlit room. Then I tried the solid door, but to my horror I found it was held tight by a mortice lock. I kept trying for several minutes and then I began to get scared and thought I had better get back out of the window and try the bell again. Suddenly I heard the front door open, and a voice say, 'He's in there officer . . . the burglar.' Then a key turned in the door of the room where I was trapped.

I was so petrified that I ducked under the bed and lay on the dusty lino, shivering with fright.

A policeman opened the door, switched on the light and the first I saw of him was his shiny black boots by the side of the bed. He looked under the iron bedstead, saw me and dragged me out by my arms.

'Hello, what have we here? he said sternly. 'What are you doing here boy?'

'I just wanted to go to the party upstairs, honest mister,' I stammered.

'Oh no you didn't, you wanted to burgle my house,' yelled the spinster's brother Wally, a balding man in his forties. 'I don't know, we let you kids in the house and this is the way you reward us.'

'Honest Wally, I rang the bell and couldn't get you to hear,' I pleaded.

Evidently no one believed me, and the stern-faced copper grabbed me by the scruff of the neck and said: 'You're coming with me - to the nick.'

By then my mates had rushed down from the festivities, some of them still wearing party hats and waving balloons. They thought my arrest was all a big joke.

The police had obviously been called after I was spotted clambering in by a nosey neighbour. And before I could say 'PC 49,' I was lifted bodily into the street by the officer and thrown into the back of a police car.

By then curtains were open and neighbours were peering out all down the street. I felt like a dangerous criminal. It was a shattering experience for an eleven-year-old.

When we got to the nick, the copper shouted at me roughly. I was in tears by then, and yet there was worse to come. The station was full of drunks, who all seemed to be cursing and yelling.

'What's your name? hissed one of the officers, above the alcoholic din. 'And where do you live?' Then with a twisted smile, as if I was a regular rogue, he added, 'Don't I know you from somewhere?'

I could hardly speak for fear. I had been frightened many times by the violent rows in my home but this was even more terrifying. I kept protesting my innocence but to no avail. Then the sadistic officer shouted, 'We know your game sonny. You broke in so you could steal an accordion in the front room.'

I didn't know what he was talking about, though I knew the musical instrument in question. We had often had a sing-song, with Jessie's father playing it as the accompaniment. 'I couldn't even lift that thing, so how could I possibly try and steal it?' I retorted. But logic didn't seem to matter to these officers, probably frustrated at having to work at Christmas.

Then they took me to a detention cell with blanked-off glass windows and a solitary light bulb. For what seemed like an eternity I sat there on a little wooden chair, and literally shook with fear. I just couldn't stop crying. All the time I could hear the drunks' yells and curses echoing down the passage. No food was brought to me and no drink of any description. I was locked in like a caged animal.

After several hours of this nightmare my mother was summoned by the police to the station, where she had to stand £10 bail for me. After a few choice words from the cops about my future behaviour, I was released to her and as she dragged me home along the dimly-lit streets she kept belting me on the back of the head.

'Honest Mum, I didn't do anything wrong,' I said.

'Oh yes you did!' she yelled as she hauled me along.

There was the predictable family row when I got home, and my parents blamed each other for my arrest. I was dispatched straight to bed and sobbed myself to sleep. There was certainly no Christmas spirit in my heart that night . . . just hate.

A few days later I had to appear at a juvenile court in front of a committee of stern-faced men and be-hatted women. After hearing the 'evidence' they sent me to a remand home called Stanford House in Shepherds Bush for reports.

It was a tough little community, a real breeding ground for London's future underworld. These remand homes are where potential criminals often learn their various future trades. Young car thieves, burglars and violent kids are all mixed up, sharing their nasty secrets. My dormitory was like a kid's encyclopaedia of crime. I soon learned that if you wanted to survive in this world, you had to adapt and become extremely aggressive. Up until this time, I had been quite a meek person, but with so many bullies at the home trying to cause me problems, I learnt to have two quick fists and a hard head.

As I look back at that spell at the remand home, I can honestly say that locking young boys up like this is certainly no solution to junior crime. It's like a club where teeny criminals are put in touch with each other. When they leave, they form gangs and associations which give society so much trouble.

In a bid to get rid of our aggressions in the home, boxing matches were organised, mainly for those caught fighting. The winners of these bloody battles would be rewarded with an orange and a bar of chocolate. I had two fights with the gloves and won both of them by TKOs.

My two weeks of 'observation' at Stanford House were a revelation to me. Before then I had been a shy child. Now, in just 14 days, I became a sort of raging animal, ready to take on the world.

I was driven back to juvenile court in the home's green van. I remember seeing the snow on the ground through the windows and thinking how cold a person I had become in such a short time. I had been branded a black sheep and so I decided to act like one.

The chairman of the court, a middle-class biddy with a plum in her mouth whom one police officer nicknamed 'Old Mother Reilly' because she was such an old fusspot, told me, 'We have heard the evidence, boy. We think you did plan to steal the accordion.' I tried to protest my innocence, but it did no good. 'Two years' probation,' she said firmly. 'And don't let me see you here again.'

My parents were in court and we were all introduced to my probation officer, Mr McGregor, a kindly Scot who over those two years did all he could to try and help me. I fully believe to this day that he knew I was innocent.

For twenty-four months I had to regularly visit his office. Mr McGregor soon realised that my family life was a nightmare and he became my first real friend. He was one of those few people who would listen to me. And, although I liked the man, I still couldn't help fostering a real hate for society. Someone had to pay for this miscarriage of justice against me.

What made life so humiliating for me at that time was the fact that I was forced to wear jumble-sale clothes and was nicknamed 'The Tramp' by other children. I looked just like Denis the Menace *, the cartoon character, because I had so many holes in my trousers and

---

* For our American readers who are used to a clean-cut blonde Dennis, the British Dennis the Menace (from a comic called *The Beano)* is a much more sinister looking character with a shock of unruly dark hair, a catapult (slingshot) in his pocket, and an equally menacing dog called 'Gnasher'.

---

socks, and my hair was unkempt. It was shattering to realise I had been brought into a loveless world and then exposed to it without defences. I was like a lion cub born in the jungle and then told to fend for itself.

I started to associate with young boys who were regularly in trouble with the police. I was drawn to the type of lads who were also dubbed black sheep. We had been labelled this way, and so we acted the part. We would break into shops, steal from cars, and force entry into homes. We would take anything we could lay our hands on.

As my life of crime began to escalate, my dad left my mother because of the constant rows. I suppose in a way it was a relief, as I hated to see the pair at each other's throats. The split didn't seem to affect my mother too much. She just continued going to the bingo most nights, and like millions of other working-class housewives, dreamed of winning a small fortune. Of course, she never did.

While she and her cronies were chasing the jackpot, my pals and I were planning nightly jobs and executing them with ruthless efficiency. The rewards for us were big - up to £ 100 a time. And we never got caught. Every penny I got I used to buy myself clothes - new shirts, ties, socks and shoes. People at school quickly stopped laughing at me. In fact I looked quite a toff. My mother would often quiz me about where I was getting these clothes, but I wouldn't tell her.

One night I had just got off a bus when I noticed a plate glass window in a clothes shop by the stop had been smashed. Inside waiting was a fine collection of women's jumpers, so I eased my way in through the jagged glass, found a plastic sack in the shop and stuffed it full of these jumpers in various pastel shades.

There were so many I could hardly carry them all. But I somehow got my swag home and hid it in my mother's wardrobe. Then an uncle from Ireland found them while nosing around the house, pinched them all without my knowledge, took them back to the Emerald Isle and sold them. I never got a penny out of the deal! When I discovered he had taken my loot, I prayed that the ferry carrying him and the jumpers would sink . . .

As the months drifted by, I became very hard for such a young kid, and having proved my toughness in the playground, I became involved in a teeny gang called the Paddington Firm. We used to fight other gangs from nearby Kilburn, Kensal Green and Notting Hill Gate with razors, knives and chains. We were such evil little monsters that our rivals would soon scarper when they saw us on the rampage.

One day I was with a friend called Barry and we were roaming around Paddington looking for mischief when we came across a film crew. 'Hey lads,' shouted the director who wore a silk cravat and smoked a cigarette through a holder,' want to earn yourselves five bob (25p)? You look like a pair of tearaways. We want the two of you to pretend to beat up this young boy. Make it look realistic, but don't hurt him.'

Willing to do anything to earn money, but deciding we'd have some fun at the young actor's expense, we gave him a beating we knew he'd never forget. When the director shouted 'Action,' we pummelled the boy unmercifully on the face and body as he lay screaming on the floor yelling, 'No more, no more!' The director became hysterical. 'What are you louts playing at? Are you trying to kill him?' he hissed.

'Sorry mister,' we chorused in innocent unison. 'We'll stop if you'll give us the five shilling.' He did and we ran off laughing. I never found out the name of the film, but one day I hope to see myself scrapping on the screen. By the way, the boy actor suffered a black eye, a busted lip and a bleeding nose . . . all with the compliments of Maurice O'Mahoney, and friend.

I was now living up to the reputation that the judiciary had given me. They had branded me a criminal, and if that's what they wanted, I decided that was what they would get. And this was only my apprenticeship. Worse, much worse, was yet to follow.

I mixed with much older fellows who were inflicting violence at school and I became a part of their gang and consequently got a part of their proceeds. Their main money-making racket was to terrorise younger children and then extract 'protection money' from them. It added up to a tidy sum for all of us each week. My take added up to about £2 every Friday. I had one particular boy from a relatively wealthy home so well trained that he would meekly bring his ten shillings (50p) contribution to my desk each week without me having to ask.

The teachers knew all this was going on, but they didn't interfere. It was anything for a quiet life for them.

Then I began stealing cars, stripping them down and selling the parts to a bent car dealer. I'd taught myself to drive at 14, and I specialised in taking Minis, which I found easy to break into. I would start the ignition by using a threepenny bit to complete the electrical circuit under the bonnet, pressing the solenoid and driving off. I would then find a bomb site and start taking all the bits off. In a couple of hours the shiny car was reduced to a shell. Almost everything, except the engine went. Usually the car dealer would give me a list of spares he needed and then I filled the order for him. What was left over I would store in a secret hideaway for future sales. At one time I seemed to have more parts than British Leyland!

I also discovered selling car radios was very lucrative. I usually got about £8 to £10 for each one. As I got better at the job, the dealer would order complete cars from me and I would then get paid £100 a vehicle.

I had many close shaves, but the nearest I ever got to being caught was when a policeman who guessed my car was stolen stood in from of me and yelled, 'Stop.' I said, 'Not f.....' likely,' and swerved and drove on. There were no police radios then and he had to find a 'phone box to report me. By then I had got clean away and sold the car.

Another day when I pinched a Mini, I was spotted by the woman owner. I heard her swearing at me as I screeched off, and a chase began which had my heart pounding. She got a friend to follow me in her sports car. Both of us were careering around Paddington Green, across bridges, going the wrong way down one-way streets and through traffic lights, until I managed to lose them. I drove through a gap in an alleyway which her friend didn't want to risk her car through. I took the car into a council rubbish yard, lay low in the back of the Mini for an hour and then sneaked out and got a bus home. I never heard what happened to the car. Actually the chase seemed funny at the time, but now I realise I could have killed somebody.

The police knew I was up to something, but could never catch me. Sometimes I was so cheeky I would pull up outside my house, take all the good parts off the nicked motor, and then dump the rest of the car nearby. I would often drive off without a boot, doors or number plates. When I got hold of a car you would think a piranha had gone through it.

Funnily enough, some of the officers who used to chase me all round London later ended up as my bodyguards. And we used to sit down in the police cells and re-live all these early experiences.

I finally got caught when three officers claimed they had seen me driving a Cooper S erratically around a corner in Elgin Avenue, Paddington. When they checked their stolen cars lists, they found it was missing. So they came round to my house and arrested me. I was later fined £50 and put on probation again for two years. But I neglected to pay the fine. One night I went for an under-age drink in the Windsor Castle, Harrow Road, and spotted at the other end of the bar my two police shadows, whom I had nicknamed Melrose and Brown incorporated. These two - Temporary Detective Constables Bob Melrose and Geoff Brown - used to tail me everywhere. They shared an unmarked blue Wolseley car that haunted me. Everywhere I went, it went. I'd go to see a film and come out, and there would be the blue Wolseley. Outside the pub where I usually drank, there was the car. They were both good cops and they knew I was up to no good, and were determined to nail me. Informants kept grassing about my escapades and they wanted to find some proof. So that night they followed me into the pub. Soon I was getting quite inebriated. 'Hello, flat feet. How's business? I said. Then they ambled over and said: 'We're arresting you Maurice O'Mahoney for the non-payment of a £50 fine.' I couldn't believe it. As they took me away they smiled and said: 'Well Mo, he who laughs last, laughs longest.'

So they took me to Harrow Road police station, locked me up, and with a smirk on their faces said, 'By the way Mo, we're just off for another drink. See you in court in the morning.'

Whenever I saw them both later they would smile and I would grin back, and then try and get away from them as quickly as possible. The pair became notorious with villains for their work in Paddington. They were good fishermen in the murky waters of crime. They always got good catches.

When I left school, I joined a large West London catering firm and began my own self-service operations. After a few months there I became a driver's mate and started raiding the other vans and taking some of their goodies. I would arrive before the other delivery men at 5 am and load up not only my large quantities of ham, pork pies, pork fillets and sausage rolls, but also part of theirs, and then sell the booty to bent butchers and restaurants. My driver was in this with me and we began to make a fortune. The management was worried about all the goods going missing, so I was asked to report in early to keep watch. Little did they know it was me who was taking the stuff! Every driver and his mate were fiddling, but not to the extent that we were. I was making about £100 a week from this meaty experience.

One of my delivery points was the canteen in a London television studio. I got to know the doorman quite well. I would give him free pies and sausages and he introduced me to various programme directors. I especially got on well with the crew from 'Ready, Steady, Go,' the rock and roll show. We used to have a great time. I would bring in a load of my stolen pies and give them to the stars. Among my customers were the Rolling Stones, the Beach Boys, the Supremes, the Mindbenders, the Dave Clark Five, Sandie Shaw, Freddy and the Dreamers, Cathy MacGowan, and Gerry Marsden. But of course no one realised the sausage rolls they were munching were stolen - by me.

I later joined a furniture company, again as a driver's mate, and stole enough to furnish two houses. We would load up the correct order at the warehouse and then add a few extras.

Friends who wanted to buy from us visited the showroom and picked out what they wanted. We would sell below the showroom price, so they were happy and so were we. This went on for more than six months, then one night it was discovered that I had taken the vehicle to load up more gear. I was reported by the driver and got the sack. I got my own back, however, because I went back after dark and threw some of the store's own chairs through the plate-glass window. I then slashed the tyres of a lorry.

I soon got a job at a London hospital, as a porter. I wanted to lie low from crime for a while as things were getting a bit too hot. While I was at the hospital I progressed to becoming a theatre porter and later a mortuary attendant. Sometimes I would witness post mortems and it made me realise how transitory life was. One day I would be talking to a man in the ward and next day I'd see him dead on the slab, cut open and looking like a joint of meat. The smell in there was so vile it would ruin my appetite for days on end. Part of my job was to collect the bodies and put them in the deep freeze. One foggy Christmas I put a sheeted body on a trolley with another attendant. As we came outside I tripped and the trolley rolled off down the hill. I lost the body for the night, and only discovered it next morning mixed up with the swill bin. Fortunately no-one there discovered my embarrassing slip.

Often I would catch policemen climbing out of windows in nurses' quarters. Obviously they had gone for a bit of 'nookie' despite the rules that no unauthorised male was allowed in staff quarters. If they saw me they would plead for me to be quiet, and I used to just joke it off. They weren't really doing any harm. One day I remember being shocked to see a well-dressed man clambering out of a nurse's window. When I saw his face I realised he was a well-known personality. I won't divulge his name, but I'm sure he was there for more than health reasons . . . I had quite a sense of humour and I loved to scare the nurses by putting a white shroud around me and pretending to be a ghost.

But I discovered, while there, that one of the wards had a real ghost in it. Apparently, many years ago, a ward sister hung herself after giving the wrong injection to a patient who died. One night when I was in the ward I saw a shadow of a swinging body hanging there. But when I looked again it was gone. It was a scary experience.

Sometimes I would break down when I saw the twisted bodies of children brought in after car crashes, fires and general accidents. I later gave in my notice as I was getting very upset. Let's face it, these weren't very nice sights to witness. I could just about cope with the dead adults, but the dead children tore me apart. I was surprised that I still had emotions, as I had become so hard as a person. I thought that this, at least, was a hopeful sign, but it wasn't.

I was then taken on as a driver for a building firm and it wasn't long before I was thieving again. This time I was helping myself to some of the items in the building trade, like bricks, cement, copper tubing, baths and tools. I'd receive bent orders from contacts and then bribe loaders to put them in a van. But then a bloke, who was about to be sacked saved his job by grassing on me. All of us in the fiddle got the sack, and he stayed on.

A printing firm was to be my next opportunity to 'print money'. Typewriters, ballpoint pens, paper and draughtsmen's tools, disappeared regularly off the back of my lorry. They would be slipped in among my normal deliveries and helped to supplement my meagre wages. I am sure they suspected what I was up to, but they could never prove it. I always knew when the iron was getting hot and would play it carefully. During this job I was introduced to a rich businessman, who was one of the biggest rogues in town. He owned some stores in west London and we started our business acquaintance when I sold him thousands of biros. He gave me a good price for them and told me to 'keep in touch'. I left that firm and went to work for one of the biggest typewriter firms in the world. While I was there it was straight back to the old habits. One typewriter for the firm, one typewriter for me, one typewriter for the firm . . .

After doing the job properly for a few days, I disappeared with a lorry load of valuable machines. I thought I would be able to sell them easily, but one dealer after another turned them down as being too hot. Finally I dumped the lorry and told the company it had been stolen from me.

 Then this businessman started putting me in contact with others who wanted to do deals, and also wanted to set up jobs for - sticking them up, we call it. They would tell me all the information I needed to know about houses and flats that I could burgle. These were the homes of friends and I would be given all the info I needed to do the job. We did a deal that we would split 50-50 all that I got from screwing these gaffs.

I used to take my typewriter van on the jobs with me, with the firm's name printed all along the side of it. It was a silly risk, but I had become so blasé.

One day I nearly got caught though. I was in the home of a wealthy Jewish family in Willesden. My business friend had assured me the family were out at a bar-mitzvah, so I took my time loading the jewellery into my pockets. Then I heard a key in the front door and the chattering family coming in. I panicked, dived through the window, landed a few feet below, and still shaken rushed and caught a bus that was pulling away. I just caught the sound of a police siren as I paid over my fare. I then reported the typewriter van stolen and when it was recovered I picked it up at the police station!

I'm sure the police officer who handed the van back to me knew I had done the job but I was confident there was no evidence to convict me. How frustrating it must have been for him, seeing the villain walk away with a smile on his face and wondering who would be his next victim.

2
Two Broken Wrists

Three swarthy men held my arms over a small wall adjacent to Kensal Green swimming baths while another repeatedly crashed a pickaxe handle down on my wrists. I screamed inwardly. It was dark, and these animals seemed to carry on this bone-breaking ritual for ever. The pain I suffered was unbelievable. Satisfied at last, they shoved me into the road where they planned to run me over in their getaway car. As I lay there numbed, I saw them driving hard at me. Suddenly another car came up behind them, its headlights blazing, so they swerved past and left me there half dead. I somehow staggered to my feet like a drunk and sat on the wall where I had been punished. When I felt some strength return to my body, I began a dazed trek to a nearby hospital.

'What's happened to your wrists?' asked a tired house doctor as put on the plaster. 'Oh, I just slipped and fell,' I said. He knew better. 'Some fall . . .' he muttered.

That was my first experience of the savage vengeance wrought by criminals who are double-crossed. The beating happened when a burglar called Tony, with whom I had been working, scarpered without paying off some tipsters who had supplied information about a successful job. They had turned up at a pub in Kensal Green to collect their percentage for tipping us off, but Tony wasn't there. I guessed he'd become too greedy and didn't see why they should get a cut. Unsuspecting, I had gone to the pub, and they took it out on me instead.

Tony was several years my senior and we had met in a coffee bar. He'd heard a little about me, but I knew all about him. He was a noted professional burglar who really knew his job. There was one flaw in Tony's operation, however. He didn't drive. So he put a proposition to me. 'Mo, let's form a partnership. You, drive and I'll show you how to earn real money. Are you willing to learn?' Was I willing to learn? Of course I was. We bought ourselves a well used Austin A55 van and were soon driving out to addresses in the stockbroker belts in the swish London suburbs. Tony wouldn't tell me where he got his solid information, but I later discovered that it was often supplied by greedy mini-cab drivers who would take clients to a show or out to Heathrow Airport, and, because they knew their passengers' properties were empty, would tip off Tony. Naturally they wanted a percentage of the take for their info.

Tony's skill was remarkable. I thought I knew something about this game, but he really opened my eyes. Tony taught me how to make keys, a skill I later found invaluable. He also showed me his automatic catapult. This was no schoolboy's toy - it would fire a piece of metal through the glass of a door so a knitting needle could then be inserted to open the lock. Tony also had a glass cutter which could take a whole pane from a French window, so we could just walk through the space where the glass once rested. My main job when I was out with this master burglar was to be his minder. That was on top of being his driver. The idea was that if anyone disturbed us, I was to clobber them. One day he allowed me to play my part in a robbery and asked me to shin up a drainpipe to get in through a window, then come downstairs and open the front door. My debut for Tony was spectacular. The pipe was rotten and it came away from the wall when I was 20 feet up in the air. I crashed backwards, hit the side of the greenhouse, and landed on the dustbins. But I got no sympathy from my teacher.

'For crying out loud, Mo, what are you trying to do? Wake up the whole neighbourhood? he whispered angrily. I did. Within seconds people peered through windows, dogs barked, and I just lay there moaning. What a choice sound we made between us. Somehow, I forced myself off the floor and began to limp away, with Tony's curses echoing in my ear. We scrambled over a five-foot wall and managed to reach the getaway van, which I had parked around the corner. We knew it wouldn't be long before we would hear the crook's national anthem - the police siren - and the boys in blue would be swarming around the area. It took tremendous will-power to drive the van that night. I was extremely worried as I thought I had snapped my spine in the fall. Fortunately, after a few days rest, it healed and I was relieved to find it was only bad bruising.

Another close shave came when Tony and I broke into a flat in a block in Willesden. We lifted £200 in cash which we stuffed into our pockets, and we were leaving through the front door when we were confronted by the occupant, a burly man in his thirties. 'What are you doing here?' he yelled. 'Spring cleaning sir,' said Tony as he darted through his arms and left me to grapple with the man. I butted him in the face a couple of times with my head, squeezed his testicles, and made my getaway as he squealed with pain.

Another night we turned up for a flat burglary after our informant told us the rich lady occupant was out. But as we often did, we rang the bell just in case someone was there, and we could 'apologise' for disturbing them. This night the lady called through the letterbox, 'Who is it?' Without batting an eyelid Tony, yelled back to her, 'Burglars you old cunt!' I just collapsed and laughed so much that I literally wet myself. My trousers were soaked. I almost didn't make it back to the van, what with my bad back and my hysterical laughter.

The last job I did with Tony was after one of our tipsters told us of a rich lady who had an incredible collection of jewellery at her home on the outskirts of London. The tip was good and we gained entry with Tony's skeleton keys - he had a massive collection – and proceeded to ransack the home. We found lots of money and valuables and then decamped. It wasn't long after this that he betrayed me, and I suffered that terrible beating which resulted in two broken wrists, a cut head - and a terrible thirst for vengeance.

I searched high and low for the double-crossing bastard, but he seemed to have gone to ground. My hatred for him, and the way he crossed me up, was there all the time and I savoured in my mind how he would suffer when I caught him. I finally flushed him out in a Club in North London. As I walked over to him in the dimly-lit club, which was owned by a former world middleweight boxing champion, Tony pretended he didn't know me. I was with a friend and I grabbed Tony securely by the arms, knocking his half-finished pint of bitter to the ground. We escorted him out to the alleyway and then to my car. 'I want a few words with you Tony,' I said.

He went white with fear as he saw hate in my eyes. 'What's the matter Mo?' he stammered. 'What have I done wrong?'

I stuck a sawn-off double-barrelled shotgun down his right earhole and said, 'You know what's up you bastard.'

He was crying and moaning, 'I got done over for the jewellery, Mo. That's why I couldn't come. The fence double-crossed me and so I got no money for it.'

I said, 'You could have come and told me that and we could have sorted the fence out. But it's too late now, you bum. You're going to die.'

I drove the quivering Tony to a river at the end of Scrubbs Lane, Shepherds Bush, where I planned to shoot him right through the nut. I was by now so full of hate for him. But my terrified mate said, 'Look Mo, I don't want a murder rap. Just hurt him, but don't kill him.' So I picked up a broken bottle lying on the river bank and jabbed it in every part of his body. 'Not my face,' he kept yelling as I made zig zags across his mush. 'Oh my God, my face, it's ripped to shreds!' he screamed. I watched gleefully as the blood oozed from wounds all over his body. I then booted him into the river and watched as he struggled in the bloodied water. I felt great relief after I had finished with him, because the urge for revenge had been eating me up like a cancer. The last time I saw the phantom Tony was a red splashing blob in the water. I presume he got out safely. But I never saw him again.

At this time I was beginning to make my mark in London's underworld. But I tried to be cautious in all that I did, because I knew that too much success too quickly could be extremely dangerous. I also tried hard to separate my violent activities from my business deals. I soon got into the brainiest of all rackets - the lucrative Long Firm swindles. This is a swindle where a phoney firm is set up, a warehouse or a shop is rented and an amount of money is deposited with the bank. The firm then gets a banker's reference and a couple of trade references, so it can start ordering goods from manufacturers. The trade reference comes from other Long Firms or respectable businesses who have been customers in the past. Then the firm begins to buy in stock. After several months, it goes broke, so it cannot pay for the stock – which by then has been sold off, and the 'directors' have made a small fortune. I was usually 'John Williams, the managing director's son'.

I joined a team of gangsters from South London for my first taste of the Long Firm racket.

Quite soon I was responsible for a lot of the buying in for their 'mini-supermarket'. One of my best buys was £8,000 worth of suede jackets from a wholesalers in Kensington. I had only gone in to buy half that amount, but the silver-tongued smoothie talked me into buying more. I insisted that I had to 'phone up my store to get confirmation as to whether we could afford it. When I got through, one of the crooks at the other end of the 'phone said, 'Buy the lot you cunt.' I said to the gentleman, 'It's OK. I can buy them.' As I signed the cheque, he said jokingly, 'Wouldn't it be funny if this was a rubber cheque?' I retorted with a grin, 'Wait until you take this cheque to the bank on Monday. It'll bounce all over London.' When I shook hands with him, his kosher voice added, 'Bless. you my son,' I thought, he'll bless me on Monday when he finds out - with a 14lb hammer!

My buying manor wasn't just limited to London. On one occasion I was dispatched with two companions to Leicester to buy from the hosiery trade there. I had already purchased about £500 worth of tights from different outlets in the Midlands city, and was making my last call at a factory there. I turned up resplendent in pin-striped suit, with briefcase, rolled umbrella and carrying my rubber cheque book. I was welcomed with open arms by the factory manager, and while my two companions sat depressed and worried in the car outside, he showed me all over the factory and then wined and dined me. I was invited to meet the directors in the boardroom at the end of the lunch. They seemed impressed with my patter, and they fitted me up with boxes of samples of various types of stockings and men's socks to take back to London to our 'mini-supermarket'. But they weren't completely stupid, and wanted clearance of my cheque before they would deliver the main order of goods. My companions were very jealous as we roared back to 'the Smoke' on the M1. I couldn't stop telling them mouth-watering stories of the delicious meal I had just enjoyed.

We sold everything we had to a London fence called Indian Joe and he paid us in cash. We were very nasty really, because as his staff were unloading our boxes for his shop, we nipped around the back of his premises and nicked two boxes of the stockings we had just sold him.

The next 'Long Firm' I joined was in south London. It operated behind the front of a cut-price shop which dealt in electrical goods. The chap running it was a man called Stan. He used to act the millionaire to salesmen, yet didn't really have a pot to piss in. He knew the spiel inside out and most of the salesmen fell for it. Once he took a representative out for a meal, and was so good with his chat that the rep ended up paying for both of them.

A notorious south London gang was behind this business, and there was friction between them and a west London gang of villains. Trouble came to a head when Stan swindled the south of the river boys out of some money and then switched allegiance to the west Londoners. The other mob tracked him down to an office in Harrow Road, burst in and stuck revolvers in his body. They proceeded to drag him screaming like a pig to a car outside and told him they were going to fit him up with concrete boots. Stan somehow managed to wrest open the door of the car as it sped along and he fell out, would you believe it, right outside a police station. He picked himself up and dusted himself down, and told the local old bill of his tale. He even made a statement against the villains who planned to kill him, but later mysteriously retracted it. Apparently they threatened his wife and child and as these men had killed before he decided not to proceed with his statement.

It was the astonishing Stan who got me involved with what I call my Towering Inferno job. He had gone into business with another firm of crooks and he approached me to burn down a warehouse they had been using as part of an insurance fiddle. Stan took me along to the warehouse, at Kingston-upon-Thames outside London and not far from historic Hampton Court. I gasped the size of the building, which I noted contained several pantechnicon lorries which were being loaded up with most of the remaining stock of ironmongery and toiletries. Stan gave me a set of alarm keys, showed me how to work them, and then outlined his outrageous plan.

'Mo, we want everything to literally go up in smoke, all the papers and the building,' he said. 'But it must be done after seven in the evening so that the 'directors' are all home and have cast-iron alibis.

This Long Firm had ordered and sold hundreds of thousands of pounds of goods, and now wanted the company to disappear in the flames of my handiwork. But it had to seem as if it was an accident. 'Do it the way you see fit,' said Stan. 'Knowing you, Mo, I'm sure you'll do a great job.'

And I did. Just after seven pm on a Friday evening, when I knew the yard of the warehouse would be deserted, I got into my Hillman car, drove to a nearby garage and bought two gallons of petrol, which I put into two cans. Then I parked the car by the warehouse and loaded it up with goods worth £600, which had been put out for me as part of my fee. I left the two cans of petrol inside the building while I drove the car to another street close to the warehouse. I then poured the petrol all over the ground floor of the massive complex, fractured a gas main, and then lit some matches and set fire to the petrol. But as I tried to run out, I found to my horror that I was almost completely engulfed in a circle of fire. Somehow I fought my way through the inferno I had created, and choking in the smoke, emerged into the yard. By now my eyes were red raw and my hair and eyebrows were singed. My befuddled mind functioned enough for me to remember to switch the alarm back on, close the door and grab the cans.

Before getting into my car, I threw the two containers into the nearby River Thames. As I went to switch on the ignition, I heard a terrific explosion which ripped through the warehouse roof. Then flames shot hundreds of feet in the air and I realised how lucky I was. I could have been engulfed in the blaze in there and sizzled alive. 'Wow!' was all I could say to myself as I drove off.

Next day I met up with Stan and his fellow 'directors' in a swish London hotel. 'It was a fantastic job, Mo, not a scrap of evidence left,' said one of the men. They gave me a fat fee for the job and, downing a large double scotch, I said, 'Keep in touch.' One of them said, 'We always keep in touch with good workers, Mo. Don't worry about that.'

Later I went back to the scene of the fire, one of the biggest ever in the town, with three Scotland Yard Robbery Squad officers - Detective Sergeants Milne and Bonnington and

Detective Constable Wreaford, and we couldn't find the shell of the building. But after a few enquiries locally we discovered it had been demolished and, would you believe it, they've built a council office on the site ...

One of my most brazen and crazy robberies took place shortly after that burn-up in Kingston. Finances were getting low for once and desperation for more cash was driving me to think up new criminal schemes. I'd just got married to Maureen, a dark-haired former nurse who I had met in a Paddington coffee-bar. She was sitting there with four nursing friends from the London hospital where she worked. I ambled up to her as she sipped her espresso coffee and said, 'What's a nice girl like you doing in a place like this?' Quick as a flash, she replied, 'The same as a nice boy like you.' I liked her cheek and we got chatting and eventually started going out seriously. In those days she had no idea of my criminal activities. I told her I was a builder, like my dad, and I worked on his properties. I always had a lot of cash to flash about, so Maureen, who had been trying to live on her meagre nurses' wages, was highly delighted with the relatively high life she got when she went out with me. I spent money on her like water. But you have to bear in mind that I was still young and very immature then. I told her my cash came from my 'rich and generous' dad. That was the biggest joke yet.

We lived together for a while and eventually married in 1968 in a West London registry office and moved into one of my dad's houses. He let us live there rent free and even gave me £50 cash as a wedding present - he still didn't believe in actually taking the trouble to select a present, but the money was still welcome. Maureen soon gave up her nursing career to become a housewife and a mother - we had two children, a boy before we married and later a girl. It didn't take her long to discover that I was up to villainy, but she closed her eyes and ears to it, and kept her hands open. She was well provided for during the course of the marriage, which started off well enough, but blew up into a gale force wind. I was so obsessed with getting to the top of the crime world and being a super-successful villain, that I just didn't seem to have any time for anybody else.

There were tender moments, like the time she needed the plane fare to fly to Ireland to see her father, who was seriously ill. It was one of the few times I had cash-flow problems, so I thought up a daring plan to rob a jeweller's shop, just down the road from Shepherds Bush police station.

On the day of the job I drove to the shop in a battered Morris Oxford estate and parked it around the corner. I had borrowed the car from a scrap dealer who had it up for sale, and had no idea that I was going to use it for a robbery. After looking in the window and picking my prizes, I walked into the shop. I was scheming up a way to get several trays of diamond rings. I looked around the shop full of sparklers. 'Can I help you sir?' said the salesman. 'Yes,' I said in a calm voice, though I must admit my legs were shaking. 'Could I see some of your gent's rings? 'Certainly sir,' he said courteously, producing a tray from the window. After studying several, I decided I had to buy one to show good faith to the unsuspecting salesman. I bought a man's signet ring for ten guineas, paying in cash, adding, 'By the way, could I look at some engagement rings?' 'Yes, sir. In what price bracket would you like them?' 'Don't worry about that. I just want to have a look.' So he went to the window again and brought out four trays of rings which glinted in the sunlight. The prices were up to £400 a ring. They were real beauties. I had done this to see what sort of security procedure he had when he brought the rings out. I noted that he kept the two front fingers - thumb and forefinger - of each hand on the bottom of the trays. After scrutinising all the rings, I said, 'I'll pop back and let you know.'

By now I had the whole situation under control in my mind. I then drove the borrowed estate car to a change-over place about half a mile away, close to the Queen's Park Rangers' football ground on the White City Estate. I walked up the road and stole a Mini, then drove it right outside the jeweller's shop and left the engine running and the driver's door ajar. Then I went back into the shop. The salesman seemed pleased to see me again so soon, and welcomed me with a, 'Good afternoon sir.' By now he obviously believed me to be a *bona fide* customer, and on request he produced five trays of rings.

He placed them on the counter and I said, 'It's very hard to choose which one I want.' 'Are you getting engaged sir?' he asked helpfully. 'Well actually, it's a surprise for somebody.' He smiled and said, 'I wish someone would surprise me.' For a second he took his forefingers off the tray, and received a surprising right hook slap between the eyes, which sent him sprawling across to the other side of the counter. I scooped up the five trays, raced to the car, threw the rings into the back seat, slammed the door and began to pull away.

By this time the man had recovered and raced outside. He desperately tried to open the door, so I jammed the accelerator right to the floor. He then grabbed wildly for my windscreen wipers and hauled himself onto the bonnet. I charged the car at a lamppost, hoping he would jump off, but he showed no indication that he would, so I braked suddenly and he went tumbling from the bonnet arse over end. Smoke rose from my tyres as I screamed into nearby Wood Lane and zoomed past the BBC television studios. He tried to flag down a passing jaguar car, but fortunately for me it contained three villains and they just drove past him. So I escaped with my valuable booty.

Within hours I had sold it. The rings were worth just under £5,000 and I sold them for several hundred pounds cash to a fence. He was a bent ex-detective sergeant who once told me he would sell out anyone for the highest bid. 'Life is too short to have friends,' he said. I learned a lot about crime and criminals from this man, but I will never reveal his name.

Maureen was delighted with the windfall and she was able to fly to Ireland. I never told her where the money came from. By now she had come to realise that if you asked no questions, you got told no lies.

3

Hospital Gang Bang

Guns soon began to figure more and more in my criminal mind. My first armed robbery came about after I met two Londoners – let's call them George and ill – while I was out shopping. They stopped me and we began to chat. This pair of villains knew of my previous record, and put a proposition to me. 'We want you to help us rob a jeweller's shop in the West End,' said Bill. The high-class outfit, they said, was in a Mayfair street close to Baker Street, the fictitious home of that famous Victorian sleuth, Sherlock Holmes. Neither of them could drive, so that's where I came in, they said. 'I'm certainly interested,' I told them, scenting big money. 'Right, we'll have to nick a motor to do it,' said George.

At that time Bill was beginning to lose his nerve, and that's why George wanted me in on the deal. In fact this was to be Bill's last job with George. It wasn't long before I had stolen a car, a Minivan, from the inner circle of Regent's Park, and parked it near the jeweller's shop, a sawn-off shotgun in the back. The getaway car was to be my own souped-up Mini saloon. I parked that a mile away from the shop. The three of us waited in the stolen van until it was near closing time and the edgy Bill said, 'It's a bit risky, let's give it a miss.' I was all keyed up for action and retorted, 'Bollocks Bill. If your bottle's gone I will have to go in there myself.' My job was to sit outside in the van with the engine running and zoom off with them to where my Mini was parked as soon as they had done the job.

After a couple of minutes of hassling, George and Bill finally agreed to go ahead, put on their stocking masks and ran into the shop. One of them held up the two shocked jewellers with the shotgun, while the other dived over the top of the counter to scoop up the trays of rings and expensive watches. But the owner, who was one of the pair held at gunpoint, kept his cool and somehow managed to press the alarm button under the counter. As the alarm bell began to ring, the pair of would-be raiders ran to the door like a pair of greyhounds, with some of their spoils. If they had not panicked they could have got a lot more. As I saw them charging out of the shop, I began pulling out with the van and they dived in. One of the jewellers chased them out and a shotgun was pointed at him. God must have been on his side that evening, for the gun went off and the blast missed his head by inches. If it had connected, someone would have had to scrape him off the wall. On the way back to the change-over car, I looked closely at the pair and they had changed colour. Their faces were purple with fright. We eventually got to the switch point, dumped the van, and then escaped in my Mini. We later sold the jewellery to a fence for a fair price.

I'll be honest, I was a bit scared on that job, but I never showed it. I believe it's bad for business if you do. Bill and George had got their courage from some large scotches before we set off, but as always, I kept well away from booze while I was working. Lots of robbers either have a good drink before a robbery, or take pep pills. But in my opinion, they are cowards with pepped-up courage. They become much more dangerous than a man with a clear head.

During this time George had been speaking to a crook called Phillip at a prison hostel, the sort of place where you live for several months when you come out of jail on licence. Phillip decided to come in with us and we met in a coffee bar. Christmas was coming and it wasn't just the geese that were getting fat – we knew there were lots of rich pickings in the offing. Arrangements were made to meet a south London team. (In the villain business, they are not called gangs.) We met in a pub called The Oliver in Harrow Road, where the south London guys called Pete and Billy, were already supping when we walked in. We downed many a foaming pint and discussed a robbery at a rent office in their part of the world. After talking it through we agreed to combine to do the job. It was planned for a Monday, and the south Londoners told us they already had acquired a stolen car for the raid. We got into it and headed to the rent office, where council tenants paid in their rents. We sat outside watching from the car for a few minutes. There was consternation, as Pete couldn't load the 12-bore shotgun. The breach was stiff. Eventually, the gun was ready and we put on our balaclavas and stocking masks, breathed in deeply and dashed into the office. A woman teller screamed hysterically as she saw several armed, masked men with coshes, hammers and sawn-off shotguns vault the counter.

One of the gunmen, I can't remember who it was, said, 'Oh shut up lady. We're rent collectors.' With that she ran into an office for safety and some of the team emptied the contents of the drawers of rent money into a plastic bag. Just as the last note floated into the bottom of the bag, a shotgun was fired, just missing the head of the bandit who was scooping up the money. It was afterwards alleged throughout the underworld that I had tried   to kill him, which, of course, wasn't true.

I later found out that the woman teller had pushed a secret alarm button, which was connected to an upstairs office. We didn't hear the bell, so we didn't panic. We got all we could, rushed out at high speed with our ill-gotten gains.

We found out late that we had left a further £4,000 in a safe. We were all pretty wound up with the tension of the job, and George told us: 'Keep your nerve. We'll be home soon! The car was dumped, and we made our own ways to our vehicles, and headed back to west London where we met in The Bridge public house, and split the dough up. Everyone was patting each other on the back, saying how well we had done, but I thought this was foolish talk. 'I knew that a lot of lives were at stake, including ours, and if we had got caught for one of these raids, it would be a minimum of ten years in a top security prison. And for what?

Because someone's mouth wanted to play canary. I was worried by the way they were boasting in the pub about the job. I told them to shut their mouths. I was amazed we weren't overheard by strangers, who could have easily bubbled (talked) on us. But we were lucky. Later we said our goodbyes and parted to go our different ways.

A few weeks later - Christmas Eve, 1968 - George came round to my house to have a chat. Strangely enough my home was in the same road where the spinster Jessie lived and where I was unsuspectingly started on my life of crime. George put another proposition to me - a job at a cash-and-carry off-licence in Kensington. After hearing what he had to say, I drove with him to the venue and saw more than 100 people queuing up for their Christmas spirits. We kept observation for a while in my car and, to our dismay, found the queue was getting longer and longer. But this also meant that the money was piling up. So we left to make arrangements, get more help, steal a car, and bring a shotgun out of retirement. We recruited two more men. The team for this job was myself, George, James and Phillip. After stealing the car and parking our own motors we transferred the shotgun into the stolen vehicle. We also had with us coshes and masks. We waited until past midnight, and shortly after Christmas Day began and the store closed we went to the side entrance where one of the team smashed a side panel of glass, opened the lock, and we went in. By this time most of the staff had gone home. The manager was still there, however, and hearing the noise of breaking glass, he came to investigate. He was savagely clubbed on the head with an iron bar and slung down a staircase by one of the team. By that time the shotgun went off and blew part of the ceiling out. We were covered in plaster dust. We entered the shop to search for the money, but couldn't find the safe keys. And what with the shot going off, and the noise that it had made, we decided to make haste and scarper. We grabbed a few bottles of brandy from a shelf and then ran to the car. As you can imagine, I was getting very frustrated at having to put myself on offer for small cash rewards and bottles of brandy - especially on Christmas Day. There was a tragic ending to that robbery: when I was arrested in 1974, I was told that the manager never really recovered from his injuries and consequently died about a year later.

Then came a big hospital job. The information for it came from a toerag (louse) whose real name isn't worth mentioning. He stuck up the information to his brother-in-law and he passed it on to us - the team. He said that there would be £14,000 at just after one pm on a Thursday in the basement of the hospital, where the wages office was. We went in and had a look at the place, and agreed to do it. By now the team had grown to six -George, Billy, James, Pete, Phillip and myself. On the Wednesday evening, I went back with two members of the team to the hospital basement and unscrewed the grill on the wages office door. I cut the screws, and put them back as if there was nothing wrong. The idea was that when we arrived there the next day, we could just pull the grill off, smash the two centre doors and climb through. The other two kept watch as I did the job. After the grill had been doctored, we met the next morning and stole a Minivan from my old hunting ground, the inner circle of Regent's Park. We then came back in the stolen van, loaded on the shotgun, iron bars, sledgehammer, stocking and balaclava masks, and then waited for the time to attack the unsuspecting hospital staff. We had one more major problem to contend with and that was a police station, which was close to the hospital. But that didn't deter us. The job was on.

Some of us walked into the hospital, while the others drove in in the van. It went in the front entrance and around the perimeter of the hospital to the rear, where it was backed up to the back door of the entrance to the wages office. We all masked up in our hideous disguises. Some members went to the far double doors and padlocked them to stop anybody coming in while the robbery was going on. A little tap on the wages window by Billy brought a response. 'Who's there?' said the voice at the other end of the room. Billy said, 'I've come to collect my wages.' The little voice said, 'Go away, and come back at the proper time.' Which was half an hour later. With that fat James pulled the grill off and George hit the two double doors, which were very brittle, with a 7 lb hammer and sent them splintering across the room. Then a shotgun was produced. There were screams, and the staff were ordered to lie on the floor. The other members of the team entered the wages office through the big hole in the door. There were thousands of pounds in wages waiting to be made up and also cash in a big box already made up in wages packets. For these people - some elderly - in that office it must have been terrifying.

We later ran to the car with the money in bags. I saw a porter lying on the floor in the passageway with a shotgun at his head. 'Leave it off,' I told the guy with the gun. The staff all kept down and we escaped by the back door entrance, adjacent to the rear door of the police station. At that time the shotgun was waving around at the back of the van doing a jig, and by the time it was passed to the front passenger seat it went off and sent a blast straight through the bottom of the Minivan and punctured a tyre. The chap handling it had put it down and the trigger had gone off. As we wobbled along the road for about a mile and a half to the change-over, the tyre began to screech. We eventually arrived at the change-over, which was by St Charles' Hospital, where I used to work. We went back to one of the team's flat in Paddington, and shared out the loot. It was just over £5,000 between us all. It wasn't long before we were out celebrating and everybody in Paddington and elsewhere knew who had done the job. Which made the police's job very easy. I know who the informant was - he was supposed to be a friend of one of the team. Within days most of us were arrested and brought in for questioning at Harrow Road nick. Only one of the team co-operated with the police, the rest of us kept quiet. At a later date, we met to discuss the matter of who had grassed us up, and someone stuck my name up. I think they realise now that it wasn't me. I had a row with fat James and I got so angry I was going to shoot him. Outside in my car, I had a sawn-off shotgun with which I was going to do the evil deed. But the governor of the pub overheard us and said, 'Don't do it in here Mo, it's bad for business.'

Fat James hadn't been questioned by the police yet – which was a good thing because he could be identified by the hospital staff. His stocking mask had split in half during the raid, leaving his face uncovered.

I had by now cooled down. I had £100 on me, and gave it to him, saying 'That will help you while you're on the run.' After a car chase up and down pavements around Paddington, he was arrested by Detective Sergeant Nicky Birch of the Flying Squad. He crashed and was taken to Harrow Road police station where he gave valuable information on the raid on the Mayfair jeweller's, and the raid on the off-licence in Kensington. I was arrested by armed detectives led by Detective Sergeant John Merrick, who is now Detective Chief Inspector at that station.

Merrick's men rang the bell in the early hours of the morning and when I opened the door, ten of his men pushed in, held me up against the wall and three searched me. Then, while a couple stood guard over me, the others ran up the stairs to see if there was anyone else there. I was immediately handcuffed and then brought upstairs, where Detective Sergeant Merrick said to me, 'I would like you to come to St John's Wood police station, where I believe you may be able to help with inquiries into some recent armed robberies.'

I replied, 'Why, are you short of men?' My distraught wife sat with the frightened children in the kitchen as we talked in the lounge. The police were very discreet in the way they searched the premises and tried not to frighten the children, for which I thank them. I was taken to St John's Wood, where I was interviewed by senior policemen about the murder of a jeweller in Great Portland Street in which I was not involved. As I sat in my cell I said to myself, 'It's the end of the road for me.' How wrong I was. It was only the beginning.

The senior police detective who questioned me in a hard, stern voice, said, 'When you come out for what you've done, we'll be living on the moon.' And I replied, 'Don't run out of petrol half way up.' He said, 'You're a witty sort of lad, aren't you?' And I said, 'Humour didn't kill anybody.' Then I was asked if I knew several people who were involved in these robberies, and I replied, 'No, I don't.' He then said to me. 'Well, Maurice, you're going to be put on identification for the murder of a jeweller of Great Portland Street, the armed robbery of a Mayfair jeweller's, and the armed robbery and attempted murder of the manager of the off-license in Kensington. Have you anything to say regarding what I have just said?' I said, 'No, Mr Merrick.'

He then said, 'You are entitled to have a solicitor present during the identification. If you haven't got one we will make arrangements to have a local solicitor here to represent you.' And I said, 'There's no need for that, I'm innocent. I have no worries.'

I was held for two days and on the third day I was taken out of the cell to be put on identification with seven other men. I was asked by a police inspector who was conducting the parade, 'Have you any objection to any members of the public who will be on the identification with you?' I looked at them and I said, 'No, sir.' He then said I could take any position I wanted to and I said, 'Can I watch?' 'No you can't,' he sniffed. Of course I knew the procedure but had to get a dig in.

I then placed myself in the first identification parade. When the witness walked in, he looked at my cold steely eyes and I fully believe he knew I was the one. But he was terrified. He got to the end of the line and he was asked, 'Have you identified anyone?' He said, 'No.' So that was one crime down and two to go. The witnesses on the next job came in - several of them - looked me up and down and passed by, because they couldn't identify anybody. Then came the final ordeal which was the jeweller's raid parade, and the man never looked at anybody. As he got to the end, he looked at the officers in charge and said, 'No, he's not there.' And the police knew full well that I was responsible for two out of the three robberies, as their informant was now in custody.

I was later put back in the cell. Detective Sergeant Merrick came in and, as the heavy door creaked open, I sarcastically said, 'Are we on the moon yet?' And he said, 'You must be one of the luckiest men breathing. It's amazing what fear can do to people, because I believe they recognised you. Do you believe that?'

I said, 'There may be something in your theory. Now go and find the answer.' He told me then that I was shortly going to be released, and I said, 'Thank you.' And soon after I was freed. Mr Merrick then said if I was to see my friend George, I should ask him to ring him, so that he could come in and go on identification. I told George and he went in on a parade with a solicitor present and was later released. The informant who grassed got eight years' imprisonment. While myself and George went free. What you might call rough justice . . .

One of my most unusual 'jobs' took place on our way to an armed robbery in Mayfair. There were four of us in the team. It was a jeweller's shop again, right next door to one of London's top hotels. We'd stolen a car and were all set, when we pulled up at some traffic lights and I saw a green Rolls Royce beside us. I noticed a lady's hand fidgeting through the window. And on one finger was a massive glinting diamond ring. I said to one of my mates, 'Hell, look at that.' And he said, 'We'll have that.' There was no traffic behind us, so I dived out of the seat, stuck the gun in the chauffeur's head, grabbed the bird's hand and tried to bite the stone out of the ring. During the struggle, she was bashing me on the head with her handbag. She swore at me several times,' and I remember her shouting to her chauffeur, 'Help me!' He replied, 'Not f...ing likely, madam.' With that the final bite took place, and with all the excitement I swallowed the sparkler. We later went back to one of our drums (homes), and they asked where the ring was. And I said, 'It must be about a foot from my rectum.' We laughed and the lads went out to the chemist and brought back a load of laxatives. Finally, after two hours of intense concentration I succeeded in delivering the prize. After a quick search in the toilet bowl the stone came to light. We sold it for £1,500, though I think it was worth somewhere in the region of twelve grand. It was a very painful experience for me I may add, but well worth while.

The days of car stealing and small stuff had come to an end for me. I was now getting involved with some of the underworld's most dangerous people. When people talk about the underworld as a jungle they're wrong. It's more than that - it's a world without end. Once you're in it, it's virtually impossible to escape. Criminals, in a way, are like birds of prey, they swoop down on society's weakest.

Pub brawls were beginning to become something of a speciality for me and with my new found confidence with firearms, a gun sometimes took over from my fists as a battle weapon. Like the time when I took on half-a-dozen paddies in a Paddington pub. I had overheard one of them insult a relative of mine and I took a swing at him. He ducked and with that the 'Men of Shamrock' pitched into me. Despite being heavily out-numbered, I fought valiantly with them for about ten bloody minutes. The place was in an uproar as tables were overturned in the melee and fists flew. Regulars abandoned their drinks and made their escape out of the door or took refuge in the toilets.

Finally, I realised that this was a fight that I couldn't possibly win, so I made my limping escape and headed for a nearby hospital.

And there, as my mainly facial wounds were patched up by a friendly nurse, I vowed vengeance against the violent Irishmen who were, by now, back swilling Guinness at the bar. After being discharged from the hospital, I returned to a secret hiding place where I stored part of my arsenal of weapons, withdrew a sawn-off shotgun, and headed back to the pub in a car I had stolen a few days previously.

All chattering and drinking ceased as I flung open the door of the lounge bar, pointed the shotgun at the paddies, and yelled, 'OK, you bastards, have some of this.'
With that they dived for cover under the table and I said, 'I'll give you 60 seconds to come outside or I blow you and this pub to pieces.'

I then withdrew to a spot across the road and pointed my shotgun at the entrance. I didn't plan to kill them, just give them a fright they wouldn't forget in a hurry.

First, one ruddy-cheeked paddy peered around the bar door like a frightened rabbit, and then the others popped their heads out. Not seeing me in the shadows across the way they tried to make a dash for it. With that I took aim just above their heads and let the gun blast away. As they hopped up and down trying to avoid being blasted, I systematically blew out all the pub windows. I could hear people inside screaming in panic as the splintered glass showered down upon them.

Then, as I went to reload, they made a dash for it and I let them scuttle off into the night.

But I wasn't satisfied with that. I then told some associates about the beating and they lay in wait one night for the Irishmen and busted them senseless in an alleyway with pickaxe handles.

Such is criminal vengeance . . .

At this time most of the team had split up and gone their different ways. But I was left with one accomplice, who introduced me to friends of his who were some of the most violent people I'd seen for a long time. But that made no difference to me. I was one of them. After I met these thugs, they put up a proposition of a robbery at a contract cleaning firm in the West End of London. After discussing the plan I was told it was an inside job. We both agreed to go along. At this time I had a brand new three-litre Rover. The new team said that they had guns and all the gear (hammers, taped-up coshes, stockings, balaclavas, etc). We then decided that we would all stay that night at one of their houses. That we did. We drank beer and talked and had quick snoozes from time to time. At five o'clock in the morning we all had a wash and tidy up, picked up the guns and then went to the car and drove to Rupert Street in the West End. It was a cold morning and the streets were deserted. We saw the name of the cleaning firm on an upstairs window and I parked around the corner - I think it was in Wardour Street. We walked through the alleyway, and the team went upstairs and knocked on the door, a man answered and he was brutally coshed to the ground. When I went upstairs, they thought I was an intruder, because at first I had been waiting in the Rover, and had decided to go and investigate.

Entering the offices, I saw a man badly bleeding on the floor, with blood pouring out of his head. Everybody was slipping all over the place in the gore. I later saw one of the men force him to open the safe. He didn't know how to do it, and was coshed again on the same gaping wound. This time the guy was knocked unconscious. Also on the floor, lying down, was a little, old lady cleaner terrified out of her wits. I said, 'Don't worry, mum. We're not going to hurt you, or any of the other women.' And she was praying to God out loud to protect them. We couldn't get into the safe as the person in charge of it had just left the building for a short time. We decamped from the job through the alleyway, taking the manageress's handbag which contained £50, and went back to a hideout, shared the money out and went home to bed. Later I read about it in the London *Evening News*. My white Rover was mentioned and I got rid of it. Just think of it; these were the risks we were taking for £50, when the total haul we should have got was £10,000. And it was in that safe - but we just couldn't get in it.

Later, I went on another robbery that went wrong, on Lady Betty Selsdon, first cousin to the Queen. She was said to have a vast fortune in jewels at her home in Chelsea. We went in a car, five of us, to rob her but she was not in. She later pulled up in her own car, which had her initials on the number plate, with a male companion. We went to stream in on her as the door opened, but a police car was patrolling through and we had to abort the attempt. Later I went back with two other members of the gang in a stolen car and carrying a bunch of flowers, to knock at the door and tell her we were from Interflora. And then we planned to knock her down. Luckily for her she was out, but a few years later she was finally attacked in her home and robbed. But it wasn't me.

The person who put up this information in the first place hung himself in prison. I believe he did it with a pair of football socks. The reason was that hidden documents were found in the Gartree Prison riots indicating that he was an informant. But I fully believe he was not a grass inside, and died in vain. He was a very brave man.

Actress Dinah Sheridan, star of films like *Genevieve* and *Where No Vultures Fly*, was to be another of our victims. She was betrayed by a show business friend who told us she carried amounts of jewellery at her lovely home in Kensington. He said it was worth at least £50,000.
Plan One to get the sparklers entailed following her to and from the West End theatre where she was starring. I believe she was then in the farce *Move Over Mrs Markham* at the Vaudeville Theatre. When we had established her route, we decided to try to hijack her in Buckingham Palace Road by swerving in front of her car, dragging her out, and pushing her in the back of our rather ancient Bedford van. We would then take her back to the flat and force her to hand over the jewels. Unfortunately, that particular night, our van was so sluggish that we couldn't actually overtake the charming Miss Sheridan.

By the way, I found out later she was born in London of a Russian émigré father and German mother, and has been married and divorced twice - to the late actor Jimmy Hanley and Rank

Organisation chief, Sir John Davis.

So Plan Two was put into operation. We decided to break in a week later when she was working at the theatre. Then when she arrived home, we would force her to hand over her jewellery. On the night we hit her place, we went in through a back bedroom window, smashing off security chains and locks. We started ransacking her possessions in the bedroom, and stuffing jewellery into our pockets. Surprisingly, the family were not alerted and there was no need to tie them up. We looked through a window and saw them watching telly.

But we had to abandon the raid suddenly before we had got everything because one of my gang thought we had been spotted entering the basement. He saw someone outside and hissed, 'The Old Bill are here.' So we tip-toed back out and made our escape, leaving the people in the flat still watching television, not realising the real life drama going on in the next room. Only as we made our getaway did we realise it had been a false alarm.

4
Call Girl Crooks

Two curvy call girls now became my best tipsters. Sadie and Sonia both hard bitten, peroxide blondes with well upholstered figures, got their information from rich clients whom they would bed and then, at what you might call important climaxes in their relationships, they would find out details of their homes and when they were usually out. They would tell me and I would do the rest. The only losers were the sex-starved clients.

I first met this deadly double-crossing duo in a Soho club, where they worked as 'hostesses'. Their job was to get important clients to spend as much money as possible on their whims in the club, like buying them over-priced drinks and cigarettes, and then do an expensive deal to have sex with them. Their prices were high but the mugs who went with them were obviously satisfied with their charms.

Sadie and Sonia were in their thirties, as hard as nails, and apparently without any feelings for their clients. All they wanted was to screw as much out of them as they could, while their customers screwed them. They knew every hustling trick in the book and upped their price before each under-garment came off. They picked their clients carefully. Those who were well-dressed and appeared to have plenty of dough to indulge their sexual whims, were always given priority. Poor punters from the provinces never got a look-in.

'Look Mo,' said Sadie one night at the club. 'Why don't we do a deal?' I thought at first she meant going to bed. 'Look love, I'm not into that. I never pay for my sex,' I said.

'No, Mo, we'll give you information, and you can burgle the places we tell you about. Then you can give us a percentage.'

These well-worn hustlers were very good at their profession - they had to be at their age to survive the rigours of their unpleasant occupation. Our lucrative business partnership lasted for several months.

This cunning pair of whores also devised a blackmail scheme aimed at key workers at Heathrow Airport, London. They had managed to bed several security officials at the massive airport, and then had threatened to tell their wives of their misdeeds if they didn't steal valuable goods from baggage passing through their hands. The frightened men did just as they were told and then received a small rake-off from the girls . . . plus, of course further favours.
Sadie and Sonia, who incidentally 'starred' in a succession of sordid blue movies and was also a lesbian, were not my only informants. I remember one burglary being put up to me by an apparently respectable businessman whom I had got to know. Over cocktails in a hotel bar one night, he told me of the gaff of a friend in Willesden. 'This chap keeps several thousand pounds there in cash,' he told me as he downed a gin and orange. 'He has it all stashed away in a bureau. All you've got to do, Mo, is get in and ransack the bureau.' He told me the man was out at work each day, and his wife loved bingo and attended sessions twice a week. I kept a discreet observation on the flat and found out that she went chasing a full house each Tuesday and Thursday afternoon.

One Tuesday I decided to have a go at robbing the ground-floor flat. I watched the bingo addict leave for a chance of winning a small fortune, and then had my own go at gaining a jackpot. As always, I first rang the bell of the flat. If there was an answer, I would, as they say in Fleet Street, make my excuses and leave. There was no reply this time, so I popped the pane of glass in the top of the door with an automatic centre punch, put my hand through the hole it made and let myself in. A quick search of the premises confirmed that there was nobody in, and it also brought to light a varnished brown bureau in a small study. Just the piece of furniture I was looking for, and I'd found it so quickly, I thought. I searched through it, but could find no sign of money. There were a lot of documents, but not a banknote to be seen. I got more and more frustrated as I hunted. Maybe my informant was mistaken.

I gave up on the bureau and looked for an exit point, just in case I was disturbed. This was always my practice - and it's one that has paid off over the years. As I looked for an escape route, I came across another bureau, this time in the dining room, I again began ransacking it, but could still find nothing of importance. I stopped work for a moment for a breather, and rested my elbow on the top of the bureau - and abracadabra! A secret cavity began to swing open. I gave the rolling bottom ledge a bit of help and resting there all snugly rolled up, were bundles of one and five pound notes. I quickly counted up £5,000. What a find. I pocketed the money, shut up the cavity and then went through to the bedroom and lifted some nice jewellery and a mink coat and jacket. I then made my escape by the rear door and slung the minks in the boot of my car which was parked nearby. I sold the furs for a total of £500 and I got a further £250 for the jewellery. But it was the cash that thrilled me. My informant got £500 for his help. With friends like him, who needs enemies?

Feeling particularly generous, I went to see some mates at a West London scrapyard. I knew the chaps there were doing bad business, so I gave the bosses a nice 'drink' of £200, plus £10 each to a few helpers. They had given me good information in the past and I was rewarding them. But would you believe it? When I left, one of the slags got on the blower to Harrow Road nick and said I was flashing a lot of money around. When I arrived back in the road in which I lived, there were several CID officers waiting to pick me up. They took me to the police station and searched me, expecting to find all my ill-gotten gains. But all they found were three pound notes. One of the officers said, 'You've just had a lot of money, where is it?' I said, 'I don't know what you are talking about. Are you winding me up?' He said, 'You know the score Mo.' I said, 'I've only got three pounds. I could do with a score myself.'

I had foolishly flashed around the five-grand that I had lifted and the police couldn't work out how, while walking the mile from the yard to my home, I had disposed of so much bread. Well, this is how it happened. On the way, I went to my secret hiding place - behind a false brick on a derelict site. I didn't like carrying a lot of money around for so long, so I would regularly stash large amounts of hot cash there. The perplexed detectives finally admitted defeat and let me go, but they got their own back to an extent by keeping me under observation for some time. I couldn't really visit my brick bank for a while, so the money went unspent. Eventually my CID shadows gave up and I was able to start enjoying the proceeds of my crime.

After this experience, I decided to spread around the false impression that times were bad. You could never be sure who was going to grass to the police on you. So I kept my criminal activities pretty quiet, except for my associates.

Through drinking club contacts, I was introduced to two notorious gentleman villains who were based in West London. We'll call them Geoff and Bert. Geoff, who was in his sixties, was a high-class professional burglar with years of experience. He was also very clever. Bert was an ex-fighter who was also a nice guy, though not as experienced as his partner. I doubt if they are now too pleased with the results of their involvement with me, because they are now serving long sentences. I worked with the pair on several stockbroker belt burglaries and found there was never a dull moment. Their exceptional skill was a revelation to me, but their choice of helpers sometimes surprised me, to say the least.

Like the so-called professional safe-blower they produced for a job at a barrister's house in Willesden. 'He's the best around, said Geoff, when I first met this wiry little man with a ferret face. 'He'll have to be,' I said when I saw the size of the safe. Rather than blow the safe in the house, he suggested we drag it to a coal shed and he would exercise his amazing skill there. We cushioned the safe as much as we could, and then he packed the keyhole with gelignite and wired it to a small battery. 'Stand back lads,' he whispered. 'I'm just going to blow it open.' With that he connected the wires and we put our fingers to our ears.

Absolutely nothing happened, so he tried again. Again, nothing. 'I thought you said this guy was a pro,' I said to Geoff. 'He couldn't blow up a rubber duck.' Geoff told me to be quiet and the safe-cracker tried another way of blasting open the safe, which we had been told contained diamonds worth thousands of pounds. This time the maniac connected the wires to an electric light socket and nearly blew himself and all of us into the next world. The blast was enormous - but when the smoke cleared the safe door was still shut. We all had a ringing in our ears for several minutes and we hoped and prayed that anyone who heard the noise would think that a lorry had backfired, as the house was near a busy main road.

We dragged the battered safe into a basement and I then got to work. I had brought a sledgehammer and chisel with me and I began banging away at the door. Chunks of metal flew off the door and cut my hands to shreds as I kept trying to smash open the safe. Finally, after about three hours, I got it open, and there inside was a sparkling collection of diamonds. We stuffed them into a bag we had brought with us, and decided to leave. We backed our van to the front door, loaded the battered safe on board and then drove off. I don't know why we wanted an empty safe - but eventually one of the lads had enough sense to realise we'd look a bit silly if we were stopped by the police and the safe was found in the back. So we waited till there was no other traffic around and then tipped it out into the road!

It was in the Regency Club, Stoke Newington, that I first met a north London hood called Pete. I was treating my two call girl contacts to a few well-earned drinks in the club, which the notorious Kray twins once had shares in. They told Pete that I was a good grafter. Pete and I took our drinks to a corner and he told me that he needed a good partner. 'Why don't we work together for a time, Mo?' he asked. So I hitched up with Pete and we had some great adventures together. He brought a sense of fun to the serious business of robbing others. And what a Casanova he was! I have never known a man who was so ugly and yet had so many women. His powerful personality just wowed the ladies. Pete would even send out his women to burgle houses for him – and they'd do it. He'd give them a good time in bed and then tell them the job he wanted them to do. He must have mesmerised them, for they never turned him down.

It was Pete who introduced me to an amazing Long Firm fraud in Plaistow, East London. It had just begun when we got involved and the guys who started it had managed to get hold of a large warehouse. On the surface the firm seemed like a genuine storage warehouse. Obviously the guys liked our faces because we were welcomed into the deal and both given offices. When I first viewed the premises, I came across a crazy psychopath called Mad Frankie, who, I noted kept a double-barrelled shotgun close at hand. I soon stuck a revolver to his head and relieved him of his weapon. This chap was later reputed to have helped burn down a prison. There was another nut-case also walking around the yard wearing a shoulder holster containing a Browning automatic (nine mm). This guy, Alan, was so crazy that I'm sure he thought he was living in Chicago in the twenties. Mind you, I don't think Alan was quite as daft as we first thought, because we later discovered that he was a police informant. Fortunately he only went to the law when he was short of money, so while he was earning - as he was then - we were all safe. He later ran a club in London's West End, which was protected by hoods ... robbing-hoods.

A front man was installed at Link Storage as 'managing director', and advertisements were placed widely in newspapers. Soon people were in contact, wanting us to store their furniture and precious items. Sadly, they never got their goods back. Although storage was our main 'business', we also had another company which specialised in buying a wide array of items. I remember once 'testing' a fork-lift truck for my managing director at an Essex firm, and then smiling as he concluded a credit deal for this gleaming monster. As soon as it arrived at the warehouse, it was sold to a rich East End wholesaler, and the money was split up between us. Goods just poured in. It was a good job that no one returned to ask for something back, because we'd have had some trouble on our hands. We usually got rid of goods on the day they arrived. We even collected items for storage in our brightly painted company vans and, of course, that added to our credibility.

During this astonishing term of big-time conning, we were all hiring expensive cars and charging them to the firm. But it didn't just end there, we started to take expensive suites in top London hotels and charge them to Link Storage. A night's bill after we had wined and dined in these five-star places often came to several hundred pounds, yet we never got caught. How was it done? Well, one of us would ring up the establishment in question and say our managing director needed a suite for the night, week, or whatever period we thought safe. They would take the phone number and then check back to confirm we were genuine. The director would then arrive at the hotel with his two bags, book in, and would receive VIP treatment. He would then go to his room and book a table for six in the restaurant. One night we were all in the Penthouse at the Royal Lancaster, where the Irish singing group, the Bachelors, were the star cabaret. They had no idea that we were a bunch of crooks, and we had a drink with them before they went on stage. We wined and dined our nights away on Link Storage's account. But although the hotels suffered, the staff never did. We always tipped generously.

This sort of thing went on for months. Every few days or so, our 'boss' would move to the next five-star hotel and the bill would be sent to the firm. Of course it was never paid. Some of those bills were even juicier than the steaks we got stuck into night after night. During our stay at Link Storage, we also made full use of the phones. We would ring numbers around the world and the unpaid bills were huge.

Although most of my time then was dedicated to Link Storage, there was also enough time for other jobs. One followed a conversation with a rich kangaroo (Jew), who 'stuck up' his brother-in-law as a good prospect for robbing. He told me the exact location of the safe in his luxury second-floor flat, the name of the man, his private and work phone numbers, and when the chap and his wife would be out. I brought in a professional burglar to help with the job and we borrowed a Link Storage van.

When we got to the flat we found it was securely protected by several locks on the front door. I remembered seeing a dodge used by a crook in a television series who was faced with a similar problem, so I thought I'd try it out. We borrowed a fire ladder from the nearby emergency exit and climbed up into a loft that went above the couple's bathroom. Then I poked a hole with a screwdriver through the floor into the bathroom ceiling then pushed an umbrella through the hole and opened it up so the bits of falling plaster wouldn't make too much noise when they fell as I jabbed the hole as wide as I could. I eventually got down into the flat by jumping down through the opening. My helper went back to the van and started it up so we could make a quick getaway if necessary.

I found the safe and was about to start opening it, when I heard a noise from outside the front door. I looked through the letterbox and saw two eyes peering in at me. Then came a scream. The woman had come home early, so I crazily jumped straight through a window and fell about 45 feet to the ground. Luckily I landed on grass but I still sprained my ankle and was in terrible pain as I hobbled to the van and we drove off. To make matters worse, a wheelbarrow in the back of the van - it was there to carry off the stolen safes when necessary - rolled forward and struck my bad ankle.

We had all had a good run with the firm, but it was becoming obvious that we had pushed our luck to the limit and when Barry had a tip-off that the Fraud Squad were closing in, we decided to pack our bags and leave, wiping the place clean of prints.

My next job was as a hit man for a greedy businessman. He wanted his partner shot in the leg so he would be out of action for some time and would be willing to hand him the business. The price for the job was £1,000 and it was arranged by a couple of professional key-men (expert locksmiths). A car was nicked, false number plates put on it and I was given a driver. I set off with him for the factory in north London where the shooting was to take place.

I was given a full description of the partner who needed 'knee-capping' and was also told what his car was like. It was a Ford Cortina. The driver took me to the gates of the factory and I waited for the man to come out. We hung about for what seemed like an eternity, and then a man fitting the description came out to a Cortina. 'There he is,' shouted my driver. 'Go and get him Mo. Shoot him and let's get out of this place.'

I grabbed a crash helmet and goggles from the back seat, took hold of my double-barrelled shotgun, and jumped out of the car. I took aim at the dark-haired man who was removing some goods from the boot of the car. He must have glimpsed me from out of the side of his eye, and quickly turned, faced me and screamed. 'Not me, not me. I stuck up the job. Don't shoot.' I didn't know if he was telling the truth or not, so I carried on taking aim. My finger pulled the trigger and he jumped about five feet in the air as the blast missed him by inches and peppered the ground. The next moment the hysterical man was on his knees praying for his life to be spared. 'Please don't let him kill me,' he requested the Almighty. It was then I realised that I had tried to shoot the wrong man. 'Come on, let's go,' I told the driver. 'It looks like he's the swine who put up the whole thing.'

When I later explained to my key-men friends, they phoned up the businessman and apologised for the mistake. He said, 'Never mind, I'm still glad to have my life intact.' However, the bastard soon recovered, and hired someone else to have a go at his partner.

A cigarette hijack worth £75,000 was to be the downfall of many of my friends, including Pete, the Casanova. A deal was done with a driver, who agreed to take his valuable cargo to an address in north London, where he would hand it over to a group of crooks and then be chauffered back to his south coast home. There, he was to say the cargo had been hijacked, and later he would get a split from the deal. The lorry which had a 40-foot trailer, was then driven to a farm near Southend - where disaster nearly overtook the whole mission. Firstly the driver went too fast up the drive - the farm had been 'borrowed' for a few days for the job - and the lorry slithered into a ditch and toppled right over, spewing boxes of the export cigarettes into the mud and a pile of manure. By now the team, following behind in a car, were getting very shaky. And as they began picking the boxes of cigarettes out of the sticky steamy manure, they saw a man on a bicycle pass by. They assumed the shadowy figure was a bobby and fled for cover. When they found out that he wasn't, they slowly came back and got stuck into the mucky task of rescuing the valuable cargo. The five million cigarettes were all stored in a barn and were collected next day in three large box vans, then shunted to a warehouse in Acton, west London, where they were put in a corner and covered by tarpaulin.

By the way, oxy-acetylene cutting machinery soon transformed the huge lorry into tiny pieces of metal, though the parts that were saleable were sold.

All had gone well for the team until a lazy so and so, who had been told to be at the Acton warehouse to let a plumber in to fix a leaky toilet, overslept. The plumber arrived and let himself in. Overcome with nosiness, he looked around the place and when he saw the tarpaulin, he lifted it and found all the fags. Instead of minding his own business, he phoned the police, who were quick to point out that if he played his cards right he would claim a reward of about £1,500. The Flying Squad soon identified the load as being the cigarettes from a lorry apparently stolen from Southampton, and laid a trap. They waited for each villain to arrive and grabbed them. Many of the team protested their innocence, saying they were cleaners reporting for work.

'That's funny, we've got nine other cleaners in the other room,' said one sarcastic policeman. 'Do you all work for Hoovers?' The villain said, 'What do you mean?' 'Well,' said the sharp copper. 'You beat as you sweep as you clean. You sweep the lorry off the road, you beat the driver on the head and you get clean away with the goods . . .' The crook smiled and the whole gang was taken to Acton police station for questioning. Later they were all transferred to a police station in Southampton, where the lorry originally came from, and charged with stealing £75,000 worth of export cigarettes.

Apparently it was the driver who had grassed them all up. Although he was in on the original deal, he changed his story three times for the police. Firstly he claimed he was at home all night and the lorry had been stolen from the yard. Then after further questions, he said he had decided to take the lorry earlier than expected and was hijacked - so he was too frightened to say anything in case he wasn't believed, and came back home and went to bed. But after more interrogation, he confessed he had given the load to London gangsters, who, he claimed, had now put his and his family's life in peril. The police promised them protection and then got him to talk, and he didn't stop. He named names as well.

I first heard of the arrests when someone told me to stand bail with him for Peter. 'With my form I've got about as much chance of being allowed to do that as Ronnie Biggs,' I said. 'Well, why don't you try?' he countered.

So the two of us took an early train to Southampton and arrived at the court. I had to go into the box at the magistrate's court to try and convince the bench that I was worth enough to be able to pay the bail money if Peter skipped off. Amazingly, I was believed, and bail was granted to the whole team.

The team were naturally worried and had an urgent meeting. It seemed as if there was no way out of it for them. But Derek put up the idea of at least gaining the sympathy of the jury by making out that a vicious 'Mr' Big' had terrified the team into doing the job and was out to gain vengeance for its failure. 'I don't mind copping 20 pellets in my leg - it's better than ten years which I'll get on my form,' Derek told the team meeting. He volunteered to be a victim of this vicious 'gangland shooting'. So it was arranged that he would be blasted in a 'terror attack' in a London pub. The hit, was to take place at the *Royal Standard* in Hackney. I and other members of the gang drove slowly towards the pub early on a winter's evening. We knew that there wouldn't be too many people supping at that time and we didn't want anyone else hurt. Derek and Don were standing at the bar talking to another fellow, who incidentally was dressed in an identical outfit to Derek. Although the pub hadn't been open for long, Derek was already half drunk. He was trying to drown his fear in large whiskies.

The shooting took place in a matter of seconds. A gunman kicked open the door - he was wearing a terrifying balaclava mask with cold eyes looking through - and turned towards the man dressed just like Derek, who had his back turned at that moment. In a split second he yelled, 'This is a message from Benny,' and fired a blast at his legs. Then he aimed the gun into the ceiling, and plaster rained down on the customers who started screaming. The gunman rushed to the Dormobile waiting outside, and the team made their escape.

Meanwhile, inside the pub, Derek, in his drunken stupor, realised that he hadn't been hit. So while the other chap lay on the floor in a pool of blood moaning, 'Oh my God, I've been shot,' he dashed into the toilet with his whiskey, swallowed the scotch, cracked the glass on the bowl of the toilet and began slashing his legs through his trousers with it.

Then he staggered back into the pub where the unfortunate victim lay writhing, and began shouting 'I've been shot, I've been shot. Oh my legs.'

The really sad thing about this farce of a hit job is that the victim's mother was working behind the bar and it must have been a terrible experience for her to witness the shooting and then see her innocent son lying in agony on the floor of the pub. By the way, the shooting was featured in all the national papers and a crew from a London television station even interviewed the shot man in his hospital bed.

The 'hijack' team were later convicted, but instead of getting the expected ten years apiece, they received from 21 months to two and a half years. The owner of the warehouse got four years. Derek had a double punishment. As well as self-inflicted wounds, he got 21 months imprisonment. But, as he said at the time, 'I'd rather limp outside after 21 months, than walk properly inside for ten years.'

By the way, I later found out that Derek was a police informant. If that had been known at the time, I'm sure the gunman would not have missed ....

5
The Day I Beat Up Nizamodeen Hosein

For many years now I've shopped at the Co-op, and I'm a big fan of their philosophy - that the public are, in effect, the owners. I've collected their dividend stamps to stick in the family book, too. After all, I'm a great believer in sharing profits - even if I had to give some people a little persuasion now and then ....

One day I got to thinking about this. Through my shopping I'd put a lot of money their way, yet as an 'owner', I didn't seem to be getting very much back. I wasn't after a few stamps or a little bonus, though, I wanted the biggest 'divi' the Co-op had ever paid out in London - £70,000. For that was the figure I and a group of villain colleagues understood would be picked up on a certain day by Security Express from a north London Co-op.

For several weeks we took turns in observing the store. We discovered from which room the money was normally collected, how many helmeted guards went on the job, where they parked their van, and what time they picked up the cash. We knew the men from Security Express wouldn't give up their money without a struggle, so we decided that a little armed encouragement would be in order. No one in their right mind would argue when a shotgun was pointed at their head. As this was going to be a big job, we armed ourselves to the teeth. Between us we had three double-barrelled, sawn-off shotguns and three revolvers, plus pickaxe handles, crash helmets and balaclavas.

Besides the deadly weapons, the choice of vehicles is vital in a robbery, so we got a Ford Transit van. It had to be in good nick the escape, so our driver spent many loving hours tuning it up. We also 'borrowed' a genuine London taxi cab from a cabby as a getaway vehicle, though in the end we never used it. The cabby agreed to say that it had been stolen from outside his home if there were any problems later on.

With our frightening collection of weapons, we all piled into the Transit parked outside a flat we used - it also doubled as our armoury - and started the tense journey to the job.

I couldn't help laughing at our driver - he was dressed as a woman. I don't know whether he was kinky or whether he just felt that his feminine outfit would be a good disguise. Anyway, those rouged cheeks and laddered tights certainly didn't do much to arouse me that day - I was too concerned with the job in hand.

Two in the afternoon was the time set for the raid. That was when we estimated the security men would be calling for the £70,000. We all waited in a side road near the busy Co-operative store. What often narked me about these times of naked tension was that so-called grown men would argue over silly things. 'Let's have a bit of hush, I can't hear myself think,' I told one of the guys who wouldn't stop nervously rabbitting on. He was obviously trying to keep his spirits up, but he was breaking my concentration - I always wanted dead still before a job. I remember once a team member so irritated me by talking that I put a shotgun to his head and threatened to blow him to hell if he didn't shut his 'bloody mouth'. He did!

In the van we were keyed up to almost breaking point, knowing that within minutes we could be killing some innocent bystander. Despite that horrifying thought, we knew there was no going back. We had the job planned and we were professional robbers. The stakes, and the risks, were high.

My task was to amble from the van to the back of the store in civvies and follow the security guards up the stairs, as if I worked there. Then I would open up a fire exit which led across a flat roof. The raiders would climb a ladder to the roof, run across it, through the exit door, up the stairs and overpower the Security Express men, shooting or clubbing them if necessary. In their escape, shotguns would blast anyone who tried to stop them. I would be just an 'innocent bystander'.

The team had given me about four minutes to open the fire exit door. Then our tarted-up driver gave the order: 'Everybody out. Off you go, and good luck.' Meanwhile I had sidled into the store, found the staircase in question, walked up slowly and opened the fire exit door. By now the guards were already in the fortified room collecting the seventy grand. I stood by the fire exit until my pals came racing in. I waited and waited . . . but nothing happened.

Outside, they had put on their balaclavas and started their dash. Up the fire escape ladder they went at great speed – and into the first door they found open on the roof. Unfortunately it led into the canteen. There were screams from the staff finishing off their lunches and plates crashed to the ground. The gunmen had it fixed into their stupid minds that they should rush through the first open door they saw. The poor chap who had the misfortune to open that door was savagely clubbed on the head by an irate team member and he later needed twenty stitches in his wound. Meanwhile the gang ran back out onto the roof.

There they spotted me walking through the fire escape door towards them. 'We've gone through the wrong f....ng door,' shouted one of the team. 'Look, there's Mo. That's where we should have gone.'

Another shouted, 'We'll never make it before the police arrive. What a cock-up. Come on, let's get out of this place.'

With that the thwarted robbers, followed closely by me, clambered down the ladder and dashed towards the Ford Transit. They were brandishing guns at everyone in sight. I had a mask in my pocket, so I put it on as I ran. The whole tragic-comedy couldn't have been worse. To cap it, the 'souped-up' van had, by now, stalled and our 'Petticoat Pirate' was desperately trying to start it. He had positioned the van right by a busy street market, and there were screams as the masked gang ran through the bargain hunters.

As the ashen-faced driver desperately fiddled with the choke, several members of the gang stood menacingly pointing guns at traders and shoppers alike. For a moment the sounds of the Cockney market went deathly still. There was no barking out of sales patter from the stall holders. It seemed like time stood still for a couple of hellish minutes.

'Get that van started!' one of the gang yelled at the unfortunate driver as the flat battery failed to turn the engine. 'You and your souped-up van. This is terrible.'

Finally, the vehicle spluttered into life and chugged off from the scene, with the shotguns pointing out of the back in case anyone tried to give chase. Fortunately for us, and them, no one did.

'What a fiasco,' I shouted. 'I've never seen anything like that in all my life. You all went through the wrong door. What were you playing at?'

'Well, we assumed the first door was the one we had to go through,' said one taking off his mask. 'But all we could see was people eating.' 'Because of that we've lost seventy grand,' I shouted.

By now we were all near to tears of frustration. 'Seventy grand down the drain,' I kept repeating.

They dropped me off at the spot where I had previously parked my Cortina 1600E, and I took some guns from the van with me. I had rented a garage in Stoke Newington where I kept the car with part of my armoury in its boot.

So I never did get my 'divi' from the Co-op. But I don't hold that against them. I still get most of my groceries there ....

Before this chainstore chaos, I had been involved in a Long Firm garage fraud in Essex. And this was to result in me arranging for an attack to be made on a learned judge. But first things first. This astonishing motors' swindle happened at what was once a straight service station and car show room at Basildon. As usual a 'director' was installed as the front man and he obtained the necessary credit references. Once the firm's credibility was established, the orders for cars, petrol and accessories would be fulfilled. Our 'director' was obviously a good con artist because he persuaded one well-known supplier to let us have £10,000 worth of cars to be put on the garage forecourt. The deal was sale or return. Within hours of the shiny cars being delivered, they mysteriously disappeared, with some of the East End's most notorious motor dealers at the wheels. I've never seen cars vanish so quickly from a forecourt! Petrol and accessories had also come on credit and so for a short time we were all really coining it in, selling everything and just pocketing the takings. As a little bonus, I always kept my car filled with free petrol.

But our luck began to run out when a senior executive of the firm who had let us have the cars, happened to be driving past one night and noticed that all the motors had gone. Next morning he phoned and congratulated us on the success of our sales team. 'We never anticipated that they would sell so quickly,' he said.

'We did,' I told him, tongue in cheek. The man said he hoped some money for the cars would be on the way to him very quickly. 'Of course,' I reassured him. 'What do you think we are? Crooks?

I had hoped that my promise of cash would satisfy him, but when, after a few more days, the firm hadn't received a penny, they became suspicious. Another phone call came from the executive. And our response to this urgent request really put the cat amongst the pigeons. A member of the Long Firm told me that his company would get paid, but would have to wait their turn. 'We have to pay off other creditors first,' he was told.

'It's not my company's policy that other creditors are paid off with money owing to us,' he snapped. 'I am taking this matter further.' With that he slammed down the receiver.

'We all realised that within hours the 'Boys in Blue' would be paying us a visit, so it was decided to immediately abandon the firm, and take as much as possible. I loaded up a lorry with all sorts of car accessories, took £275 in cash from the till, and drove off. I sold the parts for several hundred pounds and lay low for a short time, hoping the police would not identify me with the fraud.

But they did! And as always, they came while I was in bed. I faintly heard a ring at the front door and tried to ignore it. I turned over to try and sleep again, but the ringing was insistent and finally I tramped downstairs and opened the door. There stood two of the biggest men I've ever seen. I'm no midget but they towered above me. Polite as always, one of them said to me, 'Good morning sir. I think you know who we are.' Wiping sleep from my eyes I said, 'Let me guess. Are you my fairy godfather? 'No, but you're getting warmer,' said one of the giants. 'Ok Mo, we won't keep you guessing. We're your guardian angels and we're taking you to Basildon police station, as we have reason to believe you can help us with our enquiries.'

The two flat-feet came upstairs to make sure I didn't try to escape out of a window and allowed me to get dressed. By now Maureen had awoken and I explained to her that these two CID officers had come to take me over to Basildon for a chat. She gave them a cup of tea while I put on clothes. As soon as I was ready, we headed towards the Essex town in an unmarked car. They kept asking me questions which I wasn't prepared to answer there and then. So I would counter with silly remarks like: 'Am I insured in this vehicle? If not, I don't want to ride in it.'

When I got to Basildon I was put on an identity parade and to my astonishment I was picked out by two witnesses. I was charged with the garage fraud and later bailed out at Billericay magistrate's court in my own recognisance of £100. It was certainly a nice surprise to be allowed bail for such a serious charge. I was told my case would be heard at Chelmsford Assizes.

As if that wasn't enough, I then got involved in an axe incident with a man I have never got on with. One night I was standing outside a Paddington pub after a good evening of drinking with some of my friends, when he came over to me and punched me in the face. Something snapped inside me and I was determined to kill him. 'I'll chop your head off!' I yelled as he dashed off down the dark street with me chasing after him. I had an axe hidden near my home so I fetched it and went rampaging up and down the street trying to find him. If I had, there would certainly have been a summary execution. I was now twenty-two years old and as callous as anyone in Britain.

An Indian trader whose shop was still open at that late hour saw me and dialled 999. As soon as I heard the wailing siren, I tried to hide. The police car screamed up a few yards from me and out poured the officers. I ran for my life and dived headfirst through a plate glass window into a derelict house, still clasping the axe. While I lay there bleeding amidst the broken glass, they arrested me. I was charged at Harrow Road police station with possessing an offensive weapon and was given a one month prison sentence at Marylebone magistrate's court.

When the Long Firm trial started at Chelmsford - there were four of us in the dock - I was surprised to find that the judge travelled down each day on the same train as me from Liverpool Street. He would read *The Times* in a first-class carriage, while I slummed it with the *Sun* in a second-class compartment. As we boarded each morning he would nod at me and I would smile at him. It was certainly a strange relationship. As we were already on nodding terms, I thought up a scheme whereby he would actually be in my debt. And now for the first time I am going to reveal my plan to thwart the course of justice. I hired a criminal friend to try to snatch his briefcase in the morning rush-hour crowds at Liverpool Street. I planned to be on hand to jump on the dastardly attacker, scuffle with him, and then grab the judge's case, and return it to him. I hoped he would be lenient with me when my sentence was passed. I gave the criminal a detailed description of the judge and held my breath on the platform that morning as he came strolling towards the train, his briefcase in his hands. My friend pounced - on the wrong man. There was an astonishing battle going on there in front of hundreds of people with my inept friend trying to snatch the briefcase while the man beat him about the head with his brolly. In the end he ran off empty-handed - and another of my plans had gone awry.

I don't know if the judge witnessed the incident, but he never discovered what I had planned. If he had, I am sure he would have thrown the book at me. As it was, the judge was still very kind. We all got between nine months and a year for the fraud which was estimated at about £40,000.

So I was to be detained at Her Majesty's Prison at Wormwood Scrubs, that monstrosity set close to the heartland of much of west London's crime, Shepherds Bush. I decided, as those huge wooden gates clanged shut behind me, that I would try to keep out of trouble, and at the same time endeavour to make as much money as possible while I was inside. Yes, there is money to be made in prison, lots of it. It's just that you have to know how to do it. I knew the key to money-making behind bars was to become a red-band, a trusty, who has lots of freedom around the place.

One of the first capers I got up to was to become postman for some of the Great Train Robbers, who were inside for 30 years for their part in that fantastic operation in the sixties in which they held up an express train and pinched a fortune. The Great Train Robbery took place at Sears Crossing, Buckinghamshire in August 1963 when £2,631,000 was snatched by the gang. During the execution of the crime, train driver Jack Mills was savagely beaten and has since died. Most of the gang, who between them collected prison sentences totalling 365 years, are now out on parole after serving substantial parts of their 30-year sentences. Much of the money that was stolen has never been recovered.

My job was to get hold of illegal letters, called stiffs, from other members of the gang and inmates of other prisons, and get them to them. The letters were 'posted' when a prisoner was transferred from another prison to the Scrubs, and he would be given letters and messages for people. I would grab the letters for the Great Train Robbers and slip them in to them. It wasn't easy, because they were in Top Security, but I always did it. In fairness, I never read one of those letters and so I have no knowledge to this day of their contents. I would also take and pass messages for many of the other prisoners. So what with that and my contraband booze and cigarette enterprises, I was often pulling as much as £15 a week. A fortune in prison, as anyone who has done porridge will tell you.

Normally, my profits came from what I considered legitimate prison enterprises, but one windfall came from a particularly nasty con that I pulled on a nasty poof, who had committed a serious offence against a child. I was determined to get him for it and when he showed me £50 in readies on the night of his arrival, I realised he would be an easy touch. He lovingly fingered the cash and asked innocently, 'Can you buy things in here? I've got all this cash. You see I wasn't properly searched when I came in.' I said to myself, 'Mo, your problems are solved.' I asked him if he drank and smoked and he said he did. 'If you hand over the dough, I can bring you hundreds of cigarettes and plenty of drink,' I promised him. 'Would you really?' he said touching my arm affectionately. 'Oh Mo, that is so kind of you.' I kept my feelings in check - I wanted to smash him in the face - and told him, 'Don't mention it,' tucking the £50 in my pocket.

I hid the money in the grounds and tried to keep out of his way. But he managed to track me down after four days and told me he was leaving next morning and either wanted the promised goods or his money back. I thought he was going to scratch my eyes out when I said I couldn't promise either. I knew he had to be out next day by 9 am so I began sweeping up in the yard where I knew he couldn't find me. 'Oh, has the poof gone?' I innocently asked one of the other prisoners as I came in for lunch. 'He was after you, Mo. What have you done to him?' I smiled and pointed to my nose. 'Mind your own business,' I told him with a grin.

It was shortly after this windfall that I was offered a large amount of money to beat up Nizamodeen Hosein, who with his brother, Arthur, is now serving a life sentence for the kidnapping and murder of Mrs Muriel McKay, the wife of Alick McKay, the deputy chairman of the *News of the World*. Mrs McKay vanished from her Wimbledon home on December 29, 1969 and shortly after that the Hosein brothers demanded a million pound ransom. Her body was never found and the brothers have never given the police any help in pin-pointing Mrs McKay's hidden grave, which could have been taken into account when they were eventually considered for parole. Some years after the murder, Detective Chief Superintendent Bill Smith visited Nizamodeen in Parkhurst. 'What happened to her?' asked the burly bow-tied copper. He waited patiently while the dark-skinned young man considered the question. Then came a burst of laughter. It echoed round the office in the prison, and police hopes of solving the last mystery in the McKay case faded. When his outburst subsided, Hosein said with a smile: 'Oh, it's all too long ago.' His callous refusal to help could cost him years in prison. The life sentence for Mrs McKay's murder was given along with an additional 39 years for kidnapping her, demanding the million pound ransom and sending threatening letters.

Smith, the ex-police chief, who was called in after Mrs McKay first vanished from her home, said later about Nizamodeen: 'I spoke to him for about half an hour. As far as I'm concerned, he's mad - both brothers are. But he once said I was "a very nice man". So we were able to talk. We just talked around it, then I picked my time and put it to him gently. He just laughed and said it was all a long time ago.'

So the final resting place of 55-year-old Mrs McKay and the full story of her last tragic hours alive will not be revealed for years ... if ever.

I never found out who made the half-grand offer to me, but they obviously trusted me to do a good job in beating up this weird killer. The problem was that Hosein was a category 'A' prisoner, which meant he was not all that easy to get at. My break came when he was marched into the wing where I was working with two screws who for some reason sat him in a chair. They then disappeared and he just sat there grinning. Seeing my moment, I went over to him and said, 'You killed a beautiful lady.' He continued to smile like an imbecile so I then laid into him with my head and fists. I just bashed him all over the face and head with incredible fury. Cuts began appearing all over his head and face, and he screamed like a little girl as my blows rained down on him. 'Stop, please stop! You are hurting me,' he pleaded. But I wouldn't. The row brought prison officers from every direction and they dived at me. By now Hosein lay on the floor covered in blood. As they dragged me away, I yelled at him, 'Now you know what Mrs McKay must have gone through, you bastard.'

I managed for a moment to break away from the prison officers and go for him again, but they grabbed me before I could do any more damage to this pathetic, frightened killer. His limp body was carried off to the hospital wing for treatment, and I was put in a solitary cell. A message was passed, via a prisoner to the anonymous client that the job was done and the £500 in cash was delivered to an address I had given. Mind you, at that time I think I would have done it for nothing.

For such a vicious attack I was surprised that I was not charged with grievous bodily harm, but for some reason I wasn't. Instead I was given 14 days solitary confinement, which included on off number-one diet - three days of bread and water and three days on an ordinary diet - up to the end of the 14 days. I also lost pay for 28 days. Solitary is always a painful experience, but it was worth it for the satisfaction of making that man suffer - and getting handsomely paid for it. Of course if the incident had come out in the press, the public I am sure, would have been probably in my favour.

After I came out I saw Nizamodeen again in a workshop where he helped to make tents. When he saw me he cowered in a corner, but this time I left him alone.

My next bit of trouble came when I went to assault a particularly obnoxious screw. We all knew it was a matter of time until he did some sky-diving from the fourth balcony - it was just a question of who would get him. The man was an ex-marine. He said things like, 'Come on you slags, get back to your cells.' One day he was ranting and raving and I couldn't resist saying to him, 'Is your face hurting you?' He bristled and said, 'No, why?' I replied, 'Because it's killing me.' By now I'd had enough of this pig so I added, 'Now, I'm going to kill you.' He could see the evil glint in my eyes and ran to try and raise the alarm. I gave chase and grabbed his arm, but was quickly jumped on by several officers. Nicked again. It was back to the punishment block for more bread and water. I got 28 days for this and lost seven days remission. I thought I was never going to get out at this rate.

When I got back to my cell I found that some vulture had stolen all my orange juice, sugar, biscuits, soap and toothpaste. When I tracked down the culprit, he said, 'It was only a joke, mate.' With that I smashed him in the mouth, and said, 'Now laugh that off,' as four of his teeth fell out.

Eventually the time came to bid farewell to my first real spell in prison. On the last evening I walked into a surprise that I had never bargained for. I couldn't make out why everyone was staring at me and laughing as I went to get a mug of tea. All of a sudden 15 prisoners pounced on me and pulled down my trousers. As I lay there wriggling they began putting boot polish on my private parts with shoe brushes. 'Get off you bastards!' I yelled as they continued blacking me up. I didn't realise that this was a tradition inside. The idea is to prevent you having sex with a woman when you first leave. About 100 cheering prisoners clapped as I rose to my feet and hitched up my pants after the ordeal. It took hours to remove that awful stuff. I went through agony in the shower that night trying to scrub it off. I finally went to bed in agony in the most sensitive part of my anatomy.

Next morning shared out to my two cell mates what was left of my possessions, such as sugar, tea, cornflakes and soap, shook hands with them and made my way to the reception room where I was given the suit I had arrived in. I had put on quite a bit of weight inside and so I had difficulty getting into it.

Then the nasty screw gave me a shock. 'O'Mahoney, you'll be interested to hear that a policeman is waiting to re-arrest you when you get out of the door,' he sniggered.

I nearly passed out, thinking my other crimes had now been discovered. But I took a deep breath and walked out through those huge wooden gates and strode towards the officer waiting on a motor bike for me. 'Are you Maurice O'Mahoney?' he asked. 'No,' I replied, and kept walking. The bewildered officer revved up his bike, drove to the gate and saw the screw that I had already left. 'That's him,' he said, pointing at my figure in the distance. He came zooming back and caught me up. 'Are you trying to make a fool of me?' he thundered. 'Sorry,' I countered. 'I didn't realise you wanted me.'

Then he handed me a summons - for a driving offence I had committed before going inside. I was caught doing 80 mph in a 30 mph area. He couldn't understand why my face lit up and was thanking him profusely. 'People don't normally thank me for doing this,' he said. Little did he know how relieved I was.

Before the hearing at Wells Street magistrate's court, I walked into the warrant office there. Nobody challenged me so searched around until I found a file on my case. Maybe they thought I was a solicitor or something, but no one questioned me as I picked up the file and walked out with it under my arm. I disposed of it quickly and was amused with the confusion in the court later. When the officer who gave me the summons stood in the dock, his face turned red as he confessed to the woman chairman of the bench, 'Madam, er . . . all the documents relating to O'Mahoney's case seem to have disappeared!'

So the magistrate adjourned the case *sine die*. 'There's been enough time wasted on this trivial matter,' she said as she admonished the police officer.

I bowed my head towards her and thanked her for her consideration. As we left the court, the officer came up to me and said, 'I don't know you very well O'Mahoney, but how did you do it?'

I winked and replied jokingly, 'Well you see officer, the magistrate's an old flame of mine ... '

6
'Whisky A-Go-Go'

A raging toothache was to guide me accidentally to a unique money-making scheme, which not only got rid of the pain in my aching molar, but also helped me to bite straight back into the good life.

At a loose end one day, I decided to pop round to see the father of a prisoner I had met in the Scrubs and deliver a message to him that his son was fine. The old chap was very hospitable and immediately put the kettle on for a cup of coffee while we chatted about life inside.

As the kettle came to the boil in the kitchen of his council house in north London, I asked him what sort of job he did. 'I'm Chief Security Officer for an international freight company,' he said. 'I'm responsible for all sorts of valuable cargoes.'

Trying not to show too much interest, but sensing money, BIG MONEY, I said, 'Oh yes, what sort of things?'

'Well, whisky, cigarettes, perfume, all sorts of things like that,' he replied handing me the cup. As he spoke I took a sip of the hot drink and let out a yelp as it struck a nerve in a loose tooth. 'Would you like an Anadin [*] for that?' the old boy said. 'I've got lots of packets of them here.'

'Oh, that's very kind of you. Do you store them at your warehouse?' I asked as I popped a couple of them into my aching mouth.

'Oh yes, we have thousands of boxes. The warehouse is covered with them. There's enough there to knock out a town. Why do you ask?'

Not knowing whether to come straight out or not, I hedged for a moment and then took the plunge. He knew I was a villain, but I didn't know his pedigree. 'Do you want to sell any of

---

* Again for our American readers. Anadin is a brand of painkillers sold in the UK. These include several different types, but the original Anadin were Aspirin and caffeine based,

---

these?' I asked. 'Who to?' he asked. 'Well, I think I may be able to find you a few customers,' I told him.

Obviously the temptation was too much, and he told me to come up with an order and a fair price, and he'd consider it. We shook hands on the plan, and I left to visit some friends who owned a warehouse. I asked them if they were interested in buying boxes of Anadins and they said they were. I quoted them a price of £60 a box, which I believed was about half the retail price. 'I'll have ten cases,' said one of the greedy directors. 'Done,' I said. I went back to see the security boss and told him I had managed to persuade a contact to buy ten boxes at £20 a box. He was highly delighted and we agreed to go fifty-fifty on that price. He was even more pleased when I said I would take another ten boxes on top of that and try to sell them, too.

He told me the best time to collect the pain-killers was on the following Saturday afternoon.

'Things are quiet at the warehouse then,' he explained. So at one pm, I backed my car into the huge building and he helped me to load the 20 boxes quickly into the boot. I took them to my first customers and their faces dropped when I told them, 'I'm afraid I couldn't get you ten boxes lads.' But they burst into smiles when I added, 'I've managed to get you twenty instead.' Their faces lit up like the star of David as they carried them into the warehouse. 'How do you do it Mo?' they chuckled as they went to the safe and counted out £1,000 for me in used notes.

With a grand in my pocket I later met up with the security chief in a pub and handed him £200 in a plain envelope in the toilets. 'I thought I'd never see you again,' he said gratefully. 'I must say Mo, it's a pleasure to do business with you.' 'Likewise,' I said. 'I think now you owe me a drink.' He thought he had done really well getting half of my sale of 20 cases at £20 each. I think I would have needed a mouthful of painkillers if he discovered how I had double-crossed him. But that's business and he did accept my offer.

We propped up the bar that night for several hours talking through other plans that could prove profitable to us. For the time being though, we decided to stick to Anadins. So each Saturday lunch-time I would back my car into the warehouse and we would fill it with cases of the drug. Each time I drove to the entrance of the Aladdin's Cave, I thought how interesting it would be to actually have a guided tour of the place to see what other goodies could be lifted.

One day he took the hint. 'OK, Mo, come tomorrow, and I'll show you over,' he promised.

I arrived on the Sunday complete with a notebook and a sharpened pencil, and my eyes 'photographed' each part as he guided me through the bays which were jam-packed with every type of saleable product imaginable. I listed the bay numbers and what they contained. Then he showed me the fleet of articulated lorries waiting to leave with their precious loads next morning.

'Most of these,' he said pointing at about six monsters in the far corner of the yard, 'are loaded full of whisky. You'd be a rich man if you could hijack one of them. Each load is worth about

£40,000.' I smiled and said nothing.

I also met Prince, the Alsatian guard dog that day - an animal I guessed I would need to make friends with. So I took time out to be pally and spoil him. 'He only barks at people he doesn't know,' my contact explained. 'That's why I'm making a fuss of him,' I grinned.

The more I thought of it the more I realised that although the weekly Anadin run was still very profitable, I was missing out on the really big money. The thought of hijacking one of those whisky lorries became more and more appealing to me. I carefully assembled around myself a team that I felt would be capable of doing a job of this magnitude. It wasn't just a matter of doing the actual hijacking that was important. The successful selling of the booze, and disposing of the truck were also vital.

As always my security officer friend was the key. He supplied me with the full route that the lorry picked out for the job would be taking. We decided that the best spot for the foul deed to take place was a side street close to Tower Bridge. As a theatrical touch, I thought it would be good if we all wore wigs over our balaclavas. What a frightening bunch of individuals we must have looked. The articulated lorry was tailed for about 20 minutes after picking it up part way along the route, and when we came to the spot chosen for the hijack, one of our vans zoomed past and stopped. The alarmed truck driver slammed on his anchors, while the other car stopped behind and we all jumped out and aimed shotguns at his head. 'OK lads, I'll come quietly,' he said on seeing us. He jumped down to the road and was bundled into one of the vans.

A team member took the giant articulated lorry to a secret destination which we called the slaughter, while the driver was taken and dumped at the road side outside London. He was unharmed because he didn't try and cause us problems. Wise man.

I told my security man friend that I was delighted with his help, and we discussed an even more daring plan . . . to actually steal two of the whisky lorries from the depot. 'That would save us the trouble of doing another hijack in a street, which always means that someone could get hurt,' I told him.

He agreed and another 'slaughter' was found. Buyers were also alerted, and we went ahead on a Sunday evening with our cheeky plan to take the two lorryloads of scotch from the yard.
There was a major problem confronting us, however. An old man was on duty all night and he had to ring in to a security number every half hour and give a coded message that he was all right. If he didn't do this, the police would immediately be alerted.

Prince also had to be taken care of so his barking didn't raise the alarm.

A railway line ran alongside the warehouse and that night we scrambled over the top of the high wire fence and dropped down into the yard. All of a sudden Prince charged at us, but when he saw me he screeched to a halt and began jumping up at me and licking my face. 'Good boy,' I whispered as I patted him on the head. 'Good boy Prince. Now be quiet.' He suddenly broke away and began playfully chasing all over the yard. He thought it was all a game, but I knew I had to catch him and bundle him into a spare cab so he wouldn't cause us any more problems. I finally grabbed him, lifted him up into a lorry and put him in with his food and water. Then I shut the door firmly.

With all the commotion, the old man came to investigate and he was gently jumped on by some of the gang and told to be quiet.

'Look Pop, you won't get hurt if you don't cause us any problems,' said one of the gang. 'Now which way do you want it?' he was asked. 'I'll do whatever you want me too,' he sensibly replied, his false teeth chattering with fear.

The security boss had told me the index numbers of the two lorries we could take, and we soon found them. 'Come on, let's start one of them up,' I said urgently to the man deputed to drive it. But would that gleaming monster start? No fear! He tried and tried but the engine would not fire. So he got out and swung back the cab to examine it. While he was doing that I realised it was about time for Pop to report in. 'Look, I want you to phone as you normally do and say what you need to, so that they won't know something's up,' I told him. He was grateful not to have been knocked about, so he dutifully complied.

Back in the yard, my driver desperately kept trying to start the engine and finally did so. With all this agro getting the truck started, we decided to take just the one this time. I donned the old man's security hat, borrowed his keys and opened the barrier at the main gates as the truck swung out and on to a main road.

Pop was taken and dumped in Southend. He was found bound, but unhurt, on an allotment. Meanwhile the rest of us, followed the truck and quickly unloaded it at our secret destination. The bottles of whisky sold out within several days.

What made the robbery even more amusing was that we did it on the very night that television personality Shaw Taylor * was telling ITV viewers on 'Police Five' about the previous week's whisky lorry hijack. I got a particular chuckle when I tuned in the following Sunday and he said: 'Do you remember me telling you last week about the hijacking of a lorry laden with whisky? Well this week the thieves actually went into the depot and drove out another articulated lorry. And the cheek of it was that while I explained the hijacking to you, they were actually in the depot taking another one.'

He said there would now be two rewards for information leading to the arrest of those responsible and the recovery of the whisky and the trucks, I poured a drink of scotch from that second load, and lifted my glass to the screen. 'Good hunting, Shaw,' I said.

---

* Again for our American readers. Shaw Taylor (born 1924) is an actor and TV presenter, best known for present-ing *Police 5*, a long-running 5-minute television programme first broadcast in 1962 that appealed to the public to help solve crimes.

I would sometimes see Shaw, the debonair crook-catcher, in his car as I drove about London. He would give me a courteous smile as we pulled up side by side at the traffic lights and one day I mouthed at him, 'Stop talking about me like that on television.' Of course he had no idea what I was saying and grinned at me.

I know many of my villain friends were very worried by the success of 'Police Five' and one day they talked to me about attacking Shaw's wife at the antique shop she runs in London. They wanted to tie her up, but that was only stupid. 'After all he's only doing his job,' I said. 'If it wasn't him, someone else would do it.'

All I can say now, Shaw, is keep up the good work as you are a big deterrent to villains.

I'm afraid the team was a bit nasty towards my security officer friend and often didn't give him his cut for all his valuable co-operation. Like most crooks, they had become very greedy and didn't see why they should share out large percentages to anyone. It was a counter-productive philosophy, but often greed has no logic. He started to moan that he was owed thousands of pounds. 'Look Mo, I've got nothing yet from the whisky lorries. I don't think it's fair. I'm taking the risks as well as you,' he whined. I sympathised, but the rest of the gang didn't want to pay. The team began to worry that he would go to the police in spite and shop the lot of us. So I was dispatched to his home one night. He was terrified when I explained that if he did he would not only disappear but his body would never be found again.

'Not even your Anadins will be able to help you then,' I said. I felt very sorry for this whimpering nonentity, as he had been a marvellous contact. But none of us would have hesitated in killing him if he had even hinted to the police what had been going on. So far he, and we, had been kept clear of the police investigations into the robberies.

A grave-digger called Arthur was to be the next key to riches for me and the team. Arthur had worked at Kensal Green cemetery, but hadn't been too good at his job - in fact he'd been a dead loss - and was fired. Arthur, who was about 30, fat and shabbily dressed, came round to see me. He was despondent about not having a job, but I had a brainwave. Maybe I could get him in as a security officer at the depot where we had stolen the whisky lorry. He could become our new contact there, instead of the disillusioned Chief Security Officer.

'How would you like to become a security guard?' I asked Arthur. 'I'd love it, Mo. Anything would be better than sitting around all the time with nothing to do.' 'Good, I'll see what I can do,' I told him: So I helped him compile a letter applying for a job there and told him exactly what to say if and when he got an interview. Well, it worked, and soon Arthur was a trusted security man there.

I quickly explained to him that he wasn't there just to earn wages for himself, but to assist me and my team in our various forms of skullduggery. 'Here's £50 as an advance against the work I want you to do,' I said. 'If you let me down your job will be forfeited.' Arthur was to get 20 per cent of everything that we got out of the place, so he had quite a bit to lose if anything went wrong.

I left him a week or so to find his feet, and then began to lean on him. Because I knew the place inside out, I would tell him what I wanted and would turn up each week representing 'O'Mahoney Enterprises', and he would help me load up the gear - whisky, perfume, and, of course, our good old standby - Anadins, by the hundreds of thousands. The security chief had no idea that Arthur was my man, and we always loaded up when we knew he was off duty.

Over a period of months I got several hundred thousand pounds' worth of stuff from the place. Then came what was going to be the biggest robbery I had ever done. There were three articulated lorries about to go out on a Monday morning with a combined load worth nearly £100,000. 'But at the last moment, I found the guy who was to supply the 'slaughter' had gone off to America for three months. There wasn't time to find somewhere else, so I dropped this plan. It was a terrible blow to literally have to pour all the whisky down the drain.

At the same time the security chief began to get suspicious about the large quantities of goods that were still going missing from the depot. He started to suspect that someone on the inside was involved. So I decided that I had better do a 'moody' burglary there. This is a phony break-in to make it seem that an outsider has been burgling the place.

To get in that night I had to scale the 20 foot wire fence from the railway siding again, move some gear around to make a bit of a mess, and then make my escape. That would take the suspicion off Arthur for a while. I decided to take another guy with me and we put on balaclavas and were quickly over the top.

We had hardly touched down when I heard a commotion and saw a group of coppers dashing towards us. Someone had spotted us skulking around the wire and raised the alarm, so we had to quickly rescale the fence to escape. It had barbed wire on top and was quite easy to climb over if you didn't rush, but in these circumstances there wasn't time for hanging about. My mate was over first and I scrambled up after him. But as I swung myself over the top I caught my stomach on the spikes. The rusty barbs tore into my guts, but I gritted my teeth, extricated myself and then jumped the 20 feet to the floor. I fell awkwardly on a stone and twisted my ankle.

The pain of my shredded stomach and twisted ankle was something else, but at least I'd got away from the boys in blue. One of them glared at me through the fence and said desperately, 'I can't climb this.' He was about two feet away through the wire. Then he added, 'Don't you dare move. I'll come round and get you.' I put on a good Irish accent as I looked at him through the slits in my balaclava. 'Go and have it off with a duck,' I told him as I hobbled off into the night. I knew this would at least convince the people at the depot that someone had been in stealing stuff.

But my troubles still weren't over. I had to walk through a railway tunnel to make my escape, and as I was part-way through I saw sparks in the dark and heard the roar of a train approaching. I fell to the ground at the side of the tunnel and fortunately was not hurt by the roaring monster. I then kept limping until I came up at the nearest station, climbed up and walked through the ticket barrier. No one was on duty at the time. I couldn't drive because my leg was by now like a balloon. So I caught a bus home.

'When I saw Arthur on the following day, he said I had caused plenty of amusement amongst the police officers. One of them had told him, 'I've met some cheeky bastards in my time, but that guy beats them all.' Arthur told him, 'How do you work that out mate?' The officer said,

'The guy vaulted the fence like a half-starved Biafran looking for a banana. And then he told me to 'Go f... a duck".'

But Arthur's luck wasn't to last. The security chief began to realise that he was working for me and asked him to look for another employer. He was very nice about it, and even gave him references for his next job. Which amazingly turned out to be another security post …

7
'you are Going Out with One of the Most Dangerous Men in London'

My love for my wife Maureen was a flame that had by now gone out. She hated me, I despised her, and we only lived together because of our children. It was a highly volatile relationship that was always flaring up into bitter rows.

Things weren't improved by Maureen's insistence on locking me out if I wasn't in by a certain time. I often used to return in the early hours after a successful evening of villainy and find the door locked and bolted like Fort Knox. I had made the place safe now my skill was working against me. She had so many security devices on the inside of the front door that there was no way I could get in once she had locked it. I would bang it, shout and ring the bell; I often woke the whole street, but she just lay in bed, determined to make me suffer.

In desperation I would try to get a bed at a friend's house or in a hotel with rooms still empty at that time of night. It got to such a stage that in the end I wouldn't even bother going home if it was late. I would just check into a hotel and then make my way home the next morning.

I can understand that my wife resented my wicked life, but she never complained about the ease of living it brought her. Our flat was so luxurious that a film star would have been happy to live there. I once estimated that I had spent about £8,000 decorating and furnishing the place. But despite my financial generosity towards her - I was always buying her jewellery and other presents - a meal from Maureen was a rare delicacy. Usually I had to go to the chippy or munch a pie in the pub. We irritated each other beyond words.

So when I met dark-haired Susan, she was like a vision of loveliness in every way. She was sensitive, pretty and someone I fell in love with immediately.

Our first meeting was in a Fulham disco where I would go to dance off the frustrations of my marriage - and also meet villains. Susan, in her early twenties, was a cashier there and as I handed over my entrance fee I came up with my usual corny line. 'Hey beautiful, why are you working in a dump like this?' I asked her. 'I have to work because I have a child to support,' she replied. 'No husband?' I queried. 'I'm separated from him,' she said. As I looked at Susan's beautiful, but sad face, I exclaimed: 'He must be mad!'

She seemed taken aback by the compliment, and blushed as I added, 'If I had a lovely wife like you, I wouldn't let you out of my sight.' With that I took my ticket and went into the noisy, thumping, seething place, which was packed like sardines with people dancing to soul music. Strobe lights in rainbow colours flashed on and off. I watched the dancing for a few minutes and then went upstairs to discuss business with three of the bouncers who worked there. We had met on a previous visit and they had told me they were fed up only earning £6 for a night on the door dealing with the awkward customers. 'We're after some really big money. Have you got any work for us Mo?' one of them had asked me. I told them to come up with ideas for jobs themselves and then we'd talk further.

Well, this night we stood in an upstairs corner and one of the bouncers - let me call him Malcolm - who was about 16 stone and very tough looking, said he knew a place where we could do a £10,000 wages snatch. It was at a builder's firm on the western outskirts of London. They pay out to the workers early every Thursday afternoon,' he told me.

So we agreed that we would keep observation on the firm each Thursday for a few weeks. It wasn't too difficult because we knew the bank where the wages were collected, and there was a café exactly opposite it. I would have toast and coffee as I watched employees from the firm come for the ten grand at the same time each week.

Now we had a pattern established. We knew the exact times the money was collected and later paid out. I told the bouncers that the job was on. I checked the roads around the building firm and worked out a getaway route. The car to be used was a Ford 1300 Cortina which I'd stolen from Kilburn High Road, and then false number plates were put on it.

On the morning of the job we all met up at a Wimpy Bar in North End Road, Hammersmith, and talked through exactly what had to be done. I, as always, relished the job, but I could see that these muscled novices were getting decidedly edgy and I told them to just keep cool and not get too worked up. 'It's an easy job, this one,' I said, as we devoured hamburgers and chips. We then piled into our cars and drove to where the change-over point was to be. Then we got into the stolen Cortina and went the short distance to the yard.

It was one o'clock when we zoomed in through the gates, turned round near the cement lorries and screeched to a stop facing out towards the main road and next to a door marked 'Offices'. We noticed some men coming out clutching wage packets. We all quickly masked up and jumped out of the car, carrying sawn-off shotguns. One of the gang also had a policeman's truncheon.

The paddies who had just got their cash sensibly decided not to interfere with the raid and we dashed up the stairs to the office. A few seconds later a shotgun blast went off and blew a huge hole in the ceiling. There was a snowstorm of plaster. A man rushed out of an office to see what the commotion was about and he was bashed in the face with a fist. Then the butt of a shotgun sent him spinning. With that we went into the office he had come from and realised we were in the wrong place. There was no money in there.

Another terrified employee pointed to another room. 'It's the office over there, mate,' he said. 'The one over there.' There must have been at least ten people cowering in terror in the room when we entered. One woman, obviously pregnant, was shaking with fear. The money we were after was scooped up and dropped into a canvas shopping bag we had brought with us, while our guns covered the staff. One false move from any of them and a shotgun would have blasted them through the heart and into eternity.

'OK, let's get out of here,' I shouted. We ran down the stairs as fast as we could, but just as we got outside an alarm bell went off. 'Keep moving,' I roared. We piled into the car, with our balaclavas still on, put our weapons on the floor, and shot out into the main road.

Suddenly our hearts dropped a mile. A policeman was directing traffic at a busy intersection just outside the yard because the traffic lights had failed. But when he saw us he just waved us through. I am sure he must have thought his eyes were deceiving him as he saw us flash by and realised we were wearing masks.

But by the time he could collect his thoughts we were just dust on the horizon. We soon arrived at our change-over point, unmasked, jumped into our own cars and then drove straight back along the road, past the copper directing traffic. We watched with pleasure as we saw police cars with their blue flashing lights and wailing sirens pouring into the yard.

With the money from the raid in my pocket, I plucked up courage to go back to the disco and ask Susan for a date. When I was on a job I had no real care for anyone, yet I became tongue-tied when I approached her at the payment desk to ask her out.

She made it easier when she gave me a lovely welcoming smile. When I asked her if she would care to join me for a meal in a particularly expensive restaurant, she said, 'Of course I'd like to come out with you.'

When we got into the high-class diner later that week, I did something I had never done for Maureen - I pulled a chair out for Susan to sit on. I found my manners change for the better. I couldn't help myself, for Susan seemed to bring out the best in me.

'I must tell you that I am married, Susan,' I said as I sipped the champagne. 'But I'm very unhappy with my wife.' She wasn't shocked. In fact she had already guessed.

I felt as if I was discovering a completely new world as I sat with this lovely lady. She, too poured out her heart about her broken marriage. We were like a couple of lovesick kids. Afterwards we went to a party and danced closely together into the early hours. I told her that I was a successful car dealer and she believed me.

We agreed that we would start going out regularly and I already knew I had fallen head over heels in love with Susan. I even began seriously thinking of giving up my evil life of crime and settling down to a straight existence. I said to myself that I would do a couple more 'biggies' and then quit crime while I was still ahead.

We used to go for long drives in my car and discuss our respective lives. I would tell her about my children and the hellish existence I had with my wife. I would shower Susan with beautiful gifts and she would always try and refuse them. But I would tell her, 'Look, Susan, I've had a good deal with a motor car. Please take my gift. I'm only trying to show you what I think of you.'

She explained that she didn't want my money, or my car, all she wanted was happiness. 'I've had so little of it in my life so far, Maurice,' she told me. 'To me happiness is the most valuable thing there is.'

Then came a crisis point in our relationship when a crook told her, 'Do you realise that you are going out with one of the most dangerous men in London?' She couldn't understand it. All she saw in me was a kind and loving man. She had no idea of my double life. So when she confronted me with what this man had said, I felt I owed it to her to be honest, and owned up. Rather than drop me there and then, she told me she wanted me to give up my criminal activities. 'I will shortly, I promise you,' I told her. And at that moment, I meant it.

I felt concerned for her working at that particular disco, so I persuaded her to leave. I didn't like her mixing with the villains who frequented the place.

Again my violent temper got the better of me and I found myself in all sorts of trouble for attacking a relief manager in a Paddington pub. I had gone into the boozer to intimidate witnesses who were to give evidence against two friends of mine. These two grasses, instead of lying low, were spending each evening in a particular pub. So I went in and began 'accidentally' spilling drinks on them, and stepping on their toes. I wanted to provoke them into attacking me, thus discrediting them, but they kept their cool. The relief manager watched all of this and finally told me to knock if off.

'I'll knock you off if you don't button it,' I told him. Then I seized a soda syphon and smashed it down on his head, leapt the counter and began grappling with him. At the end of the encounter we were both in quite a bad way, in fact two of his teeth became embedded in my head during the no-holds-barred fight. Police were called and I was charged with GBH (grievous bodily harm). The two witnesses to the incident were the pair I had previously tried to intimidate. So just before my trial at the Old Bailey, I found them in another pub and asked the shaking pair to join me in the toilets. As they walked in I produced a revolver and asked them, 'Are you going to testify against me? Because if you do, you will both die.' They knew I meant business and managed to say, 'We wouldn't give evidence against you, Mo.' I gave them both £100 to spend a day at the seaside on the date of my trial.

At the Bailey I smiled to myself as I watched the police desperately try to find their two key witnesses. Finally they had to admit defeat, and I was acquitted for lack of evidence. The drunken pair returned to London that night, and I got off. The police were very angry.

Someone else came into my life about this time. As I mentioned earlier, I never got on well with my parents, so I was more than thrilled when I met up with a villain and his wife who became, for a time, substitute parents. I'll call them Jim and Jennifer. They were much older than me and made me part of their family. I spent many hours at their north London home, enjoying Jennifer's tasty meals and the sense of belonging I got from them. They were particularly good at the times when I was on the run from the police. I didn't dare go near Maureen as the police were watching the flat all the time.

But because of my evidence, Jim is now serving 15 years in prison. He hates me with all his heart. In fact, at his trial at the Old Bailey, he leaned over the dock and said to me, 'I'm going to kill you and your kids.'

Jim doesn't realise how lucky he was to survive that remark. I nearly grabbed the revolver from my police bodyguard's holster and shot him dead. Although I was a brutal man I never would harm anyone's wife or child. And I would expect others to do the same. Our war is with each other. Kill or be killed - but only involve villains. I don't think the public realise even now how dangerous it was for me to make my decision to turn Queen's Evidence. I had good reason to do it and I'll go into that more fully later. But one thing I want to make clear here is that I didn't do it for spite, or to gain a lenient sentence. I did it because I was betrayed by my own people. At first I was prepared to go to prison for them and even give them their freedom, because most of the evidence was against me. But as you'll find out later, they wanted to kill my girlfriend Susan, whom I loved very much and also to maim one of her family. I think I could take anything that they could do to me, because deep down I know there will be assassination attempts, but they should never dare to threaten any woman or child. That's not part of the code for the criminal world.

In a way Jim's sentence broke my heart. And as the judge passed sentence on him I thought of the good times we had had together. I always called him, 'Big Jim, the Gentle Giant'. But his threat to me was far from gentle that day.

However, it wasn't always like that. Jim was one of my closest friends. He was over six feet tall, weighed about 16 stone and was as strong as an ox. I know when he comes out he will not be satisfied until he has hunted me down and killed me. But he'll have to find me first.

I met him on a job I was to do with a team at a jewellery wholesaler in the Clerkenwell district of London. Five of us met up in a mini-cab office on that Saturday morning for the job. I thought Jim was a copper when I first met him. He had that sort of physique. When we arrived in Clerkenwell, we checked the area for police. It was surprisingly quiet around the wholesaler's, so two of the team broke into the building to try to de-activate the alarm bells. Jim positioned himself outside while I waited with another man in the van at the rear of the building. We knew most of the gear was kept in an upstairs room, so it was that alarm they were working on. Suddenly the bell went off and kept ringing.

I said to the guy with me, 'We'd better get them out of there and scarper.' He kept cool and said, 'No, Mo, they're all right.' He looked at his watch and started counting, 'Ten, nine, eight. . .' And by the time he got down to two, those frightening bells stopped ringing. 'Oh, they're quicker than usual,' he observed. The pair came out of the wholesaler's, made the doors look as if they were still locked and walked around the block for about 20 minutes to see if any police came sniffing around. They didn't, so we all dived into the building.

We went up the back staircase and into the room and began carrying down boxes of watches, worth about £500 a box, to the van parked at the rear. After one run, we went to get more. I heard tiptoeing up the stairs, and hissed, 'Someone's coming.' We all braced ourselves, and then Jim steamed out and hit this poor guy in the stomach. I heard the whoosh as the wind came out of his inside. A man who was with him turned and fled down the stairs into the street. We began to make our escape but as we passed the winded man he grabbed my leg - which was the worst thing he could have done in the circumstances. I swung my boot into his stomach again and he gave up the fight. Silly man. We ran out, down the alleyway and into the van, which as yet had hardly any gear in it.

We had driven about two miles before anyone spoke. 'Cor, we were lucky there,' said one of them. 'Lucky,' I said. 'We've left nearly empty-handed. Call that lucky? I'm going back to get more gear. That's what we went for.' The others didn't like the idea and one of them said, 'No, Mo, it's on top. The police will be there soon.' But I had made up my mind. I was going back. And Jim said OK, and then they all agreed to go back with me. 'We went to get a prize, so let's get it,' I said. Big Jim agreed, 'You're right, Mo. Let's go back and get more gear.'

There was no sign of activity outside the building, so we forced the front door and crept in. I went upstairs first with Big Jim following me. I carried a load of boxes of watches down while Jim seized a sackful which must have weighed at least three hundredweight, and hurled it over his back. We got outside, shut the door, and put them into the back of the van. We waited for 20 minutes and then I went back in on my own and brought more boxes out while Jim waited with the engine running. In all, we had got nearly forty grand's worth of watches. We put the stuff in a slaughter and later the team met up in a pub to discuss the disposal of our valuable haul. The others were full of praise for the risks I had taken on their behalf and Jim said, 'You did well, Mo. You've surprised even me.' We sold the watches for £10,000, so all that risky work was worthwhile.

Jim told me to keep in touch and gave me his home 'phone number. I kept all my numbers in code in my diary, and his went in that way too.

Soon this tight-knit team was involved in an astonishing range of activities. It became a joke each Sunday night when 'Police Five' came on television that we would predict what stolen goods Shaw Taylor would feature that week. Quite often most of the programme would concern our stuff! Jim and Jennifer and I would chortle as we watched Shaw do his best to try and thwart our enterprises.

One week we'd have fifty grand's worth of whisky, the following week it'd be fifty grand's worth of radios, cigarettes or razor blades, anything that was saleable. The size of our operation was staggering. Most of the goods came from daring hijacks, and the police were getting very concerned with the number of armed lorry grabs that were taking place on the streets of London. They didn't know where or when we would pounce next, but pounce we did.

We set up a network of buyers who would give us a fair price for the goods and then sell to their own contacts. Occasionally those rogues would cause us a few problems by not paying up on time, and then we had to teach them a lesson.

The first one we picked out to be an example to the others got his fright one evening as he was watching 'Softly, Softly' on television. And I planned to be far from that with him. It was to be my personal pleasure to hurt him. I rang the bell of his home and he came to the door with his slippers on. As the toerag peered through the darkness at me we grabbed him by the throat and dragged him down the path to a waiting car. We slung him into the back seat and put a gun to his head. His eyes nearly popped out with fear and he did something that used to happen when I was a young boy in school. He wet his pants. The driver took us to the bottom of the road and I asked this quivering jelly of a man to comment on the fact that he had been overheard in a pub telling people that he was 'doing us for our dough'. He had also been heard saying we were 'all mouth'. I asked him for an explanation, but he was too scared to even talk. He just sat there shaking.

'We want all the money you owe us by Friday,' I told the man. I produced a hammer and crashed it savagely into his face. Then I bashed both his kneecaps with it. At a signal 'my driver did a three-point turn and sped back down the road towards the man's home. As we passed his front gate, I opened the door and hurled him out. His scared wife, who was watching through the window, collected him from the gutter and called an ambulance.

On the Friday I was on the doorstep again and he hobbled to the door with all the cash he owed us. 'Now why didn't you do that in the beginning?' I asked him. 'It would have saved all this trouble.' He said nothing and handed it over in silence.

Another slow payer got a similar warning from us. We grabbed him on his doorstep, too, and dragged him to the car, where I asked him for the £500 he owed the team. 'I've got the money at home,' he squealed. I hit him on the head with my hammer and said to the driver, 'I think this one's an Epping Forest job.' Holding his bleeding head he said, 'Please don't, please don't. I've got the money at home. It'll never happen again.' So we went to his house and he produced £500 in cash, plus an extra £100 which I insisted he paid for a prior load.

This was a side of me that Susan never saw - thank God. It was part of my old Jekyll and Hyde existence, something that has now gone for ever - unless someone ever harms her or my kids.

It was certainly true, however, that she was going out with one of the most dangerous men in London.

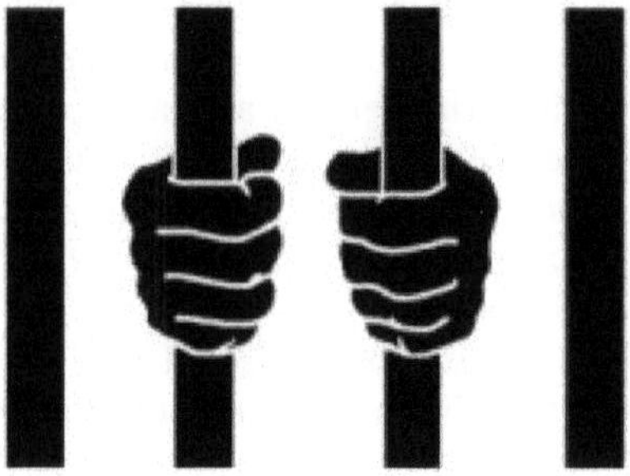

ABOVE: O'Mahoney with his double-barreled shotgun

LEFT: Mo, later in his life sitting in the garden of journalists Barrie and Pat Tracey

OPPOSITE: Rick Wakeman and Maurice O'Mahoney posing for the camera
ABOVE: Mo leaving one of his homes

Maurice O'Mahoney living the high life at his 'home' in Chiswick Police Station

Mo in one of his many disguises

'P.C.' O'Mahoney in his cell at Chiswick Police Station

Maurice O'Mahoney enjoying the spoils of his life as 'King Squealer'

ABOVE: O'Mahoney 'resting' in his police cell

OPPOSITE: The frightening figure of Maurice O'Mahoney as he would dress for one of his many armed robberies

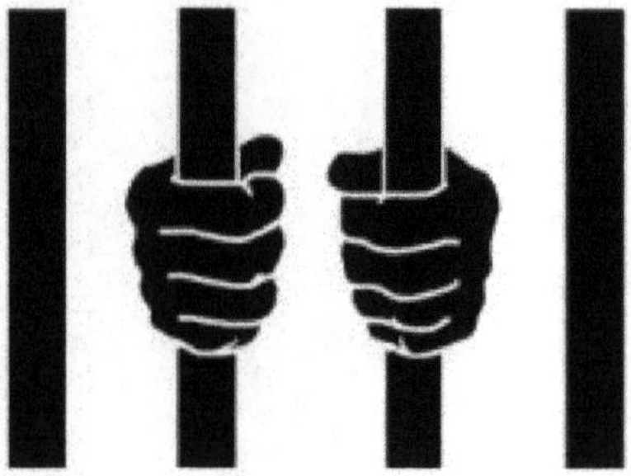

8
Cain and Abel

I am not a keen student of the Bible, but one thing I do recall from my Roman Catholic upbringing is the story, in Genesis, of Cain and Abel. They were the eldest sons of Adam and Eve. Cain was a farmer while his younger brother Abel became a shepherd. At harvest time Cain offered God some farm produce, while Abel brought the fatty guts of meat from his best lambs, and presented them to the Lord. God accepted Abel's offering but not Cain's. This made Cain both dejected and very angry, and one day while the brothers were in the fields, Cain attacked Abel and killed him. He killed for envy. When the Lord said, 'Where is Abel your brother?' Cain uttered those famous words,' 'Am I my brother's keeper?'

Knowing this Old Testament story quite well, I labelled two of the most hateful men I ever knew as Cain and Abel. This modern Cain didn't actually kill his brother, but he went as far as he could to destroy him. As for Abel, the Biblical name signifies vanity and this one was just that. Vain, conceited, yet a much more likeable person. This Cain and Abel have certainly contributed a chapter in my Bible of crime.

I first met Abel in the Scrubs, where he was serving a sentence for arson. He was a 20 stone lump of blubber, who had got fat through good living. We shared a cell for a time and I decided to cash in on his riches. I supplied him mainly with tobacco and toothpaste, and he paid handsomely for it. You will recall that I attacked a prison officer while inside. Well, this was partly through the way that screw kept picking on Abel and I decided to take action. I thought the officer was taking things too far.

You'll remember that I got 28 days. After I returned from solitary Abel said to me, 'Mo, I don't know how I'll ever be able to repay you.' I smiled and said, 'I'm sure you'll find a way.' That way came soon after I left prison. Abel had supplied me with his equally fat brother's address. 'He'll give you some money,' said Abel. 'I'll get a message to him asking him to do all he can to help you.' When I met Cain in the jeweller's shop in north London he owned with his brother, I thought I was looking at Abel. They were so alike.

'Oh yes, Mr O'Mahoney, I've heard all about the way you stood up for my poor brother inside,' Cain told me in the shop, which was dripping with sparklers. 'Here's £25 to keep you going,' he said, dipping his hand into the till. I took the money and told him I'd be back next week for the same. He seemed a little surprised, but when I returned seven days later he cheerfully paid up.

One pay day he asked me if I'd like to earn a little extra on top of my weekly £25. 'It depends,' I said. 'What do you have in mind?' The fat slob leaned over and outlined a plan in which he wanted to collect an outstanding debt from a man who wouldn't pay up, and also frighten him. The victim owned a high-class hairdressing salon in central London.

Never one to turn down a contract, I went out and bought myself a dark wig, put it on and headed towards the salon. As I walked through the door a young girl receptionist asked me, 'Have you an appointment sir?' I replied in the affirmative and before she could say any more I walked downstairs to the office where Cain had said this man usually worked. I didn't bother to knock, but flung open the door. His secretary, who was taking dictation, dropped her pencil when she saw me. But she quickly gathered her composure and said sternly, 'Who are you?' I ignored her question and told her, 'Get out,' As she scuttled through the door I turned my attention to the terrified salon owner. He spluttered as he asked, 'Who are you and what do you want?' I grabbed him and yanked him towards my face and said, 'Five hundred pounds.' Then I threw him across the office.

'My heart, my heart,' he whined. 'You ain't got no heart,' I told him. I then slapped him several times across the face and told him to open his wallet. He meekly handed it over to me and there I found £200 in notes. I took them out and threw the wallet down on the floor. 'That'll be the first instalment of the money you owe my client,' I told him as he lay there. 'And if you open your mouth to the police about this you're liable to meet with an unfortunate accident.' He just lay on the carpet shaking with fear as I stalked out. His secretary had disappeared and no-one made any attempt to stop me.

Although I didn't recover all of the money, Cain rubbed his lands with glee when I told him of the fright I had given the toerag. 'That's lovely Mo, tell me the whole story again my boy,' he said to me. Afterwards he added, 'What a good debt-collector you make.'

I had obviously made a big impression on Cain and I thought it time to make an even bigger mark. I saw my chance when he suggested that I 'do' his jeweller's shop; he'd claim the insurance and buy back the goods that I, and my associates, had taken, at a lower price. 'I'll weed out the good stock Mo, and you just take the rubbish,' he said. 'The insurance company won't know what you've nicked.'

Cain wanted a week's notice before the evil robbery was to be done, but I decided it could be more profitable for me if I surprised him and got some of the good stock as well. Cain also insisted that the 'raid' had to be carried out on a Monday morning so he could sort out the best goods on the Sunday morning, so I decided we'd hit him just as he arrived.

So, unknown to him, my team met up at nine am on that particular Sunday at a member's flat and then collected a previously stolen Ford Escort van and Mini. Both had false number plates. My Bedford van was also to be used. The three motors went to the shop and were parked in different positions. The Ford van was parked almost outside the shop, while the others were at the rear. I stayed at the back by an alleyway as I didn't want Cain to know of my involvement in the crime.

We waited until Cain arrived in his swish Bentley with a teenage boy who turned out to be his son and had had time to switch off the alarms and open the main safe.

Those at the front were parked by the alley and one of them gave me the thumbs up sign. Then I told the team to 'move'. I gave one of them my Luger to stick to Cain's head - though it couldn't have done any harm because I had taken out the magazine.

My plan was even cheekier than a straight forward theft. I decided to pretend to Cain, that I had heard of his misfortune and promise to do all I could to get his goods back - for a price.
Cain was dumbfounded when these villains burst into his shop and a revolver was pushed into the side of his balding head. 'What's going on?' he spluttered as he was roughly searched and his wallet taken. 'Just shut up fat man and you'll be all right,' he was told. 'And that goes for the boy as well.'

The terrified pair were then herded down a dark cellar and pushed in through the door which was then locked from the outside. Cain and his son knew the place was rat-infested and that made the experience even more horrific for them.

Then the gang began loading boxes of expensive watches and other jewellery into the Escort van outside. They moved at amazing speed and cleared the whole shop within ten minutes. About £40,000 worth of stock was crammed in. But one of the team got too greedy and binned (pocketed) a gold watch worth about £1,000, plus £800 in cash. In the share-out, he only declared £200 cash, but I got him to admit he had also taken the valuable watch and confiscated it. I gave him a serious warning and he lost part of his share of the profits.

Cain and his son finally managed to force open the cellar door and make their escape. He went white when he surveyed the empty shelves and display cabinets. 'My life, I'm ruined,' he told his son. 'What will I do now? I'll never get over this.' He was sensible enough to call in the police, and next day I sidled into his bare shop and commiserated with him over his unexpected misfortune. Cain was most upset because he hadn't had time to organise an insurance policy and so he stood to lose everything. 'I'll do everything I can to recover the goods,' I assured him as he wiped tears away from his puffed cheeks. 'Thank you Mo,' he said. 'I knew you would come to my aid.'

My 'investigations' ended quickly and I returned to the shop with the good news that I had recovered the whole load. Delighted, Cain made me an offer for several thousand pounds, plus a personal commission for my good detective work.

I suggested it might be nice for him to loan me his Bentley to go round to the slaughter and pick up the stolen goods. 'Take it, Mo. Anything, as long as you can get my stock back,' he said.

It was at great feeling gliding around London in such a fantastic motor. I even toyed with the idea of taking the car and the jewellery. But then I thought of my promise. So I turned up with the car and with the help of the team, loaded it, with the stock. Before returning to Cain's shop, we all went in the Bentley for a slap-up celebration meal in Hammersmith.

Cain made an astonishing recovery from the shock of the robbery as he watched me bring in the boxes of watches and jewellery. He was so overwhelmed that he didn't even notice that a few boxes of watches were missing. I had taken them to help pay off a friend who helped unload the haul in the shop.

Cain was even more grateful when I produced the missing gold watch. 'Here you are,' I told him as I dangled it in front of him. I knew it was of great sentimental value as his mother had given it to him. 'I've even recovered this for you,' I told him. He said words couldn't adequately express his gratitude. I said, 'Money could, though.'

As the memory of the robbery receded in Cain's mind, he began thinking of more ways he could cash in on his planned insurance fiddle. Then one day he told me, 'Mo, could you arrange for me to be done again and I'll give you five grand. I've now got the insurance situation sorted out.'

Somehow, I never got around to that job.

When Abel came out of prison he decided he needed compensating for his painful experience. Cain didn't agree, so Abel, who was legally his partner, began 'weeding' the business. This means he was helping himself to the stock and money and also cooking the books.

A friend of Cain knew of this and really wound him up, urging him to take revenge for his brother's misdeeds.

He suggested to Cain, 'Why don't you get Abel tied up to teach him a lesson? After all he's been double-crossing you.' Cain thought for a moment and said, 'Who will do the job?' The friend who by now had Cain seething with anger replied: 'Mo will do it. And he'll do it well.'

I met Cain and his advisor and we discussed how the job should be done. Cain was very agitated and told me, in a voice quivering with emotion, 'You know Mo, my brother's a real bastard, having me over like that. You would think you could trust your own flesh and blood. I can't forgive him for such behaviour,' I wasn't impressed with his snivelling and told him so. 'Cain, you've been having Abel over for years.' He replied, somewhat illogically, 'Well, that was business.'

As a further incentive for me to take the job, Cain said I could keep any 'weeded' stock I found in Abel's house and sell it back to him later.

He suggested a date for the job at Abel's beautiful detached home outside London, while his brother's wife was away on the Continent on holiday. I agreed the date and a team of five of us set off on a dark winter's night for Abel's palatial house.

I wanted to keep a low profile and remain outside for a time, because |I didn't want Abel to suspect I was involved in the job. I planned to come in masked later and not open my mouth.

Having spent so much time together in the Scrubs I knew Abel would immediately recognise my voice and could later have me nicked. The other four put on their masks and tiptoed down the drive to the front door. One of them rang the bell and when Abel came to the door and saw the masked men standing there looking menacing, he tried to slam it shut. One of them managed to keep it open with his foot and shoved my revolver through the doorway. The door was then forced open and the team jumped on Abel, tied his hands behind his back, and then dragged him into his large lounge where he was blindfolded.

I waited for the commotion to die down and then went into the house. As I walked through the open door I was shocked to see a woman standing completely naked at the bottom of the hallway stairs. She was shaking with fear, not quite knowing what to make of these masked men in her home. Obviously this was Abel's wife, who hadn't yet gone on her holiday. She was about to take a bath when the raiders struck. I could see her great embarrassment at being stared at by five masked men, so I indicated to one of them to get a blanket and wrap it around her ample frame. I didn't want to speak within Abel's earshot. She was taken to the lounge and I called one of the lads into the kitchen, where I gave him an instruction. 'Tell them that no harm will come to them if they don't cause any trouble.' I said. The message was relayed.

As one of them kept watch on the terrified couple, the rest of us ransacked the house. As Cain suspected, we came across quite a bit of 'weeded' stuff from the shop. So Abel was double-crossing his brother. But it wasn't that that shocked us, it was the discovery of a sleeping baby in a bedroom. The kiddie was deeply asleep as we switched on the light to check the room. I didn't know Abel and his wife had a child and sent one of the team down to ask whose baby it was. As I waited for him to return I could hear a row developing between two of the team.

I ran down the stairs to the hallway to find out what it was all about and discovered that one of them wanted to rape the wife. 'If you touch her or the child I'll kill you,' I hissed. 'We're here on a job and nothing else.' With that I rescued my gun from the maniac and tucked it into my trousers. He knew that I wouldn't hesitate to use it, and cooled his ardour.

Just as I was ticking off the potential rapist, the front door bell rang. 'That'll be the au pair,' said the shivering wife in the lounge. 'You'd better let her in.' With that one of the team opened the door, snatched the amazed girl and shoved her into the lounge with the other victims. 'I don't understand . . .' she said as she saw her employers there. 'You don't have to understand, darling,' she was told roughly. 'Just behave yourself.' With that she was bound and gagged.

Abel kept making gurgling sounds through the gag and finally one of the team removed it and asked him what was the matter. 'I want to make a deal with you,' he said. 'You see, that baby upstairs isn't mine. I'm looking after it for the night for a rich friend.'

I came to the side of the lounge door to listen to Abel's outrageous proposition. 'Look, all you have to do is take the child to a safe place and I'll get in touch with the father and say the baby's been kidnapped and you want £50,000 for its return,' he said. 'Go on . . .' said one of the team. 'Well, then I would take £20,000 for handling the negotiations and you could split the remaining £30,000.'

I thought my ears were deceiving me, but they weren't. I couldn't stand this shocking suggestion any more and still wearing my mask I stormed into the room and began kicking the fat louse in his stomach. There's nothing I hate more than anyone wanting to hurt children in any way. I was so full of revulsion for Abel at that moment that I would have probably shot him to death if the others hadn't pulled me away. The gag was put back in his fat mouth and we continued to ransack the place. All I could hear was his muffled moans as we began to unearth more and more loot from the shop. I recognised it all from a description that Cain had given me of missing items. With all the sparklers in our pockets, we left the shocked Abel, his wife, and the au pair, and headed back to London. As we raced through the dark I told the others that I was still disgusted with Abel's kidnap suggestion. They agreed, though they thought the money might have come in useful. I then anonymously 'phoned the police and told them of the tie-up.

The tragedy of that tie-up was that shortly afterwards, the shock of the incident drove Abel's wife to a nervous breakdown. She was admitted to a mental institution for several months for treatment and I understand that she still hasn't fully recovered. For that I'm very sorry. I have often wondered why she was still there when Cain assured me she would be away on holiday. Now I'm convinced that Cain didn't hit it off with Abel's wife and wanted her hurt. So he invented the holiday story, because he knew how I hated to hurt women in the execution of my villainy. I most probably wouldn't have taken to job if I'd have known she would be there.

Cain beamed next morning as I told him in the shop that the job had been done successfully. 'Let's go to the café up the road and talk more,' he said as I quickly outlined what had happened. But then his expression changed to feigned shock. He said sternly he was horrified that I would do such a dreadful thing to his beloved brother and sister-in-law. The evil fox, he was obviously becoming scared that I would link him with the job. But when I told him we had got back quite a bit of the 'weeded' stock he made a quick recovery, and he made an offer for the return of it. We did a deal and the goods were fetched from behind a secret panel in the flat of one of the team.

Shortly after this Abel 'phoned me to say he had been raided and the crooks had taken quite a bit of stuff. He obviously didn't know I was behind it. 'I know you have your ears close to the ground Mo,' he said. 'If you can get the stuff back for me and not tell Cain about this, I'll make it worth your while.' I told him I'd do what I could.

People talk about honour amongst thieves - but believe me, it doesn't exist. For these double-died bastards then went to the police and reported me. I discovered this after sleepily hearing a thumping at my front door at 6 am one morning. I looked out of the window and saw about five burly men and one particularly savage looking Alsatian all staring up at me. I guessed they had come to see me so I went down to the front door and asked through the letter box, 'Who are you looking for?' One of the flatfeet replied, 'Are you Maurice O'Mahoney?' 'Yes.' 'Well, we're looking for you.' 'Oh no,' I said, 'have you caught me parking on double yellow lines again?' The copper ignored that comment and asked me to open the door. I knew if I didn't he and his giant sized 'pandas' would smash it down, so I let them in.

Each officer stood over six feet tall and they all appeared to weigh more than 19 stone. They all looked very menacing so I decided not to argue with them. One of them told me, 'We are from Golders Green police station and we have a warrant to search your premises.' The giants then bounded up the stairs and into my front room. When I joined them, one said, 'What a lovely pad you've got son.' I said, 'Years of hard work . . .' Pull the other leg,' he said. 'I would but I doubt if I could lift it,' I replied.

Maureen wiped the sleep from her eyes and emerged from the bedroom in her dressing gown. 'What's going on Mo?' she asked as she saw the policemen in the room. 'Oh they're just trying to give me some agro,' I told her. Then the officers went into action. They went through the flat with a fine toothcomb but fortunately found nothing incriminating. They did everything bar pull the floorboards up. After a thorough search a detective inspector who was leading the raid said, 'You will be accompanying me to Golders Green police station, as I have some further inquiries to make and I believe you can help with them.' I said, 'Can I get this straight. You'd like me to help me to convict myself?' He said, 'In a nutshell, something like that.'

I put on a suit and we went away in unmarked cars to that wealthy area of north London. I was escorted to an interview room and surrounded by about eight men all with pens and notebooks at the ready. Before the stern-faced detective inspector came in to the room, I asked one of the other men, 'What's it all about?' He said, 'You tell me.' I told him I hadn't got a clue. I somehow suspected that Cain and Abel had something to do with this, and my fears were confirmed when one of the policemen actually mentioned their surname.

The detective inspector then joined us and began his interrogation. He got straight to the point. 'O'Mahoney, we first want to talk to you about a tie-up job in Golders Green concerning some Indians. We have reason to believe you were involved.' I had heard of this job, but it was nothing to do with me. 'Oh, it's funny you should mention that because a couple I know suffered a similar treatment recently,' I said. 'But that doesn't concern the case you are talking about, does it?' He said, 'Carry on,' so I decided to play along and tell them the whole shocking story about the way my friends Cain and Abel had suffered from an amazing number of unfortunate incidents and I was trying to discover who had perpetrated these deeds and bring them to justice. 'But officer, we are not here to discuss these two fine gentlemen are we?' I said. 'You wanted to discuss Indians. Well, I don't know any Indians. The only ones I can think you're talking about are the ones I've seen on television fighting with cowboys. I certainly haven't tied any of them up.'

The cat and mouse questioning was exhausting, but it always seemed to come back to the Cain and Abel saga. But then he appeared to lose his patience and told me sharply that I was being detained for the time being 'compliments of the Metropolitan Police'. I said, 'I never knew you had self-contained flats here.' A quick check of the cells revealed that they were full up, so I was transferred to Hendon and then apparently forgotten about. The only bit of fun I had there was on the first morning. When the key-man came in with my breakfast and I said, 'Is it free?' He said 'Yes, of course.' So I said, 'Can I have two then, please!' He went mad and didn't see the joke at all.

Just as I was beginning to think I'd never see the outside world again, five CID officers came into my cell. I hadn't shaved and I felt pretty terrible. An officer didn't help matters when he said, 'Come on Mahoney, the day of judgment is at hand.' I had to wash and then I was taken back to Golders Green to see the DI again. He didn't beat about the bush this time. 'It's all rubbish what you have been telling me,' he said in a firm voice. I looked pained and replied, 'Officer would I lie to you?' He ignored my act and said, 'OK, I'll put my cards on the table and tell you why you are here. I have more than reason to believe that you robbed a jeweller's shop belonging to two men and I've also more than reason to believe that you tied up one of these men and his wife. Both men have been in here and made statements to that effect.' I felt the colour drain from my cheeks and really thought my number was up. But then he added, 'For some very strange reason, they have retracted their statements.' I felt myself mutter, 'Thank God for that.' 'What did you say O'Mahoney?' 'Nothing sir. All I want to say is that I've been locked up for three days for nothing. I'm innocent.' The officer scratched his head and murmured, 'Something stinks about this case.' He asked me if I had anything further to say and I said I hadn't, except that I was sorry that these people had been wasting his valuable time. He told me I was free to go and on the way out a detective sergeant, who gave me back my property and had been observing the questioning, said, 'Just between me and you, did you do it?' I gave him a lovely cherubic smile and said, 'That's what you are here to find out.' And on the way out, I added, 'Don't put C11 on my tail.' (They are the people who put you on a target. They report on certain criminals who they believe are particularly active.')

I went home for a lovely soothing bath and then went to see my girlfriend, who had been worried stiff. Susan didn't know where I had been and cried when she saw me. I told her I had been to Ireland on some business and when I 'phoned to tell her at her flat she wasn't in. She felt relieved and then we went out and I got drunk on champagne. I somehow drove home and fell asleep on my sofa. I couldn't even get undressed, I was so paralytic.

Next day, fighting off my hangover, I 'phoned up both Cain and Abel and thanked them, for my 'holiday at Golders Green and Hendon'. I promised them that they would both pay dearly for the experience.

Remember that Bible lesson? After Cain killed Abel, God told him he would be banished from his homeland and would be a fugitive and a wanderer on the earth for the rest of his life. And Cain said: 'My punishment is greater than I can bear.'

All I hope for this pair, who are so hateful in all their dealings, is that their mental and financial punishment for their double-crossing in life is more than they can bear. And it will be a punishment that they will thoroughly deserve.

They have already suffered at my hands. I had them blackmailed and also began to arrange for them to be gunned down.

Here endeth my Bible lesson . . .

9
My Plan to Kidnap Elton John

ne of the biggest crimes we ever planned was to kidnap pop superstar Elton John and demand a two million pound ransom. I had long been a fan of the bespectacled rocker and thought it would be interesting to have a chat with him - and also make him pay for it.

The information on how to do it came from an associate of the singer. He had already fed us quite a bit of information on Elton's movements and we were waiting for his tip on when it would be best to actually capture him.

The idea was to grab Elton at his home and hide him in Scotland until the ransom money was paid. The operation was all set to go when our luck suddenly ran out. The police were tipped off about an armed raid on a Securicor van near London's Heathrow Airport, and I was arrested. But more of that later.

I am still a pop fan though, so when I was offered the chance to protect some superstars for good money, I jumped at it. The job was to assist with security at a pop festival at the Oval cricket ground, home of Surrey County Cricket Club. Under the shadow of that famous gasometer, stars like Frank Zappa and Jeff Beck were to wow the fans.

For this two day festival I was asked to provide a team to protect some of the stars on and off stage and also help carry cash from turnstiles to the counting room. During a lull in the proceedings, I noticed a whole row of turnstiles at one side of the ground not open, although outside there was a long queue of fans waiting to get in.

Obviously, I thought, I would be performing a public service if I opened my own turnstile and let them in. Maybe the organisers wouldn't get the money, but I would certainly help the fans. So I got three other guys and we managed to open up the gate and get the turnstile clicking. As the gate swung open, one fan said to me, 'About bloody time, mate!' And as they poured in, the turnstile was getting almost red hot with the speed I was getting them through. Those that had already bought tickets didn't pay me, but I took the tickets and some of my team went outside and sold them again as touts.

We nearly got sussed, however, when one of the organisers spotted our gate and came over. 'Hey man, what goes on here?' he asked. I explained that we had been asked to open the gate because there was a bottleneck at the other entrances. He obviously didn't believe me and began scratching his head. I encouraged him to believe my tale by adding, 'Look, mate, if you don't leave us I'll be forced to call an ambulance.' He said, 'What do you need an ambulance for?' 'It's for you,' I said. 'Why? There's nothing wrong with me.' I retorted, 'There will be by the time the ambulance arrives.' He scuttled off and I decided that I had better close the gate quickly before he returned with the police. Anyway by now the queue had shrunk into a mere trickle. We shut up and went to a quiet place to count up our spoils. In less than two hours we had clocked up a profit of about £1,500. I split it between the four of us and I then had to think of another plan to make some more money at the festival.

I noticed a small army of hot-dog men around the inside perimeter of the ground, and I thought that they could obviously do with a bit of protection. So I went up to the first and threatened him that if he didn't pay up I would turn over his van. He paid up. We then went around the ground using the same technique, and it proved highly successful. And, as an added bonus, the hot-dog men supplied us with free hot-dogs and cold drinks.

I must admit that we were a bit mean in some of our dealings during that festival. Like the time when one of the team was asked by a press photographer to give a shivering fan who had queued up all night a steaming plastic cup of coffee, so he could take a picture. When the photographer had finished, my mate took it back and emptied the contents down his greedy gullet.

One of the most important jobs we had was to carry money, accompanied by the group of four security men, from the turnstiles to the Oval's counting room. I would carry a box brim full of cash while these men, wearing crash helmets and with their sun visors down, walked each side of me. Later I would carry the boxes of money to the security van. I did this so I could get a glimpse inside the van and see its layout. I gained a lot of valuable information that day, much of which was accidentally supplied by the men in conversation. They liked my style and we became good buddies. Little did they realise what I was up to.

Near the end of day two of the festival the organisers were hearing tales about the activities of myself and the team. One said sarcastically, 'We have reason to believe that you'll soon be able to hire the Oval yourself if you carry on at this rate.'

So I decided we should quit while we were ahead. I collected my wages for the two days of hard slog and we left, well happy with the deal. By now I could hardly walk, there were so many notes crammed into my pockets, but I somehow made it to my car.

In the sub-culture of the underworld, violence is the main coin of the realm. If you can instil fear into people, you can usually get your own way. But like the old fashioned cock-of-the-school you have to earn that title. You have to be prepared to take on all situations to rise to the top.

I earned a lot of my 'war' medals in stupid pub brawls, and most of them were pretty vicious. There were no holds barred when I did battle with my opponents.

Almost anything would set me off. But the beating I am going to tell you about now was not with a villain. Nevertheless I think it was thoroughly deserved by the victim. It began when a long-haired hippie sauntered into a pub where I was drinking with some friends. I am dead against drug-taking and when I see a pusher at work I see red. This one was blatantly touting his killer merchandise around the pub, and one of my friends, who was minding the place, went over to him and told him to leave the premises. He smiled and said, 'Sorry man, I'll leave it out.' He left and came back a few minutes later.

'We were carrying on with our conversation when he re-appeared at the bar and asked for a drink. Knowing that some hippies would sometimes quickly down a drink and run out before paying, the attractive young barmaid requested money before she poured the drink for him. All of a sudden he freaked out, picked up a whisky glass, broke it lightly on the side of the bar and jabbed it in her pretty face. She was screaming hysterically as blood poured down her on her white blouse.

I went absolutely crazy when I saw this and dashed over to this animal and smashed my fist as hard as I could into his face. As he crumpled and fell to the ground I stood over him and rained in punches, breaking his nose, cracking several ribs, and cutting his face in many places. I dragged the unconscious slag outside and noticed several of his teeth embedded in my right fist. I then began banging his head against a wall. No one attempted to stop my rage. I was completely out of control for those shocking two or three minutes. I left him for a few seconds and then heard him say, 'No one can hurt me.' I heaved him a short way down the road and hurled him through the plate glass window of a Laundromat. He lay there ga-ga, half in and half out of the window, as an ambulance arrived to take the barmaid off to hospital. I was back in time to see her carried out on a stretcher, her face a jigsaw of bleeding cuts. By now she had passed out and lay there quite still.

Police arrived from everywhere and I got chatting to one of them, who said, 'What a horrible thing to do to a young girl.' I agreed and told him that the man who did it was just up the road. 'He's hanging around a window just up there,' I said pointing towards the Laundromat. He was also rushed to hospital and then charged with GBH. There are some nice hippies, but this one was definitely from the bottom of the barrel.

My next fight was with a 14-inch knife with a double-edged bacon slicer blade. I did most of my drinking in pub discos and I always told the bouncers in these places that if they ever needed any help they had an extra man here. They appreciated this because I was always ready to pitch in wholeheartedly when trouble reared its ugly head.

This particular night I was in a disco close to the Western Avenue at Northolt in Middlesex, celebrating a relative's release from prison with him. There was a group of us standing around in a semi-circle by the bar when I noticed two clowns taking a liberty with one of my friends. They kept reeling about pretending to be drunk and spilling beer over this chap's suit. I asked one of the bouncers to tell the pair that if they didn't stop they'd get a clump.

He did and they just laughed at him. I tried to keep my temper as I watched the 'deadly duo' continue with their games at the expense of my friend. In the end I stalked over to them and said, 'It's quite funny, isn't it fellas? You throw all the beer up in the air and everybody around you gets wet.' They grinned like Cheshire cats as if to say, 'What are you going to do about it, mate?' So I let fly at one of them with a right hander that would have done Muhammed Ali proud. He went down for the count and with that his pal took flight. I chased him through the screaming dancers, caught him and let fly with rights and lefts. He lay there in the semi-darkness of the disco moaning and groaning. The music just kept thumping out.

Then an uncle of this man decided to join in. He whipped out a glinting knife and shouted to me, 'Do you know what I'm going to do with this?' Before I could answer he said, 'I'm going to cut your bollocks off.' I then jumped over the pub counter, grabbed a knife there which was even bigger than his, and said, 'That's funny, I thought of doing the same to you.' Then I began chasing him all over the room and into other bars of this monster pub. Tables went crashing as I lunged at him and stabbed him several times in the backside. He staggered forward and kept repeating, 'Oh God, please let me live. I'm sorry.' But I wasn't giving up that easily.

I chased him out into the road and he dragged himself along with blood pouring down on to the pavement from his wounds, trying to escape from me. By now my pals had caught up with us and then I spotted police cars arriving at the pub car park. I told them that I thought we ought to leave. One of them saw how wound up I was and tried to take the knife from me in case I decided to lunge and kill the wounded guy. I whipped it away and the double-edged blade shred my friend's hand. I didn't mean to hurt him, but I still needed that knife for protection. We jumped into our cars and one of the group took the chap with the bleeding hand to hospital for stitches.

I never found out what happened to my stabbed victim, who just lay bleeding out there on the pavement. All I know is that he never made a complaint against me, and again the police could do nothing to curb my uncontrolled violence. I discovered later that the man was no angel himself. He had recently come out of prison after serving a sentence for stabbing a policeman. The only trouble with these sort of fights was that they didn't bring in money. They helped you gain respect from villains, but didn't pay the rent, so to speak. But successful big-time armed robberies did.

One biggie we were to attempt was snatching a £35,000 pay-roll from a west London firm. We had a contact inside the huge factory who told me that this amount would be distributed one evening in the factory canteen. Clerks would hand out the money, guarded by five security men, he said. Our contact drew us a map of the place and showed us where we should drive in and then make our exit.

The plan was for him to go into work as normal, than as soon as he knew what time they would be paying out to 'phone one of the team, and then we'd move quickly. We gathered in a flat, waiting tensely for that 'phone to ring. It did. 'It's on at 9 o'clock tonight,' said our man tersely. With that the 'phone receiver was replaced and we rushed to our cars. The four double-barrelled shotguns we planned to use were already on the floors of the cars, which we drove to the change-over point. They were the Ford Escort van used for the Cain and Abel robbery and a stolen white Hillman Imp.

We drove through the 'In' security gate at the front of the factory as if we were night workers, and then went around to the large car park. The plan was that we would wait for our contact to come over and give us the nod when the, cash started flowing.

We waited and waited and he didn't show. I don't know what went wrong, but there was no sign of him. So I said, 'OK, let's go in anyway.' We put on our masks, got our shotguns ready - I had a pump action model for this job - and then we dashed towards the back canteen entrances. One of the team followed us, carrying a couple of sacks for the money to go in and wielding a police cosh.

To our horror we found the entrance was padlocked from the inside. And as we were desperately trying to heave it open in the darkness, a security guard showed up. I pointed the sawn-off shotgun at him and he fell to the ground and held his hands to his head, thinking I was going to blast him.

With that I yelled, 'Everyone back to the car and let's get away.' As we dashed back to the vehicles I saw people coming towards us. I pointed the shotgun at them, then raised it into the air and fired some shots. They took the hint and ran for cover. Three of us got into the Escort and the other two into the Imp. The driver of the Imp was so scared that he froze at the wheel and held up the second car's getaway for valuable seconds. His mate kept yelling at him to 'move' until he did just that. When I heard this later on I pointed a gun at his head and told him, 'I've a good mind to blow your stupid head off.' He said he was sorry and wouldn't do it again.

My car screeched through the grounds and rammed a Mercedes Benz on the way down to the service crescent, and I went to the 'In' entrance at great speed. There was no barrier, so we zoomed out into the dual carriageway straight across the low concrete dividing barrier and away. The others went out of the correct exit and the security man actually raised the barrier for them.

There was a heated session that night when we held a post mortem on what had gone wrong. But we concluded that no one could have guessed that the door to the canteen would have been locked like that.

I was still frequenting the disco where I had first met Susan, but as I previously mentioned she was no longer working there, and I had persuaded her to give up her job and become an ordinary housewife. I began transforming her flat into a luxurious palace, fit for a princess, and helped to fill the financial gap that giving up her job had caused.

While I was at the disco, one of the bouncers there stuck up another wages job, this time at a south London engineering firm about two miles from Clapham Common. I took one of the team to keep an eye on the factory and discovered that Group Four Security Ltd were the people who brought the wages. I noticed the men carried the money into the factory in bags chained to their wrists. My plan was for us to pounce the following week when they arrived, shoot the security guards in the legs, cut off the bags with wire-cutters and make our escape. I said this was the quickest way of getting the money. When we had a conference about the plan, the others were scared and said they didn't fancy the idea, so I bowed to the majority verdict.

On the day of the robbery, we had a final briefing and then I went out and hired a brand new Ford Transit as the getaway vehicle. And sadly this was to be the last raid in which the by now famous Ford Escort van was used. Three sawn-off shotguns were to be our weapons that day and our masks were thick sleeves cut off two of the team's jumpers, tied at the top and with eye slits cut into them. Both vehicles were driven to Clapham Common and then we got into the vehicles we were using for the actual raid. By the time we pulled up outside the factory, one of the team's bottle (nerve) had gone. He had freaked out with fright and said he couldn't go on. His bum was stuck to the seat. So I gave him a little encouragement by pointing a gun at his right earhole and saying, 'Get out of the car or I'll blow your head off.' He was shaking like a rubber sausage, but the gun did the trick, and he jumped out, put on a mask and ran into the place with us. We tip-toed past a telephonist who was deeply engrossed in a telephone conversation and didn't notice us. But as the gang made their way upstairs to the wages room, a man saw us from the top of the staircase and shouted, 'What are you doing?' He got his answer when a shotgun was fired at him and the blast missed him by three inches. He dived to the floor and we ran into the wages room. A male clerk who was sitting at a desk was attacked and knocked unconscious with the butt of a shotgun.

My men desperately searched the room for the wages and got one person there to admit that the money had been taken to a security room which was now tightly locked. By that time the alarm bells had gone off and people were lying all over the floor, terrified out of their minds. It was decided to wait no longer and make our escape. The gang rushed-down the stairs and out through reception, by that time the telephonist had finished her conversation with her boyfriend and was dialling 999. A shotgun was pointed at her and she froze, put the 'phone down and screamed as a blast crashed into her switchboard. Everyone made for a door we thought would give us a short cut to the outside, but we couldn't get the door open, so we had to smash it in with the butts of our guns. Then we jumped through the splintered hole in the door and dashed to our vehicles. What had happened was that there had been a delay in the paying out of wages and the money was still being put into packets in the security room when we struck.

I could have cried with frustration after this raid. It all seems so easy in the planning stage, yet nothing is ever like that. The problem in every robbery is the human factor . . . and that's something you can never actually predict. We'd done a vicious robbery and two people were nearly murdered. What for? Nothing.

Most of our raids were successful though, and when things went well, we were cock-a-hoop with joy. We really cleaned up around Christmas 1973 at a West London bathworks. This job was stuck up by Arthur, my up to then faithful security guard. He had been working there for some time and had found out all the information I needed for a robbery. So I could personally check on the place, he arranged for me to have a night tour. It was fascinating to see how they made the baths, how they were painted and treated. But I was much more interested in the size of the payroll. Arthur had done his research well and even took me into an executive's office where there was a double-door safe in which he told me the money was deposited when it came in on a Thursday.

We got most of the team assembled and well-briefed. On the day of the raid, Jim 'phoned someone who said, 'Don't go, it's a fit up. The police know of your plans and will be waiting for you.' He asked him where he had got the information from and he said from a policeman. 'He's always selling information to the underworld,' the contact told him.

We decided to postpone the raid until our man had had a secret meeting with the policeman in a pub. This bent copper had been giving criminals information for money for years. He has since had another reward - he was drummed out of the force after an A10 investigation.

When we decided that the policeman's information was good, we decided to call off the job for a few months, then try again when the heat had died down. This time it went without a hitch. We drove up outside the bathworks and then jumped out, ran around the front, drove sledgehammers through the doors and dashed into the office where the safe was. Terrified staff were made to lie on the floor and a 'phone was ripped out so no one could try to 'phone the police. A shotgun persuaded one of the staff to hand over the safe keys and we loaded many thousands of pounds into wooden and metal boxes, and made our escape. The whole raid couldn't have taken more than three minutes.

As you can guess, we were full of Christmas cheer when we arrived back at a flop (flat) in Fulham where we were to divide the money. But I was in for a Yuletide surprise that I hadn't bargained for. For some unknown reason, my security guard had shopped us to the police and made a statement to the local police. But strangely I never heard any more about it.

As I have said before, a bent copper is a disgrace to the force. But they have some terrible tricks played on them. Each day a good copper walks through a minefield of trouble and is easy prey for framing.

One copper who was framed was a detective sergeant investigating an insurance fiddle that I was a party to. I had been asked by the manager of a wholesaler's - let's call him Moisher – to burgle the premises so he could claim the insurance. I had already done quite a bit of business with him in the past, mainly selling him stolen goods, and decided it was a job worth doing. Moisher promised to give me the keys for the building and its alarm system. So on the surface it seemed relatively easy to execute.

I had hired a lorry for the job from a rental company in Park Royal and took the team along to do the job. We reversed the bright yellow truck into the premises and loaded it up with Anadins, radios, tape cassettes and players, perfumes, hairsprays, tights, and Wilkinson Sword razor blades. It took us hours to load up the gear that Saturday afternoon. The plan was that Moisher would pay us for the haul and we would then return it to him. He would also pocket the insurance money. I decided to sell off some of the stock, which I did for several thousand pounds.

But I made a silly mistake in letting the team have some of the gear to take home as presents for their wives and girlfriends. One of the chaps was going out with a brass and unfortunately the police raided her place and discovered some packets of stolen tights. She confessed and told them everything and they raided my pal's drum and found other goods valued at about £200. Underneath the sofa were revolvers and shotguns, but fortunately they didn't find them.

By now there was panic in the team and one of them shopped me to the police. They arrested me, but he then refused to make a statement against me, and I was freed. It was a very fraught time for all of us.

The police officer was by now piecing the whole job together and knew Moisher was behind it all. He told Moisher that he would soon be arrested, and this made the drowning rat think up a desperate plan to destroy him. For not only would this policeman thwart the insurance payout, he would get us all locked up. The plan was simple. Moisher 'phoned up the copper, said some forged money had been passed to him, and asked if he would like to come and pick it up.

A10 officers had been stationed in the warehouse so they could hear and see what was going on without the detective realising. He turned up and asked Moisher, 'Where's that money?' Moisher said, 'Here it is.' Then the policeman said, 'If there's any more, I'll be back for it.' So Moisher said, 'If there is any more, I'll ring you up and you can have it.' The policeman looked sternly at Moisher and said, 'This isn't going to get you off the burglary you organised.'

The ploy worked like a charm and as he left the premises, the officer was arrested by the Scotland Yard men, who had observed the whole thing. He was immediately charged with receiving a bribe and suspended from duty. He knew he could receive up to seven years if found guilty, and naturally he was going out of his mind with worry. Meanwhile Moisher was rubbing his fat hands with glee at the officer's misfortune.

Two days before the case was due to be heard at the Central Criminal Court in London, I made contact with A10 and was interviewed by officers. I told them the whole story and at the end of our chat, they were convinced that the officer was framed and all the charges were withdrawn. The man, who had five children, must have thought I was an angel out of heaven. But it was something that I felt I had to do.

I know A10 has done a good job in weeding out bent coppers, but you can take it from me that it has also served the purposes of the criminal world very well. As soon as a villain is caught, he arranges for relatives to lodge complaints against the arresting officer. I would say about 99 per cent of allegations against the police are wrongful and only about one per cent are genuine.

I don't condone the actions of a bent copper. But I can understand some of them. For they are only fighting fire with fire . . . but, of course, this often results in getting burnt.

10
Four Hours in the Buff

Nightwatch, Laurence Harvey's last film before his tragic and untimely death from cancer in 1973, was jinxed by a chain of calamities. For a start, the Lithuanian-born star was rushed off the set with a burst appendix, holding up production - at enormous expense - for a whole month.

Then the beautiful screen goddess Liz Taylor, who was playing Harvey's rich and bored wife, broke a finger, and Brian Hutton, the director, had severe 'flu. The trouble seemed to be over when Laurence Harvey was well enough to resume his role.

But then Billie Whitelaw's son, Matthew - Billie played a sinister house guest - was stricken with meningitis. Matthew was in a critical condition for 16 days and Billie and her husband, writer Robert Muller, took turns to watch over him. During that time Miss Whitelaw was also suffering from severe stomach pains caused by a grumbling appendix. Fortunately, Matthew was soon on the mend and Billie was able to have her appendix out.

Having heard about these problems, I thought the film makers would hardly notice if I added to them. So I and my associates began working on a daring plan to kidnap, or, at least rob, Miss Taylor. The snatch was to have taken place in a London street while Miss Taylor was on her way to a film location. We knew she had been provided with a Rolls-Royce and we planned to hijack it and grab her from the back seat. We would then have put her in a fast car, tied her up, gagged her, and hidden her away. Our ransom demand would have run into millions.

The guy who put up the job was a technician working on *Nightwatch*. He kept feeding us details of her movements and told us she was carrying her favourite jewellery in a safe box in the Rolls. I began going to locations and watching as the filming was done. When her chauffeur went off for a bite to eat or a 'Jimmy Riddle', I would peer through the windows of 'Diamond Liz's' flash car to see if there was any sign of the jewellery box. But I saw nothing. The more I saw of her chauffeur, the more I realised it would not be an easy task to spring the much-married lady from the car. He looked the sort of bruiser who would battle to the end to save her.

And as for the safe box, our informant meanwhile told us that he had heard Miss Taylor often carried substitute sparklers around in it to fool potential crooks. The risks for us were high and the chances of pulling the kidnap or robbery off seemed remote so we decided to shelve it all for the time being. Instead we began drawing up a list of superstars who might be easier to kidnap or rob. We were going to pose as an overseas terrorist group like the Baader-Meinhof gang later proved to be in West Germany.

Big money was always the only object of my crimes. I knew in the back of my mind that one day it all could go wrong and if I was caught I would face a long sentence. So I decided that if that was the case and I did get picked up it didn't really matter what I'd done. I might as well be hung for a sheep as a lamb. So I began to think really big. And I was given a taste of big money one day at a farm where I was shown six million pounds … the snag was that it was all in forged fivers. But this forger was brilliant and had even been able to insert a genuine-looking line through the notes. All the fake money was packed neatly in cardboard cartons and kept in a barn.

We were asked if we could distribute this lot throughout the world by the forger's agent. 'We know your firm have the contacts and we'd like to do business with you,' he said.

I marvelled at these immaculate forgeries and knew they would certainly fool most people. In fact I could hardly tell the difference myself and I know something about forged money. 'What an artist your client is,' I told his representative. 'I'm sure we can do business.'

I had begun to find eager buyers when I was arrested. While I was in custody I was later able, via the police, to tip off the Bank of England about this forged money being circulated. Come to think of it, they still haven't yet had the decency to thank me.

I know I am called 'King Squealer' for all the information I have given to the police, but there was a time when I despised police informers. One I was particularly out to get had shopped some of my team over the hijacking of a load of spirits and he was marked down for a sharp lesson. This tough gangster had once worked as a 'minder' for the notorious Kray twins, Ronnie and Reggie, now serving life sentences for murder in Parkhurst Prison. But the grasser's Kray credentials didn't worry me. He had betrayed my friends and he was going to pay severely for it.

'I think we ought to shoot him and then cut his body into little pieces and throw them into the Thames,' said one of the boys during a discussion. It was what he deserved but I felt this would be too dangerous for us. I knew the law would immediately link us with the killing and that would have brought them down on us like a ton of bricks. So we agreed on a compromise - that he would be badly hurt and made to think twice before ever doing such a thing again.

Plan One was for me to go to the informer's furniture store in the East End and blast him away with a double-barrelled shot gun, damaging him and his precious shop. He was not to be killed though. I put the plan into operation and wearing a brown wig, headed east. Heavy evening rush hour traffic held me up though, and by the time arrived at the shop he had locked up and gone off.

Plan Two was completely unofficial and not agreed to by the team. One of the boys was so incensed with the grass that, without telling us, he went around to his house with a shotgun. He rang the bell, ready to blast him when he opened the door. But the squealer obviously checked the caller through his spyhole and when he saw the gun, the door stayed firmly shut. We used a woman in our third plan. We got her to 'phone this grass up and say her husband had just died and she wanted to sell her furniture. 'Will you please come and give me a quote to clear it all out?' she sobbed dramatically down the 'phone. He fell for the trap. We knew his route would take him past the rear of Pentonville Prison so we lay in ambush ready to capture and give him a beating he'd never forget. Two cars were waiting for him that morning with me in one and Jim in the other. When we spotted him, I overtook Jim's car, got behind him, blocking the rear. Then we both dashed to his motor and Jim began savagely beating the grass while my fists went to work on the driver. We pummelled away unmercifully for about two minutes, but then the drivers who were being held up by our ambush began blasting their horns. I don't think they were worried too much by our brutal actions - they just wanted to get to their destinations! So we left the battered pair and made our escape. No one tried to follow us.

My life of villainy wasn't all grim, however, it also had its funny moments. One incident which gave plenty of laughs, was caused by my bad driving. We had a farm which was regularly used as a slaughter and I was waiting there one day for a lorry load of stolen goods to arrive. When it came I took over the wheel and tried to back the monster vehicle through the barn door. I slammed it into reverse and put my foot down. But as it shot backwards it caught the side of the door and part of the flimsy building. There was a terrible creaking sound and the whole place began to crumble and literally fell apart. As it crashed down, there was revealed to any inquisitive visitor an Aladdin's cave of stolen goods.

When everyone had stopped laughing we covered up the contents the best we could and began trying to shore up what was still standing of the barn.

The irate farmer complained bitterly when he saw what I had done. But when I had paid him for the damage he was quite happy. After all, his original barn wasn't up to much anyway.

It's surprising how many barns are used for villainy. There are bent farmers who will rent out buildings to crooks to stash away their goods. And some will even, for a good price, allow a body to be buried in one of their fields. A large farm is the perfect place to dispose of a corpse. If it was ever possible for the police to make a major roll-call of villains each year they would be astounded to discover how many go missing without trace. But don't believe all those stories about bodies hidden in concrete motor pillars - most are dumped in rough graves, on remote farms. These bent farmers have learnt that it pays to ask no questions and just accept the fees.

Of course, I knew that one day this could happen to me. So when one bleak winter's day I saw a rough field it really gave me food for thought. I was told that the victim had been done away with in a gang-land battle and his bullet-filled body had been wrapped in polythene. I later told the police where the body was lying, but when they got there armed with their shovels, the corpse had been moved. I must emphasise that most farmers are not bent, but just a few who have serious financial troubles sell their souls to the underworld.

Although I was getting more and more into big-time crime, I never turned up my nose at more bread and butter forms of villainy. Like the job at a grocer's who lived over his shop that was put up to me. I was to steal £17,600 in cash. It's one thing to employ a crack safe-blower, but to actually wheel out a bulky safe is another. And that's what happened on this occasion. The job entailed manoeuvring a four hundredweight safe from a back room and out to a waiting van. We had been told by a trusty informant that the occupier and his wife loved dog racing and regularly went betting at London's White City track. To make sure that this night they followed their usual routine, we parked down the road and waited for the couple to leave. Then two of the team followed them to the stadium, checked that they went in and returned to the scene.

It didn't take long for us to break into the house with a jemmy and find the safe we had been told about. But I had the fright of my life when, in the darkness, I stepped on a cat which ran shrieking to another room. Then a growling Alsatian dog appeared from nowhere. Fortunately I was able to make friends with it and patted it on the head so it didn't cause us any trouble. The safe itself looked absolutely immovable as it stood majestically there on legs in the corner of the room. One of the team vainly tried to move it. 'We'll never get this out of the place, Mo,' he moaned in frustration. 'Want to bet?' I retorted.

I told the lads to follow me upstairs and get some mattresses downstairs. I got everyone to heave away at the safe until it toppled over onto the bedding with a dull thud. 'OK, let's start dragging,' I said. We began pulling the mattresses with the safe on top to the back door, where our getaway van was parked. We were pouring with sweat as we dragged it into the back of the van. We went to an address in Fulham and unloaded it, and I went to work with my hammer and chisel which I had wrapped in old clothes to deaden the noise. It didn't take me long to get the safe open, and there were the diamonds and cash. So far, so good. But then everything started going wrong. I later had a blazing row with my associates over the jewels because they claimed a fence told them they were fakes and worth virtually nothing. At the time I didn't know whether they were genuine, and this so-called expert had handed over only a pittance for the diamonds. I later found their true value - and hit the roof. By then the crooked valuer had gone to ground. I also found out that we had missed £40,000 in cash in a shoe box in the loft. To many people a haul of £17,000 must seem a lot but I had, by then, begun to expect much more. And when you share out that amount amongst a team there isn't too much for each person.

The safe? Well, that got hurled out of the back of the van next day on to Barnes Common. I often wondered what people thought when they came across one of our battered safes.

Sometimes these burglaries were committed with a full team, while on other occasions I took out only one associate. And it was on one of these double acts that my next arrest came. Each week we were breaking into beautiful detached houses and ransacking them. I suppose the problem was that on this occasion I had become too blasé and forgot to listen out for the occupants. We were busy in an upstairs room when the couple arrived back from a night out and realised someone was there, so they tip-toed to a 'phone and dialled 999. Within minutes sirens were wailing and lights flashing up the drive and we were trapped like rats. I told my colleague to escape out of one window and I'd try my luck out of another. He wasn't as well-built as me and was able to slither down a drainpipe, vault a wall and make off. I made it to ground level but unfortunately I hurt my back clambering over the same wall. I was in agony when a copper spotted me and I was soon surrounded. I went quietly. I never grassed on my friend and so they were never sure whether anyone was with me on the burglary.

I was taken to Wembley police station for questioning and while they were going through my belongings they found a spare key. I never told them what it was for - in fact it opened the door of the garage where I kept a lot of my stolen goods. At that precise moment it was chock full of nearly 15,000 stolen albums that I had taken during a burglary on a record company warehouse. I had already begun to sell them at cut-price to record shops, but there was still a mountain of them waiting to go out. They were mainly Donny Osmond, James Last, and *New Seekers* LPs. But there was something more incriminating in the garage - a terrifying collection of some of my deadly firearms.

After several days of questioning I was taken from Wembley nick to the local magistrate's court - minus my socks and shoes. They had all been sent off to the police laboratories for forensic testing and so I was barefoot. I felt quite embarrassed as I shuffled into the dock with my naked 'plates of meat'. I complained bitterly to the magistrate and later a policeman gave me a pair of unpolished black prison shoes. My lawyer was very competent and managed to get me bail, something I was highly delighted about. That was not just because I valued my freedom, but also because there were a couple of very big jobs in the offing . . . .

I was committed for trial at Middlesex Sessions at the Guildhall, London, which is opposite Parliament. As soon as I was out I began discussing ways we could intimidate members of the jury. But as my trial got nearer I tried to forget all about its outcome and continued to work flat-out on planning two big jobs. One was to rob the Allied Irish Bank at King Street, Hammersmith, and the other was to raid a Securicor van in Heston, Middlesex, close to London Airport. Both were daring and dangerous assignments which could have yielded us big rewards.

Our bank plan was to have vehicles waiting outside full of armed men. When part of the team pounced the other part would block odd the one-way street. After the guards had unloaded the money into the bank, we would then dash in, smash down the protective screens, vault the counter, run into the vault and grab the cash before the huge door swung shut. If it had been closed we would have forced the manager or a senior member of staff to re-open it at gunpoint.

But there was something else exciting on my mind. My lovely girlfriend Susan was about to have our first love-child. We spent many happy evenings together at her flat discussing names for the baby. I would often rest my hand on her tummy and feel the child - OUR child - kicking. I even spent quite a bit of time in shops like Mothercare selecting clothing for the tot.

It's hard to imagine a hardened villain like me being so caring, but that was the other side of my bizarre life. This pretty girl had taught me what love was all about.

I became really excited as the time approached for the baby to be born. So when Susan went out shopping one Saturday afternoon and I went off to tail the Securicor van we later planned to ambush, I couldn't have been happier. But little did I know the tragedy that was about to come to us both. Susan was slowly walking along North End Road in Fulham when her waters broke and she fell to the ground. Embarrassed shoppers scuttled by as she lay there crying out for assistance: 'Please someone help me,' she cried for several minutes. Just as she thought no one would ever come to her aid, a kindly taxi driver saw her predicament and stopped. 'Come on luv,' he said as he helped her to the cab. I'm taking you to hospital.'

Susan was in deep shock as she was wheeled into the delivery room. Doctors worked desperately hard to save the baby's life. But sadly the child - a girl - was born dead. Her name would have been Michelle.

The first I knew of this was next day when I went around to Susan's flat. My marriage was completely on the rocks but I still lived in my flat home with Maureen. We slept in different rooms. I had gone straight back there after following the security van and had an early night. When I arrived at Susan's flat and found it empty, I panicked. I picked up the 'phone to call her mother, but just then her sister arrived. She looked pale and drawn and said to me, 'Mo, Susan's in hospital. And your baby's dead.' I dashed out in panic and drove like mad to the hospital. I raced into the ward and caught a lump in my throat as I saw Susan lying there in bed crying. I put my arms around her and hung on tight. We were like a couple of statues. It took several minutes for her to tell me what had happened. Then a doctor called me over and explained that the child had been stillborn. 'Can I please take Susan home, doctor?' I asked. 'I promise to look after her.' He agreed. Susan got dressed and we left with my arm around her still-shaking body. It was hard for us both to hold back the tears. This tragic end to a time of great hope had brought us even closer.

As the weeks went by I felt I was changing. Susan was desperately trying to reform me because she knew that if I continued as I was she would lose me for many years behind bars. As it was I had the Guildhall trial to contend with.

But despite her pleas, I somehow couldn't stop my life outside the law. I had to get the Securicor raid out of my system. I had spent so much time on it already, and maybe when that and the Allied Irish Bank jobs were over, I'd settle down to a more normal life.

The planning for the Securicor job was probably the most thorough we'd ever done. By using contacts I had been able to see inside several of the firm's armoured trucks. By now I had an intimate knowledge of their interior layout, and I even knew how to get in through the rear of the truck while it was locked. I can't say how I did it because this would only encourage more callous crooks to have a go. And that would probably mean more deaths for security guards.

Our informants included not only Securicor staff but ex-policemen. I would like to take the opportunity to give a stern warning to all security men - it might save their lives. Never put up jobs to crooks. They might say they will cut you in on the deal, but you can take it from me that there is a good chance that either you or a colleague will get shot dead during a raid. Even if you are working with the villains, they are so callous they will have no hesitation in gunning you down if they think it will help them. Because if you are still alive there is always a possibility that you could betray them. You could be the last link in the chain of evidence for the police.

I remember the weather was changeable that day in June 1974, as we gathered at my West London flat for what was to be our last robbery. One moment the sun shone brightly, and then it would cloud over. We had high hopes that this job would net at least £200,000. This was D-Day for me, a day I'll never forget as long as I live. Sitting there all tensed up in my flat smoking and chatting nervously were some of the most dangerous men in the country, men who would have no hesitation in killing anyone who stood in their way. We waited anxiously for the time to leave in our amazing collection of vehicles. They included an articulated low loader, a Daimler XJ6, two Cortinas and a Vauxall Viva XL. And at the last moment we were to steal a Commer van. I felt quietly confident, but then I didn't know that there had been a major breach of security. For some of my stupid colleagues had been asking other villains to take part in the job and through this, half the underworld knew of our plans.

One of the villains who had been approached was a slag called George du Buriatte, who despite his French sounding name is as Cockney as jellied eels. I later found out that this Judas of the underworld was working with the Flying Squad and was able to inform them of every detail of the job. This man, like myself, is hated by the underworld. He has been given a new face by a plastic surgeon and a completely new identity - just like me. (in fact I've got a new identity now.) There are contracts out on his life, just as there are on mine.

My bone-headed colleagues had been asking du Buriatte to take part in the robbery and he crafttily kept pretending to hedge, and kept asking for more information about it. For many crooks, du Buriatte had good credentials. He once moved in the same criminal circles as the Krays, Richardsons and the Nash brothers. He was the boss man in and around London Airport - planning graft, protection rackets and armed robberies from his house in Chertsey, Surrey. Then he suddenly decided to change sides and act as a double agent. His new friends, the police, had to maintain elaborate security, as du Buriatte was still going on jobs with his old criminal comrades. It had its funny side, too. Villains du Buriatte had informed on were often held at Chiswick police station, where he met his CID contacts. So to preserve his incognito role, he would adopt a disguise. On the way to the nick he would stop at a public lavatory and put on a wig and false moustache. Then he went through the back door of the police station. Inside, a PC would grab his arm and twist it up his back as if he was arresting him. This little show was to fool any villains, or their friends, who might be present. Then du Buriatte would be taken up to the third floor to talk. His information helped to solve one of the Yard's biggest headaches: the escalating number of bank robberies and wage hold-ups.

If I'd known at the time what du Buriatte was up to I would have killed him there and then. For he was the man who brought my life of crime to an end. I had a suspicion that he was up to something, though, and queried him with one of the team, who said, 'I know George, he's as sound as a bell.' Little did we know that he was dead right about the bell - it was the one ringing in the Flying Squad office . . . But, as I suspected someone might be informing, I called off the job and then put it back on again. Du Buriatte was asked by one of the team for a final decision and he said that he couldn't really take part because he had cartilage trouble and would probably collapse if he had to run.

Keeping du Buriatte in the back of my mind, I set the date for June 1, 1974. We moved off to a road along which the security van came, and as 6 pm approached we began to mask up, and get our shotguns, revolvers, sledgehammers and axes ready. Then it happened. Around the corner sped the armoured security van. Our articulated lorry shot forward and rammed it, and in seconds we had it surrounded. A sledgehammer and an axe smashed through the window, then we fired shots through the gaping hole, just missing the two terrified guards. As we got into the back of the van, one of the team pulled out a guard from the cab and bashed him savagely on the head with a hammer. He slumped into the road in a pool of blood. As I got in through the back doors, I found an elderly man. He was obviously another guard, though he looked too frail to be doing such dangerous work. 'Please God, don't hurt me,' he said. I told him, 'Don't worry pop, no-one's going to hurt you.' Then I began throwing out boxes of money, and mentally photographing the interior again for further use.

When we had removed all the money, we loaded it into the boot of the XJ6 and made our escape in our various vehicles. We had our problems. I gasped as we screeched in convoy along service road and a young girl stepped out in front of one of cars to pick up her purse. It swerved crazily and just missed her. Then we found ourselves snarled up in a traffic jam in the next road. Some of the team were so anxious they wanted to fire out of the window so other cars would let us through. But I convinced them that would be the quickest way to get caught. We eventually got out of the jam, reached our change-over point and transferred all the money into a Cortina, ripping the registration plates off the XJ6. Then everything was taken to my flat and we split up our rich pickings. Later I hid the guns and some of the gear in another flat. We were in a jubilant mood that night as we celebrated with a few drinks. Other jobs were already being suggested to us, like a £300,000 raid on a security truck heading for Lombard Street in the City, and a £150,000 raid on a London bank, and I liked the sound of both of them.

Shortly afterwards I thought it would be nice to take Susan out to a show at the Victoria Palace, a theatre in London. I booked a box for us to see Sid James and Barbara Windsor in a 'Carry On' show. I think I disgraced myself a bit, though, because I turned up in my jeans, instead of wearing a black tie, which would have been more suitable for the occasion.

As I kissed Susan goodnight I never realised that within hours I would be involved in another incredible drama. I got home quite late and settled down to sleep on a sofa. I hadn't known that for some time C11 at the Yard had me on target. They had been watching my every move and knew exactly where I was at any time.

I was soundly asleep when at 6 am a terrific row started downstairs. I jumped out of my make-shift bed stark naked to see through a window what was going on. A whole posse of police was down there, beginning to smash down my front door. I grabbed the gun I always kept by my pillow and jumped through a rear window on to a small roof, and from there clambered onto a larger one. Then I began vaulting across to other buildings until within seconds I was five houses away. There I lay in my birthday suit and watched the activity down below. I was freezing. My teeth were beginning to sound like a Black and Decker hedge trimmer and I had the biggest goose pimples you've ever seen. I spent four traumatic hours up on the roof before I felt it was safe to return to my flat. By then I was so cold that I felt really ill.

The police had searched the gaff thoroughly but hadn't found any stolen money or arms - they were safely hidden away somewhere else. I was still shaking with the cold as I clambered back into the flat and quickly got dressed. My wife had come to expect these raids and said very little. I told her I was going out for a while and said goodbye to her and the kids. I knew the law would soon come back for me, so I had to try and make a break for it.

I got into my Cortina GT and sped down the road, but when I turned right at a junction I could see a brown Triumph full of men. It was obviously the Flying Squad waiting for me, so I put my foot down to the ground and an incredible chase began around the roads of Paddington. At times we were touching 80mph and people were scattering everywhere to get out of our way. Fortunately I knew the area really well, and finally lost the police.

When I got to Susan's, I could hardly walk, I felt so feverish. She put me to bed and I just lay there shivering and wondering what on earth was going to happen to me next. I knew the game must be up, and was in no condition to run any more. Before leaving the flat I had 'phoned up some of the team to warn them and found they had already been arrested.

I guessed that under heavy police questioning one of them who knew Susan's address would tell the police that I was there. I certainly can't blame du Buriatte for that, because he didn't know where she lived. Only three people in the team did, and one of them sang.

It was 4 pm on June 11, 1974, when they finally came to get me. Susan answered a knock on the door and a squad of police heavies rushed into the bedroom where I lay, still feeling terrible, and pointed guns at my head. Somehow I summoned up enough strength to try to resist, and leapt out of bed and had a go at one of them. I heard one copper shout. 'He's mad. How can anyone have a go when guns are pointed at his head?' Then another PC called a halt to my token resistance when he aimed a gun between my eyes and said, 'Move and you're dead.' The double handcuffs clicked shut . . . and my life of crime was finally over.

11
Why I Became King Squealer

As I lay in agony on a bed in a Hammersmith police station cell, I little realised that my team were singing their heads off as if they were on stage at Covent Garden. And their appreciative audience as they went through their paces was a group of detectives with notebooks. The police surgeon had diagnosed my condition as gastro-enteritis, and he insisted that I must have no food for several days. I was certainly not in the sort of condition to face up to heavy questioning.

But my misery didn't end there. I found out that my girlfriend and her child had been pulled in to Hounslow Police Station plus her mother and father. I just couldn't believe that they were also being questioned and going through such a terrible ordeal. As I lay clasping my stomach in the cell, a policemen came in and showed me a statement Susan had made. In it she told everything she knew about the Securicor robbery, implicating other members of the team. I knew she had given the statement only because she felt I should make a clean breast of everything, and also because of the expertise of the police who had convinced her that she was doing the right thing. Susan meant me no harm and didn't realise the repercussions of what she was doing. The officer gloated as he watched my crestfallen expression. Then he added to my agony by reeling off every tiny detail of the raid. Obviously my so-called friends had all been grassing on each other to try to secure a deal with the Flying Squad. I was sickened with all of this.

I groaned in both mental and physical pain as he left. Then another officer walked close to the cell door and shouted, 'Guess who's shopping early for Christmas?' I couldn't raise even a weak smile as he peered through the observation window for my reaction. Finally at midnight on June 13, 1974, I was charged with the Securicor robbery. I made no reply and refused to make a statement. That morning I was taken, under heavy armed escort, to Brentford magistrate's court where I was put in a cell with some of my double-crossing colleagues. We looked an incredibly dishevelled bunch. Our hair was unkempt, there were dark lines under our eyes and our clothes were all wrinkled up. We just glared icily at each other and said very little. Then we were handcuffed together and ushered into the dock, which was surrounded by armed police with their shooters at the ready. Not surprisingly the police objected to bail and we were remanded in custody for a week. Off we went to Brixton Prison where we were told we would be category 'A' prisoners - which meant that we had screws with us everywhere we went.

It was in Brixton that everything really began to get on top of me. I could hear these worms telling each other in loud voices that I had done the grassing. Then during visiting hours, their wives began to wind them up by saying that Susan had helped me in grassing them up. They told callous lies against us both.

After one particularly nasty visit from these women, we all trooped back to the recreation cell, where category 'A' men can mix freely. There I heard one of the team say they were arranging to have Susan murdered. 'We've got they guy who's prepared to do it,' he said gloatingly. I flew at the bastard and began raining blows down upon him, but I was overpowered by another team member who tried to cool the situation.

The story was true. I have since discovered that a £2,000 contract was taken out on her life with a well-known criminal. I later heard one of them shout out that he was arranging for someone to kill one of my kids. 'We'll cut him up in little pieces and post his limbs one by one back to Mo's wife,' he said smugly. That really terrified me because I love my children and I didn't want any harm to come to them. It's surprising how many villains really do love their kids, though these unfeeling animals didn't appear to.

The troubles just mounted up for me. One day I was attacked by several members of my team who threatened to gouge out my eyes with a toothbrush. These savages, some of them weighing 16 stone, were hardened criminals and meant every nasty word they said. I managed to get free from them that time, but I knew they would eventually get me. I certainly didn't want to lose my sight for something I had never done. Later I found out someone had even smuggled a cyanide capsule into the prison and planned to slip it into my tea. But before that happened I had decided to take the most momentous decision of my life - to turn squealer. The pressures had built up to an unbearable pitch and I started to think about these criminal so-called friends of mine. If they could do this to me, why should I be loyal to them? I mulled over the matter for some days. Then I called a screw and said, 'I've had enough. Get me a high ranking officer from the Yard. I want to confess.' I told the warder that I wanted to reveal many important matters. 'Something like Bertie Smalls is it?' he asked. 'Bigger,' I said.

The message was flashed to the Flying Squad at the Yard and soon I received visits from several detectives. I told one that I had many things that I wished to talk about and they showed great interest, but at that early stage I don't think they grasped the full significance of what I wanted to do. I was taken to Brentford court again for my weekly appearance, and there I spoke to Terry Wrefford of the Sweeney Todd (Flying Squad). When he realised the full magnitude of what I was willing to say, he told his superiors.

The previous week I had appeared with the rest of the team in the dock, but in view of what I wanted to do, the police arranged for me to appear on my own. And they asked the magistrate to let me be remanded into police custody, rather than to Brixton, as they believed I could 'help them with certain important inquiries'. He agreed and I was taken downstairs and guarded by ten Squad officers.

The word soon got around those buzzing cells that 'Mo's gone QE.' (Queen's Evidence). And that sent my ex-colleagues into absolute panic. They had unjustly accused me of being a grass, well new they would really see what sort of grass I could be – THE BEST. In the days and months ahead I was to become a walking, talking, living, breathing encyclopaedia of crime. And my information was going to spell trouble, big trouble, for a lot of people, including those who had threatened to kill Susan and her son.

I was bundled out of the court, a blanket over my head, into a green prison van with dark tinted windows. I noticed through the glass as we sped away that there were crowds of people on the pavements watching this drama unfold. Police cars with their blue lights flashing and sirens wailing accompanied us front and rear as we drove to nearby Hounslow police station. I think the police were being a bit melodramatic - we screeched around corners and even mounted pavements as they rushed me through the streets. Maybe they felt that there was a danger that someone would try and ambush the vehicle to stop me squealing.

When we arrived at Hounslow police station, I was binned (locked up) and given a meal. When the talking began in earnest, the officers sat there open-mouthed. I think they thought I was just going to talk about the Securicor raid and a couple more jobs, but I couldn't stop speaking. Astonished members of three top Scotland Yard branches - the Flying Squad, Robbery Squad and C11 (Criminal Intelligence Branch) listened to my inside stories. I spoke of lorry hijackings, highly professional burglaries, bank raids, wages snatches and murders. I informed on more than 200 crooks involved in crimes totalling more than £2 million. And I personally admitted 102 offences, including more than 13 armed robberies and over 65 burglaries, involving more than £197,000 in cash and property. The officers just couldn't keep up with me. Not surprisingly the top brass of the Yard were soon at the station to talk to me. Like Robbery Squad chief,' Deputy Assistant Commissioner Ernest Bond, plus other top officers like Commander John Lock, Chief Superintendent John Swain, Chief Inspector David Dixon (now head of the Robbery Squad) and Chief Inspector Michael McAdam. They took turns in grilling me, but each time my stories were the same. It was very taxing mentally but my photographic memory stood me in good stead and I was able to go back many years and still recall every tiny detail of a job.

Fortunately Ernie Bond was prepared to accept me and my evidence, and decided that what I said should be acted upon. Ernie Bond, OBE, has now retired after a distinguished 30-year career, but he was then operational chief on the Yard's 3,500 detectives. Mr Bond had already been involved in the case of another arch squealer from the underworld, Bertie Smalls. The Yard had wanted to talk to Smalls about a bank raid but he vanished from his £30,000 home in Selsdon, Surrey. Then one day he turned up again - with an astonishing proposition. He wanted to talk. What he told the Robbery Squad not only led to the conviction of twenty-one top robbers, but was responsible for Scotland Yard setting up a new crime-fighting pattern that provided police protection for me and a string of other criminals prepared to 'shop' their former accomplices. After Bertie Smalls, I was the next big-time 'Judas of the Underworld', followed by people like Billy Williams, Jimmy Trusty and Charles Lowe. Between us we have helped to put away some 400 crooks. As with most of my squealing, the men Smalls informed on were his former friends. And like myself he was no fringe man. He actually donned a mask, carried a gun and went on the raids. He told Bond that his price for the talking was immunity from prosecution.

The Yard considered the case with the Director of Public Prosecutions, Sir Norman Skelhorn, and it was agreed that Small would go into the witness box and give evidence against the main figures in the bank robberies he had talked about, instead of standing with them in the dock. After Smalls' former accomplices had been sent away for jail sentences varying between three and twenty years, Sir Norman faced criticism from the legal profession and MPs. His opponents said it was wrong that Smalls, who was as guilty as his colleagues, should walk free. So it was decided that in future cases, no squealer would escape charges if he played a major part in the crimes. I know Mr Bond still thinks that Sir Norman's decision was right because from the public's point of view it is better to see several crooks locked up while one escapes justice than have them all avoid punishment. In Smalls' case the Yard saw they had been offered a great opportunity to break up organised crime. But they knew that Bertie's life was now in great danger, so a day-and-night guard was put on him and his family. Today, they are living respectable lives in total obscurity.

Since that case, despite the fact that none of us squealers was given a guarantee that we would not be prosecuted, we still went ahead. We gambled that co-operation with the police would be taken into consideration when jail sentences were passed on us.

I was kept at Hounslow for 21 life-changing days. I made statement after statement and every day I was taken out in an unmarked car to go over routes used for the robberies I had described to the police. Gradually I was able to supply telling bits of information which were later to prove vital to the police. The officers couldn't have been kinder to me during this traumatic period and I was staggered to discover their real humanity. My previous encounters with Old Bill had always been rather unfriendly, but these guys treated me with the utmost respect. They even allowed me, every second day, to go into Twickenham police station. There armed guards stood by as I had a lovely warm shower and trimmed my bushy beard. Back at Hounslow they now allowed me to have a radio in the cell, and in the evenings I would lie on the crisp clean sheets of my wooden bed and listen to pop music, or talk to my guards. The hell of Brixton was beginning to seem a long way off. As I let my thoughts wander, I began to fear for the safety of my girlfriend, and my wife and children. But the police assured me that they had moved them all to safety. 'They're all OK,' I was told. After 21 days at Hounslow, the Yard realised that this was a much bigger operation than they had first thought and decided to move me to another station, Chiswick. Shortly after I moved in, they formed a new Robbery Squad based there.

One day at Chiswick I was summoned before a very special committee of leading Yard officers, led by Chief Superintendent Jack Slipper, who is a man who has been much maligned for his handling of the Ronnie Biggs affair in Brazil. But he is someone I deeply respect and admire. He's a truly great copper who did a marvellous job in even getting to Biggs's South American front door. There was no way that he could have known that the slippery Mr Biggs would avoid extradition to England by a technicality, ie, putting his girlfriend Raimunda in the family way. Anyway, back to the committee.

Mr Slipper said to me, 'Well Mo, I must make it perfectly clear that there is no way that you can do a Bertie Smalls.' I told him that I knew I had to be punished for what I had done. He said, 'Well then, what do you hope to gain from all of this?' I replied, 'Nothing. But I have my reasons for doing what I am doing.' He knew of the threats to my girlfriend and family and patted me on the shoulder. 'Mo,' he said, 'it takes a lot of guts to do what you are doing. And I admire you.'

All the senior detectives in that room knew that my actions meant I had quite literally signed my own death warrant. That for the rest of my life I could never walk easily. For in a split second I could be wiped out by an assassin's bullet. 'I can take the threats on myself Mr Slipper, but I can't accept these evil men threatening to maim and kill my loved ones,' I said.

After the 'committee meeting' I was taken back to my cell by my faithful armed guards - Detective Sergeants Trevor Binnington, Billy Milne and Terry Wrefford. These were the men who guarded me with their lives and took down many of the statements I made regarding large-scale crime. The main cell at 'Costa del Chiswick' as I later nicknamed it, was brand new and L-shaped. It was very cosy. It was in a little cell block and I had access to another cell. I was allowed my door open all the time, though the passage door was usually locked. There was a sink in the block and I could use that freely and also walk about so my limbs didn't seize up. Sometimes I would see that the passage door had accidentally been left unlocked. I could have made a break for it, but that would have been pointless because by now there were people on the outside who would have done anything to kill me. I was much safer confined in a police station than if I was 'free' on the outside, a certain prey for London's savage underworld. In that strange little world at Chiswick, we all became matey. It wasn't long before we were on first name terms, and I even called the top Yard men by their Christian names. They always called me Mo.

A routine was soon established which usually included making statements and correcting them, pausing for refreshments, and then going out for walks by the River Thames at Chiswick bridge. It was decided that if I was not allowed out for a while each day, I might become stale and not able to recall all the information I had for them. So I was handcuffed and then driven to the river. There we would walk up and down the towpath and talk about almost everything. Sometimes they would let me do a bit of fishing. It was all very crude and I would use a bit of string and a bent nail with a little worm on the end. I didn't catch much, but it was really relaxing. On hot days we would sit on the river bank in the baking sunshine and I'd close my eyes and drift off into an uneasy sleep. We would all get really tanned. At least one of them always had to be on the alert in case of trouble, though most of the time they all kept watch while I snoozed. I would talk to my guards about my life and they would tell me about their families. It was strange, but these men were spending more time with me than with their wives and children. We became very close and had a real respect for each other. One of them told me one day, 'Mo, I never thought I could really like you, but I do.' And I told him he wasn't so bad himself!

I discovered later that I wasn't being taken out just so that I could keep reasonably fit, but also because the police didn't really want it known that I was at the station. Villains were being brought in all the time and placed in nearby cells, so the law wanted me out of the way for long periods in case the crooks recognised me.

I particularly enjoyed walking around the local parks. One day we were strolling through one when I suddenly realised it was the place where an elderly park keeper had been savagely coshed to the ground after he noticed some of the team putting false number plates on the getaway car in the Securicor raid. The brutal attack had happened so quickly that I hadn't been able to stop it, but I was so angry with the maniac that I threatened to put a hammer through his head. What animals we all were at that time. I asked my police guards if they had received any news of the poor old man, and they said they had heard that he had recovered from the beating. Apparently he was so afraid that he didn't report the attack to the police, and they didn't hear about it until much later. It just shows how frightened people can be when villains explode uninvited into their lives. I wonder how many attacks like this are never reported to the police because of fear of reprisals.

When we got back to Chiswick, my guards used to troop into the canteen and bring me double helpings of everything. I made a real pig of myself, but this was such a contrast to my harrowing life in prison that I couldn't help stuffing myself. I knew it couldn't go on for ever, so I decided to make the best of it while I could. I usually had a refreshing Pepsi Cola to go with my meal and then to follow, a nice cup of tea and some biscuits to dunk in the cup.

After my food I would lie down for a while to let it go down or we'd sit round and play cards before going out on to the streets of London so I could point out more locations of our raids. After the claustrophobia of prison, this was so wonderful. Anyone who has never been locked up will never understand how terrifying it can be. Even a normal villain can find it torment but for me, a person who never knew if each day would be the last one, it was absolute torture, both mental and physical.

I longed to see Susan again. She was always on my mind. So one Sunday I asked if there was any chance of speaking to her on the station 'phone. The police didn't see any problems, so I was able to dial her number. Naturally, she was amazed to hear my voice and she broke down and sobbed her heart out with happiness. I think she had believed we would never see each other again and that I didn't love her any more. After she recovered her composure, I said, 'Darling, could you bring me some Sunday dinner? I'd love to taste your cooking again.' I don't know whether she thought I had escaped from prison or not, but she asked me where I was. 'I'm at Chiswick Police Station, Chiswick High Road. Go to the front counter and just ask for Mo. They'll let you into my cell.'

It wasn't long before she arrived at the nick with a lovely roast beef dinner covered by a tea cloth. The amazed station officer didn't know what was going on when she announced, 'I've brought Mo his dinner.' He scratched his head and checked with my guards. They said it was all right and Susan was heralded into my cell. I cuddled her and she again broke down and cried. 'I thought you'd be happy, not upset, to see me again,' I told her. 'I am happy Mo, that's why I'm crying,' she explained, wiping her eyes. I tucked into my tasty meal, and as we talked she cried once more as she told me of the threats she had received from villains.

'They say they are going to kill me and my son,' she said. I tried to reassure her that it was me they were after and not her, though, of course, I knew these violent men would stop at nothing to hurt me - even if it was through innocent people.

After just over an hour she left and I said, 'I'll see you tonight dear.' The police officers nearly collapsed with shock but eventually they reluctantly agreed that she could come and see me again that evening. Soon she was thoroughly screened for security and was able to come and go when she liked. Not all the officers at Chiswick approved this freedom I was being allowed. One told me, 'You will only be able to see your girlfriend once a week.' I shouted, 'She'll see me day and night!' 'No, she won't,' he retorted. So I told him that if that was so I wouldn't co-operate any more, and I would just go back to jail. His face turned every colour of the rainbow when he realised the repercussions of what I was saying and he said he would consult the chiefs at the Yard. They agreed with me and so I would look forward to her visits, sometimes two a day. The officers were very discreet and she would be left alone with me for up to two hours at a time. The door was shut and the guards used to remain outside.

I must point out that this situation had never been allowed by any police force before, and so there were no rules. I was a man who was helping to smash some of London's most violent crime, and knowing full well I could go to prison for a long time, so they had to make sure I was kept in good spirits and retained my sanity. I was an important missile to use as a warhead against the underworld, but if I cracked I would be useless in a witness box. They knew that Susan kept me sane and so they allowed her to be with me. I was marked 'Handle with care' and I hope I didn't really abuse too much the VIP treatment I was receiving from the world's greatest police force.

One day I decided that I was missing some of my home comforts, and so I asked my guards if there was any chance of us going to my Paddington flat to pick up 'a few items'. I'm sure they didn't realise what I had in mind as we went over there in three unmarked cars. When we arrived I began carrying things down - first my portable colour television set, then my eight-track stereo, and loading them into the cars. The wide-eyed officers didn't quite know what to do as I went back for more food, money, shoes, shaving kit, after-shave, scissors and even my three-bar electric fire - anything that I felt would make my stay a little more comfortable.

One of the officers laughed nervously and said, 'The Yard ain't going to believe this.' Then another added, 'I don't know about the Yard not believing this; I don't, and I'm here watching it!' The poor bloke scratched his head and said, 'I think God's got a grudge against me.' But soon they were joining in the fun and one actually said, 'Why don't we take your 26-inch colour telly, so we can watch the horse racing?' If we could have got it in the car we would have, but it was just too big. . . . Then I asked them if any of them had a roof-rack. 'I may as well take my bed.' 'You've got to be joking,' said the cop. I wasn't . . . but they had no rack.'

When we arrived back at Chiswick we went in a back entrance, hoping that no-one would see what was going on. My guards checked all my gear for arms and then brought the home comforts through to my little cell block where I showed them where to put everything. 'You look as if you're just coming in off a burglary,' I joked with one of the sweating coppers as he staggered in with goods in both hands. When the senior officers from the Yard came on a visit and saw what I had, they couldn't believe it. We gave you permission to bring in a little gear, but we didn't say you could bring the whole house,' said one of them. The uniformed branch at Chiswick couldn't believe what was going on either. A prisoner with a colour television and stereo was unheard of! They thought I must be pretty important to get such treatment, so for a joke I put 'VIP' on a piece of cardboard and displayed it outside my door.

I'm glad I did get that stuff out of my flat because shortly afterwards it was burgled and goods worth more than £2,000 were stolen. At least I had saved some of the stuff. By then my wife and children had been whisked away by the police and were under armed protection in a safe place. What made this blow even more shocking to me was the fact that the insurance company who issued a household policy to me - the Prudential Assurance Company - refused to pay up. They said they would not honour my £20 document because of my record. I have considered legal action against the mighty Pru because I told the agent who sold me the policy that I was a criminal. When I took it out at the end of 1973 there was nothing on the form about having a record. I lost diamonds, fur coats, gold jewellery, a tape recorder, tapes and some other clothes. I felt I should have been treated like any other person insuring himself.

When I was freed later I spoke to David Pallister of the *Guardian* newspaper. He ran a story under the headline 'Master criminal to sue the Pru.' Part of the story read:

> His flat in Ashmore Road, Paddington, was broken into in July or August shortly after he had been arrested and held, for his own safety, in a Chiswick police station cell. It was there, on the instruction of the Home Secretary, Mr Jenkins, that he spent the greatest part of his sentence - a practice so unusual that questions were asked in the Commons about his apparently privileged position.
>
> Mr O'Mahoney's sense of injustice is unlikely to be appeased. A claims official for the Pru said that their repudiation of his claim was based on sound legal precedent. 'The client signs a declaration which includes the words that "nothing materially affecting the risk has been concealed". The courts have ruled that any reasonable person reading this would deduce that a criminal record ought to be revealed,' the 'spokesman said.
>
> 'If a fellow had only an isolated incident against him and an otherwise clean sheet the underwriters may accept the risk. In this case our agent denies that Mr O'Mahoney told him about his record. We do not turn down claims without a very good cause.'

I don't care what the Pru say, I'll never insure anything through them again. And if a salesman ever comes to my door trying-to sell me another policy, I'll rip it up in front of his eyes and boot him out. Talk about having the strength of an insurance company around you. . . .

But back to Chiswick. I was jolted back to grim reality twice a week when I was taken to Brentford court to be remanded yet again to the police station. We would set off in convoy and the whole court was searched before I was allowed in. When I arrived all the surrounding rooftops were covered by police marksmen and I would be rushed in from the van and down into the cells. I would be kept well out of the grips of former associates. But they were within earshot and would make jokes such as, 'Here comes Mo, the grass.' I'd smile and tell them about the lovely food I'd been enjoying. 'How's the lumps in your porridge?' I'd gloat. And one of them would shout, 'You'll have lumps in your head when we get hold of you.' I said, 'Now, now, gentlemen, you mustn't talk like that.' And the police would break it up and tell us all to be quiet. 'How can you keep animals quiet?' I said one day.

I would always appear in the dock on my own and the remand would go through quickly. As I appeared I would look straight ahead, but I could see out of the side of my eyes that the place was packed with relatives of the men I was shopping. I could sense the hatred in their eyes and I'm sure if they could have got at me they'd have tried to tear me limb from limb. I would just smile and say nothing. I could hear them making obscene remarks about me under their breath and this would make me and the detectives with me seethe with anger. One of the cops cheered me up one day, when he whispered to me, 'See that one there, well I don't know what she's laughing about - she's getting nicked in a minute for intimidating a witness!' And she was . . . along with two others.

Those trips to Brentford were quite hair-raising, because none of us knew what was going to happen. I was the number-one target for many vicious villains and the police were taking no chances with me. So the tension for all of us was quite electric.

Each time I got back to Chiswick, we all heaved a sigh of relief. And what made it even nicer was that each evening Susan would arrive with beautiful meals, like curries, steaks, and casseroles. I used to sit there in my 'harem' with her, feeling like a Sultan of Baghdad. She would often bring in a bottle of wine and we would enjoy that with the food. The officers were marvellous and they left us alone to talk and listen to my stereo or watch the late night movie on television. One of them would pop in from time to time to see I was all right but he would always knock first. They were very discreet. Often Susan would stay until 2 am and then get a taxi home, or if an officer was going her way, he would give her a lift in a police car. They were absolutely marvellous to us both.

A man who was to become a real friend was soon brought into Chiswick - bank robber Billy Williams. Billy was kept segregated from me, for a while, but we later shared cells at Brixton and back at Chiswick. He too had turned squealer, because a policeman's heroism had changed his life. He told me it made him sick of his criminal ways and gave him the inspiration to go straight. The cop was PC David Clements who was shot at the wheel of his panda car as he chased a getaway car after a London bank raid in July, 1974. Billy admitted taking part in the job in which PC Clements was shot. He saw the policeman flinch as the bullet hit him and watched as the panda car crashed into a roadside skip. But the young policeman reversed and continued the chase.

After that, Billy went straight - with a vengeance. He gave full details of major crimes committed in London after 1965, with the names of those involved. Later, he pleaded guilty at the Old Bailey to taking part in three armed raids, two at banks and one at a brewery, in which a total of £37,653 was stolen.

In a bid to wipe the slate clean, he also asked for thirty-six other offences of robbery and conspiracy to be taken into consideration. In return for his help, the police agreed to protect his family from underworld reprisals. Like myself, Billy made no bargain with the Old Bill and he eventually got a similar sentence to me. When he was at Chiswick, Billy was also allowed a television and other home comforts. It wouldn't have been fair if I had got them and he hadn't. And during his stay Billy, then 24, was actually allowed out of his cell to marry secretary Barbara Stanikowski, aged eighteen. The only witnesses at this bizarre wedding were two Flying Squad officers - both wearing carnations. One was Chief Superintendent Jack Slipper, who had arrested Billy. Mr John Saxby, superintendent registrar at Brentford registry office, performed the brief ceremony in a drab interview room there. Then the couple were driven back for a 'reception' at the nick, where, surrounded by detectives, they cut the wedding cake and were toasted in champagne. After a lingering kiss from his bride, Billy was taken back to his cell, leaving Barbara on her own. The Home Office had granted special permission for the wedding, mainly because it had been planned before Billy's arrest. His previous marriage was dissolved, and his address on the new marriage certificate was 205 High Road, Chiswick - the police station.

The man charged with actually shooting PC Clements, salesman Philip Trusty, then 24, was put in the next cell to me at Chiswick. I got talking to him over a period of days and found out he was frightened. I suppose because I was a villain he confided in me, which was the last thing he ever should have done. He obviously didn't realise that I was now a squealer and coughed to me all about the robbery, actually naming names. I 'was called to give evidence at his trial and he got very nasty with me in court and threatened to cut my throat. But my squealing was nothing compared with that of his double-crossing brother Jimmy, whose evidence was partly responsible for putting Philip in jail for life. During the two-month trial, 30-year-old Jimmy went into the witness box to tell how his brother nearly killed 23-year-old PC Clements who at six foot eight inches is one of the tallest men in the Metropolitan Police. He said it happened during a getaway chase after an £11,000 raid on the St John's Wood branch of Barclays Bank. The gang, with Jimmy at the wheel of a Jaguar car, escaped after the police car went into a skid when PC Clements was shot. After the case the brave copper - who was praised for his 'conspicuous gallantry' by the judge - told how he was taking home an old lady who had collapsed in the street when he drove straight into the bank robbery. After challenging the crooks in the bank and being told at gunpoint: 'One step more copper, and you are dead,' he went off in pursuit of the gang.

Besides 'life', Mr Justice Nield also gave Trusty 20 years for three robberies involving nearly £40,000 and 15 years for conspiracy to rob. 'Squealer' Jimmy, who admitted his part in the Barclays robbery was given a sentence of two years nine months earlier in the hearing. Sentences totalling 80 years were handed out to the whole gang.

But the time was now fast approaching for my own trial at the Old Bailey. Naturally I wanted to look my best so I asked for permission for my Mayfair hairdresser to be allowed to come to my cell and cut, blow dry and style my hair. Quite a few stars use this salon, including Irish singer Dana, whom I often used to talk to when I was there. My barber said he would be happy to come and soon arrived with all his equipment. We went into the gent's toilet and he went to work. He did a marvellous job and trimmed my beard as well. An armed guard stood by the whole time. We had a nice chat and he charged me £10 for his work, which I thought was very reasonable.

Then Deputy Assistant Commissioner Ernie Bond came and had a chat with me about my trial and thanked me for what I had done to assist the police. 'It's very brave of you,' he said. 'And only you can do it Mo.' By now tension was building up inside me and the police did all they could to keep me calm. I would sometimes go out with my guards to a police centre to kick a football around. Jack Slipper would pop in late at night for a talk. 'Don't worry about anything Mo, it'll all be all right,' he would tell me. But I would admit to him that I wasn't so sure. I said I was worried I would get a long sentence and that it would be a killer for someone like me in jail, 'With your courage and determination and the assistance you've given the police you should get a good result,' he said confidently. 'But, as you know, that will be up to the Judge.'

Hours of snooker in the nick's recreation room didn't really take my mind off that fast approaching trial. Soon that day, the nineteenth of September, 1974, arrived. To me the night before it was like awaiting my execution. The guards tried to cheer me up and keep me going, but I felt terrible, confused, wondering what was going to happen to me. My girlfriend stayed with me until one am and we just held each other tight not knowing what to say when it was time for her to leave. Then I played snooker and cards with the officers all through the dark hours.

At nine am next morning my escorts arrived. I had packed up all my 'goodies', which were to be taken over to my girl's secret hideout. I was then allowed to 'phone her. 'Good luck darling,' Susan whispered. 'I'll see you in court.' Then, accompanied by three armed guards, I got into the prison van and we sped out of the police yard, in a long convoy, sirens blazing. We were off to the Old Bailey . . . and my DAY OF JUDGEMENT.

12
I Sign My Own Death Warrant

Maurice, you must be prepared for a seventeen year sentence.' Those shock words from my counsel left me stunned and sick. Seventeen years . . . in solitary. It had to be solitary because I needed to be protected from the evil men who would try and kill me at the first opportunity. Seventeen years . . . of talking to bare cell walls, because no-one else would be allowed to share my hell with me.

I felt the blood drain from my face as I sat in that detention room at the Old Bailey. My police guards were as shocked as me by this warning. They were well aware of the help I had given the police with my squealing and were hoping for a much shorter sentence for me. But this was a killer.

Even as we had zoomed along the London streets to this famous old court - put up in 1834 and rebuilt between 1900 and 1907 on the site of the notorious old Newgate Prison - I had felt the inside of my mouth go dry with fear. I couldn't remember ever being so nervous before. Part of the Bailey - the word means wall and the court is built next to the old London city wall – was still damaged from the IRA car bomb attack in 1973 in which one man died and many people were injured. But it was the scales of justice on top of the court that caught my eye as we arrived. I wondered what sort of justice I would get . . .

I was in a daze as I sat waiting to be called for my trial before the man known as 'the sporting judge', Sir Carl Aarvold, by now in his sixties but in his youth one of the greatest rugby players of his time and captain of Cambridge University and England. He won 16 caps and skippered the national side seven times. It's hard to explain the fear that comes into a criminal's mind when he faces a long stretch. It's bad enough for an ordinary crook, but if you know you are going down for many years and you could spend it all in solitary . . . never-ending solitary . . . well, that can send you up the wall. Those years and years stretching before you. . . . Well, I told myself, I'd rather be dead than endure that.

As my mind began to register the full horror of this prospect, my thoughts were interrupted by the call, 'Bring up the prisoner.' I felt like I was walking to the gallows as I was ushered along the passage, guarded by ten Old Bailey officers and six Flying Squad men. I walked up the cold, dark, stairs until I got to the side door of the court. An Old Bailey officer went before me to see if it was all right for me to be let in. It was, and he said, 'OK Mo, in you go and good luck.' As I walked into Court Seven, I saw the place was packed with people - reporters, prison officers, inquisitive members of the public and more than 20 armed Flying Squad heavies. I looked into the public gallery and saw my girlfriend Susan there, along with my father and her mother. In the well of the court I noticed top cops like Ernie Bond, John Lock, John Swain and Jack Slipper, all tensely awaiting the start of the trial. They knew what happened to me could affect the decisions of other potential squealers. If my sentence was too harsh it could stop them coming forward. So it was an important day for all of us.

Sir Carl - he looked regal in his wig and red robes – stared straight into my eyes and I looked back. I didn't flinch as I knew he was obviously trying to weigh me up and see what sort of man I really was. I must say he couldn't have been more courteous during the trial, and I was genuinely sorry when I heard that shortly afterwards he retired as Recorder of London and the Old Bailey's senior judge. He had been Recorder for eleven years and at the Bar for 43.

I couldn't help myself, but as the case opened, I found my eyes going out of focus and my mind reflecting on how this nightmare had all begun with a miscarriage of justice all those years ago on that terrible Christmas Day in 1958. If I hadn't gone through that experience, maybe I wouldn't have become such a vicious and heartless villain. Maybe . . . who knows? I don't really blame anyone for what happened so long ago. It was just one of those quirks of fate that happen and change the whole direction of a person's life.

I noted the jury box was empty - there was no need for those so-called 'Twelve Just Men', because I had pleaded guilty to taking part in 13 armed robberies, 65 burglaries and various offences of conspiracy to commit crime - a total of 102 charges involving cars and property valued at £197,000. It's strange, but the whole theatrical scene didn't seem to be happening to me. It was if I was an onlooker to it all. Yet I was the unwilling star on the stage.

You may wonder why I said so-called 'Twelve Just Men'. I know many people in Britain are convinced that our jury system is the best in the world, but I know from first-hand knowledge that it is sometimes open to serious question. Before my arrest I, along with other gangland leaders, was involved in capturing and frightening jury members. In one particularly nasty case, a juror was pounced upon by two men who pointed sawn-off shotguns at him. He froze in fear as they told him: 'If our pals go down, you and your wife and kids are going to die.' The terrified man was told to keep walking and not look back. The following morning he had the courage to stand up in court and tell the judge what had happened, and he was allowed to stand down. But, unbeknown to the judge, other members of the jury had been bought off by crooks. The accused got off. Could the 'bought' jurymen have been responsible?

I supplied the police with the evidence on this case, and two men were arrested - the pair who had pointed their guns at the jury member. His description of them exactly fitted these two villains, but when they were put on an identification parade, the man was too scared to put his hand on their shoulders and indicate these were the ones. He kept telling the police, 'I can't.

My family. They'll kill my family.' He said the men knew where he lived and where his kids went to school, so he daren't co-operate. I couldn't blame the juror for his action, because these were desperate men, but I can only hope that others who have been threatened or approached with bribes will have the courage to bring these thugs to book. Otherwise British justice, the envy of the world, will just be a mockery.

Incidentally, a special squad was set up at Chiswick to investigate jury rigging after I told the police what I knew about it.

But back to the trial. Mr Michael Hill, prosecuting, described me in court as the 'most-guarded man in Britain'. He went on to say, 'O'Mahoney began talking months ago and has not stopped since.' He explained to the judge that many of the men I had named had been arrested, but many more were being sought. He said my assistance to the police had been 'incalculable'. Mr Hill told how I began my disclosures about my criminal associates after being attacked and threatened with having my eyes gouged out with a toothbrush while I was on remand at the Scrubs. He said it would not be right to divulge anything in open court, and handed the judge a list of documents containing names and details of crimes.

My defending counsel, Mr Kenneth Machin, said apart from offences in which I had been personally involved, I had warned detectives about planned robberies, including one which it estimated would have been worth about £1 million to the participants. I had also given information for an attempted murder investigation and assisted in clearing the name of a detective framed by the underworld.

'The total amount of money of crimes that have happened, or have been planned, prevented or avoided, because of him, runs into seven figures,' said Mr Machin.

He said that in prison I would have to be kept in solitary confinement. That I feared death for myself and my family from 'a number of very dangerous and violent men who would kill him at the first opportunity. And he added: 'By his action he may effectively have signed his own DEATH WARRANT.'

During the mitigation, the police officers who guarded me were called to the box. To my amazement they all spoke highly of me. I was choked when I heard what they said. Detective Sergeant Trevor Binnington said: 'I have been with him more than I have been with my family. I am convinced he is completely genuine in his attempts to win back a place in the society he went to war with.'

Detective Sergeant Billy Milne told the judge that he echoed the words of his colleague. They both came back to the dock and stood with me.

Then Detective Superintendent John Swain went into the dock. This man, who then headed the crack Robbery Squad, was obviously important to my case. I held my breath and waited to hear what he would say about me. Mr Swain told the court that it could well be that I had given police more information than self-confessed Wembley bank robber Bertie Smalls. I could hear my heart beat faster when he said this, because I knew that if my sentence was to be shorter than the predicted 17 years, I had to have the verbal support of top policemen like John Swain.

Sir Carl then asked me if I had anything to say before sentence was passed. I looked straight at him and said. 'I know that what I have done in the past is wrong and I believe that what I am doing now is right. I was brought up to believe that the only thing worth anything was money. 'I will take my own life rather that let the scum and trash of the criminal world do it. I have been put here today because of their influence.

'It's about time some people in this country spoke out against them and I hope they follow my example. I want to hit right at the heart of the criminal underworld.'

I also told the judge of the threats to Susan, her parents and son, and then I added: 'My girlfriend Susan has never conspired with me or anybody else in any robberies or any crime whatsoever. I love her very much and will marry her in due course. She has kept me going and gave me the courage that I have needed to be here this day. . '

'On the other hand, my associates have threatened to gouge my eyes out with a toothbrush and have put a contract to kill out on my family. Criminals have one loyalty, that's to themselves. They don't care who they hurt or what condition the victim is left in. I do not wish to make 'excuses for my behaviour, as I am to blame.

'I have not made a deal with you or anybody else for a lenient sentence. I am emotionally upset because of the large sentence you are about to impose on me, which I know would be an appropriate one.'

I told the hushed court that I planned to be back at the Old Bailey to 'bring these other callous criminals, to justice'. I said it was about time these criminals felt what it was like to bleed themselves.

I sat down and waited for the worst. The judge looked solemnly at me and said I should have got 20 years for these 'grave and terrible crimes' but was entitled to credit for my courage and determination in bringing other evil men to the attention of the police.

I swallowed hard as he said: 'I therefore sentence you to FIVE YEARS imprisonment.' I could hardly speak as I said, 'Thank you.' Then I found I couldn't control my emotions any longer and broke down and wept with relief. It may seem strange that a hardened criminal like me lost control, but I had been led to expect 17 years, and I was so relieved it was so much less. By now I was completely surrounded by my armed guards and Old Bailey officers in case of attack. With tears in my eyes I stood up and mouthed to my girlfriend, 'Don't worry love. It won't be long.' Then just as I turned to go down the dimly-lit stairs I heard to my horror the clerk of the court shout: 'Stop. My Lord there's a small matter of a suspended six months' sentence outstanding.' (That was for the attack with a soda syphon on a publican.) The judge looked sternly at him and said, 'Oh, very well, make that concurrent with the five year sentence.' I heaved a sigh of relief and then, as I glanced up at Susan, I noticed she too was crying and was being comforted by her mother and some Flying Squad officers.

'Don't worry love, why don't you go down to the cells and see him?' said one of the men. She was brought down to a special cell that had been set apart for me in the women's quarters, so that none of the male prisoners could get at me. We cuddled each other for several minutes as my armed guards looked the other way. I told her not to worry as it was all over now. At least we knew what the length of the sentence was. 'It may not even be five years,' I said cheerfully, 'If I keep my nose clean they could give me parole after a third of the time.' That seemed to reassure her a little and as she left she turned to me and said, 'I love you darling. Please say you love me.' I told her, 'Of course I do.' As she left I felt completely full up with emotion.

I was then escorted to the front gates where, as is the normal practice at the Bailey, I was formally told that I had been given five years. I suppose this is done because so many prisoners are in such a state of shock when they are sentenced that they don't take it in what the judge has given them.

Next I was handcuffed to a prison officer and helped into a green Transit prison van with dark windows. In the yard of the court I could see the convoy of police cars getting ready to accompany it out. Then the huge doors of the Bailey opened and away we went to the accompaniment of banshee sirens and pulsing blue lights. Policemen were stopping traffic outside the court and turning the nearby traffic lights red, so that we could have free passage. I gazed out of the window and could see Susan amidst the crowds, looking dazed and holding the arm of her mother. Members of the Flying Squad were standing on the street corner to watch me and they gave me a wave.

'It's Oxford Prison for you O'Mahoney,' a prison officer told me as the van raced through London. By now I could hardly think straight. I felt dizzy and sick. The van was full of armed policemen and I pondered on how I would be protected when they delivered me to the prison - and then left. Surely it would not be impossible for some slag to have a go at me inside.

It was getting late when we finally arrived at the grim jail in that famous old university city. The doors swung open wide and I was taken to the reception office. A friendly officer guided me to the shower and then I was given a fantastic meal of bacon, eggs, sausage and tomatoes. Well it would have been fantastic normally, but I couldn't finish it. I was too shocked to eat properly. Then I had my finger prints taken and I was asked to sign for my property. I had to swap my expensive suit for the drab prison garb of a blue and white striped shirt, green tie, black shoes, and grey socks, and grey trousers. My number, I was told, was to be 132668. I was then taken back to a waiting cell with my Flying Squad guards and I said farewell to them. They had been my friends for so long now that I knew I was going to miss their company. 'We'll come and see you next week, Mo,' they promised.

Then I was led along a badly-lit passageway and fell over the wing cat which ran squealing along the corridor. That brought a smile to my face as I thought of the times I had done that before on jobs! But the grin soon faded. The tiny cell looked cold and frightening. Several windows were broken and at times the draught was gale force. The furniture certainly left something to be desired. It was a far cry from the relative luxury I had become used to at Chiswick. There was a bed, table and chair, a dirty old bowl, a piss pot and a plastic jug. The prison officer said, 'Would you like to get some hot water before I lock up?' I nodded and went and got it, and some drinking water in my plastic jug. Then I was locked in. The bolts were drawn, and I was alone ... completely alone.

I must be honest, I felt really bitter that someone who had tried to help society by attacking the underworld at it's very heart was now being humiliated by being kept in solitary confinement. People who have never experienced it don't realise what it's like to be all alone. Your mind plays tricks on you, it taunts you and sometimes it sends you completely insane.
I wondered if I was going to be able to stand up to it ...

13
The Day Ian Brady Got My Dinner

I t didn't take long for the word to get around Oxford jail that supergrass Maurice O'Mahoney was there. I knew that no-one could actually get at me, but the mental anguish from the taunts hurled at me soon began to unhinge my mind. I would hear the slags screaming abuse in my direction from their cell windows. Things like, 'You're going to be poisoned you grass.' If I could have got at any of them, I would have torn them apart. But they were shouting their insults from a safe distance and I just had to take it.

Then threatening notes started coming under my cell door. I could hear the prisoners, who had somehow got that close, running off. I don't know what on earth the prison officers were playing at, allowing this to happen, but they did. The secret messages threatening a cruel end to me and all my family kept coming under the door and as fast as I tore one up, another would be slipped through.

My exercise period totalled an hour a day - 30 minutes in the morning and 30 minutes in the afternoon. Several grim-faced officers marched me off to a piece of ground right by the prison's old hangman's tower. In view of the threats, it couldn't have been in a worse place. The tower is in a corner of Oxford jail which has a beam jutting out from the wall. Close by is a mound - full of bodies, the last remains of those executed there. In olden times, the condemned man or woman would be taken up in the tower and have the rope tied around their neck. Then they were just kicked out into space and dangled there until they could dance no more. This morbid place was my only contact with the outside, or should I say the inside world. I would sit down, surrounded by officers, and inhale the fresh air and look at the beautiful flowers in that plot of ground I called the garden of death.

It soon became obvious to me that the authorities didn't know how to handle my case. They were certainly keeping me from physical attack, but my mind was under constant pressure and this, in many ways, was a more dangerous condition. I had always had an active brain, but now there was nothing to do with it. I counted the bricks on the wall like some people count sheep before going to sleep. I would think about my girlfriend for hours and I hoped and prayed that this time nothing would go wrong.

But the taunting of the slags finally got to me and I asked to be taken to the hospital wing. I was still kept in solitary there, but it somehow seemed a bit more cheerful. There was more going on. Anything was better than 23 hours every day in that cold, dank cell I had been given. As I lay on my hospital bed one day, a prison officer came to the door and said, 'Get dressed, O'Mahoney, you've got a visitor.' A visitor? I couldn't believe it. I had almost come to believe that I had been completely forgotten by the outside world. I dressed quickly -I was in my prison-issue pyjamas - and was taken to a private office where I was delighted to see my old friend and guard, Detective Sergeant Trevor Binnington. I could see his face drop when he saw my pallid complexion and the heavy lines under my eyes. 'What's happened to you, Mo?' he asked with great concern. When I told him of all that had been going on, he was disgusted. 'You know I can't personally do anything Mo, but I'll pass all this on to my senior officers,' he said.

It was really great to see Trevor again, but the best was yet to come. He revealed that he had a nice surprise for me. 'I've brought Susan along to see you,' he said. With that she came running in and flung her arms around me. We both broke down and cried as we hugged each other. 'I'll be all right,' I tried to assure her, knowing deep down that if I carried on in this way, I wouldn't be. She had brought me some paintings to decorate my cell, a transistor radio, some fruit and a few sweets. 'I'm sorry O'Mahoney, but you can't have any of that,' said a sadistic officer who was standing near by. I tried to explain that long-term prisoners were allowed these things, but he wouldn't have it at all. I went back to my hospital cell with a nasty taste in my mouth, and Susan and Trevor returned to London.

My stay at Oxford was short-lived and I was soon moved on to Winchester Prison. I had begun to cling on to straws,' thinking maybe this would be better, and my spirits lifted for a few hours as we zoomed along in a heavily guarded Transit van towards Hampshire. But my depression quickly came back. The taunts began as soon as I arrived. I was taken to the hospital wing and interviewed by a lady doctor. I was so despondent that I had refused to go out on exercise. She asked me why I wouldn't go and I said: 'I don't want to be involved with criminals. I'm afraid that if one of them says something to me I'll break free from the screws and hurt him bad.' She then said something which made me despair of the medical profession. 'Look O'Mahoney, I know that during your exercise period there are 21 murderers out there at the same time. Don't be afraid of them, only one is dangerous.'

I wasn't very polite to the lady. 'How the hell do you work that out then?' I asked, adding: 'Are you a nutter, madam?' She got quite annoyed. So I punched home my point. 'How can you say only one's dangerous? 'They've all killed, that's enough for me.' The doctor said, 'But some of them didn't mean to kill.' I made it clear that I believed once a man had killed that meant he had tasted blood and was perfectly able to do it again. I just didn't want to be the victim. 'If you don't mind, madam, I'd prefer just to go back to my cell and mind my own business.'

I went back all right, and refused to get out of bed - for 40 days. I just lay there in a state of mental shock, not wanting to do anything. I ate the occasional meal and went to the toilet, but that was all. And I know the prison authorities were getting desperately worried about my behaviour.

Finally the principal officer decided to take a stern line with me and came storming into my cell shouting, 'O'Mahoney, get out of that bed and go out on exercise.' Something snapped inside my brain and I jumped out of bed and rushed at him. 'It's Mr O'Mahoney to you,' I yelled. 'And if you attempt to take my bed from me to get me out I'll wrap it around your head.'

I told him, 'I'm minding my own business. I'm not interfering with you and your staff, so don't interfere with me.' He protested, 'But you've been in bed for 40 days.' I interrupted him and said, 'And 40 nights. And I'll be in bed another 40 days if I choose so.' He told me that the medical staff were getting very worried about me. I said sarcastically, 'Is that why they wanted me to go on exercise with 21 murderers, then?'

As you can imagine I was beginning to bitterly resent having co-operated with the police. 'What sort of treatment was this for having done it?' I thought. 'Some reward!'

Word began to filter back to the Yard that I was deeply distressed with what was happening and they too began to worry about me. So they sent some officers to see me with my girlfriend. I was led along yards and through the terrorist wing, where the IRA were on one side and the UDA on the other. We all met up in the same cell that Blackpool police killer Frederick Joseph Sewell used for his visits while he was at Winchester. Susan again brought the radio, fruit and chocolates. This time they allowed the sweets, but the radio, for some reason, was again confiscated. I began to wonder if I was actually in England, and not in some labour camp in Siberia. The regime was so strict and unbending.

But, I was delighted when I heard that I was to leave my hell for a time to give evidence at Brentford magistrate's court during the committal proceedings involving several of my former associates. I knew it could be unpleasant and possibly dangerous to see them again, but even that was better than what I was going through in prison at that time. At 6 am next day I was awakened by a prison officer and after a quick wash, I was taken to the green Transit van with darkened windows for my trip to Brentford. Inside the truck were seven prison and police officers and as the big jail doors opened I saw two police cars were there to escort me - one up front, the other at the back. As we changed police areas, another two cars would take up the convoy duties and the others would fall back. I felt quite excited as we hit London and I saw all the people scurrying about their business. Being locked up like an animal you forget what freedom is really like. If only those busy Londoners realised how lucky they were to be on the outside. . . .

I was thrilled when I realised that we were going first to Chiswick police station, and as I clambered out of the truck there, I burst into a big smile because the Flying Squad had turned out in force to greet me. I felt like some sort of celebrity, and more important, I began to feel like a human being again. I was taken into the canteen and given a lovely breakfast of bacon, eggs, sausage and tomatoes, with cups of steaming tea to wash it down. It was fantastic. As we sat around the canteen table I told the cops of my prison treatment and they were absolutely horrified. I also spoke to senior officers about what had been going on and they were just as shocked. The prison officers who had travelled up with me sat quietly trying to figure out why an apparently common or garden prisoner was being treated like a VIP by the police. But they kept quiet and just observed it all.

Then Susan arrived and we sat and held hands in a cell for a few minutes. Then I held her tight. We kept trying to reassure each other that everything would be all right, though by now we both had great doubts about the future. 'I don't know how I can cope with going back to Winchester,' I told her. 'It's destroying me.' She looked so helpless and knew what I had said was true.

When I arrived with my heavy escort at Brentford, I again noted that police were everywhere, streets around the court were sealed off and there were armed marksmen on the roof. The court was full of my former friends and their relatives. I don't think they realised how important my evidence was going to be, and my ex-accomplices all sat there smirking as I went into the witness box. But when they heard what I had to say, their smirks turned to black scowls. And then their anger broke out into threats to me from the dock. Several times the magistrate warned them to be quiet or they would be removed from the court. While I gave my evidence, they would make signs indicating they were going to cut my throat whenever the magistrate wasn't watching. Then they would shout 'imbecile' and 'Judas', and try and make me laugh by screwing up their faces at a crucial moment in my evidence.

Once they cracked me up and I burst out laughing. One of their counsel looked very serious and said, 'What are you laughing at?' I replied, 'The monkeys in the dock, sir.' The whole court burst into laughter. During cross examination one counsel got quite annoyed with me and said: 'I haven't come here to be insulted.' So I calmly replied, 'I'm terribly sorry about that. Where do you normally go to be insulted then?' He sat there looking very angry. I don't think I was very popular with those learned men, mainly because what I was saying wasn't putting their clients in a very good light. The charges against my former accomplices included robberies and conspiracies to pervert the course of justice.

The hearing lasted several days and each lunch hour I would go to a special room in the court and tuck into a lovely dinner. I remember one day it was roast lamb, roast potatoes and greens followed by a plum pudding and glasses of Pepsi Cola. There were incredible scenes outside the court as I left to return to Winchester each afternoon. The police received several threats that I was to be assassinated. They were trying to do everything they could to protect me, and they wanted me to wear a bullet proof vest. But I wouldn't. 'If I'm going to die, I'll die like a man,' I told them.

One afternoon I went to Chiswick and had a long discussion with senior Yard detectives and complained about my treatment at Winchester. By my performance in court they knew I was going to stick to my promise to help them yet, as I pointed out, I was being treated worse than the criminals I was shopping. I could see they were concerned, but what could they do?

The journeys back to Winchester were usually uneventful, but one day I gathered something was up when some cars seemed to be tailing us in London. The driver of the prison truck radioed for help, and soon police cars appeared from everywhere. If anyone was trying to capture the truck, they were quickly frightened off. They weren't going to silence KING SQUEALER this time.

The committal proceedings were held up when the magistrate was involved in a serious car accident.

However I was soon back in London. It was decided that I should be transferred from my private cell in the hospital wing to Wormwood Scrubs' segregation unit. I was confined there under rule 43 of the Prison Regulations. Shortly before I left, however, I was nearly involved in a serious incident. A prisoner was let out at the same time as me to 'slop out' and we got talking. He asked me what I was in for and I told him burglary. He said he was in for murder. 'I burned down a house and killed the landlord and family,' he gloated. 'I'm glad they're dead, I never liked them.' Something boiled up inside me and I was just about to lay one on him when four burly prison officers pounced on me. They had realised I shouldn't have been with anyone else, and they escorted me back to the cell - just in time.

I bade farewell to Winchester, not realising that my next port of call was going to be even worse. I was immediately installed in a cell at the Scrubs where I had previously stayed years before, now part of the infamous segregation wing. The whole place was like a zoo . . . and the animals were the prisoners. My outside exercise period was actually conducted in a small cage so that no one could get at me. I'll never forget the first day I went out and walked past a tiny cell. The small-framed man inside glared back at me as I peered in. It was spotlessly clean. I noticed he had a picture of Adolf Hitler on the wall and wondered who the 'fruit cake' was. Then I looked at the name on the cell card. It read 'Graham Young'. Young, as many of you will remember, was the notorious poisoner who was allowed out of Broadmoor, and then killed by poisoning again.

Guard dogs surrounded me in my special cage and I began to realise that around me in that unit were some of Britain's most notorious killers. For instance, above me was the Moors murderer, Ian Brady. Brady, who was in solitary confinement at his own request, was a child killer. I would think it fair to call him the most hated man in Britain. You may recall that Brady's lover, Myra Hindley, lured ten-year-old Lesley Ann Downey and watched Brady sexually assault and kill her. Together they buried the girl's body on Saddleworth Moor near Manchester where the grave of twelve-year-old John Kilbridge was also found. The couple were also convicted of killing a 17-year-old youth at their home. I understand Brady spent much of his time in his cell at the Scrubs reading Dickens, Wordsworth and Dostoyevsky - author of *Crime and Punishment*. But his favourite was Tolstoy.

I have always hated people who attack children and Brady became my number-one target. He had already been assaulted by several prisoners and I waited for my chance to show him what I thought of him. One day I was carrying a tray of food with me when there was an administrative slip-up. A door that should have been locked was left open, which meant I could confront him. I hurled the tray of hot food at Brady but it missed by inches and he made a dash for it. Naturally I got a ticking off from the prison officers for my action and missed my meal that night. But it was worth it to personally register my hatred to Brady.

Ever since his imprisonment in 1966, Brady had been regularly going on hunger strike. While I was there, he was protesting about the refusal of his request for a transfer to a prison where he could mix with other inmates, and he was being fed artificially. But even if the Home Office ever did agree to his request, I doubt if other prisoners would want to mix with him, anyway.

There were many more crazy and dangerous prisoners there, but this deadly trio were the most notorious. No wonder I was depressed, living with such evil and disturbed men. The place got me down so much that I literally wouldn't come out of my cell for weeks on end. I'd just go to the toilet and then straight back to my hellish room. I couldn't even bear to go out for exercise . . . if you could call it that. I was given powerful drugs and would sleep for hours and hours. I hardly spoke to anyone, I just couldn't be bothered. I was on the verge of complete insanity.

One day Commander Don Measham, who at that time was liaison officer for the Home Office between the police and the prison service, saw me and he was very disturbed about my condition. I told him it was impossible for a man to give his mind fully to giving evidence while being kept in solitary confinement, as I was. I was now in no fit state to do anything, especially stand up in a witness box for hours on end.

Mr Measham asked me to try and hold out as long as I could. I heard later there were many top level meetings involving the then Home Secretary, Roy Jenkins and Police Commissioner, Sir Robert Mark. This was obviously a very tricky situation, because I had been sentenced to five years, and prisoners always spend their time in prison and not in a police station. What was to be done? Well, one day I was lying on the bed in my cell in a fit of black despair, when a prison officer came in with my clothes. 'The police want you to go to Chiswick to identify some men,' he said. I was out of bed and dressed like a shot. 'Anything to escape for a few hours from this place,' I said.

When I got to Chiswick I was told that there would be a parade and I was asked to pick out men who had been on certain robberies I knew about. I picked out several suspects and then I met Jack Slipper. As we talked, I let all my frustrations come bubbling out. 'Mr Slipper, the pressures are getting too great for me. I don't think I can hold out,' I told him. We continued to talk and I suggested maybe I could come out of prison each day to go over statements, just to let my mind begin to return to some sort of normality. I know Jack Slipper was concerned about my state and he said he would try to find a solution. Soon I was called in to see the Governor at the Scrubs, Mr Norman Honey, and he said it would certainly be a good idea if I went to Chiswick each day to help with the statements. I was delighted and so, each weekday from ten am to four-thirty pm, I was at Chiswick. When I wasn't being interviewed by police, Susan would come and we would spend hours together. She would bring lovely tasty food and we would have our meals together in my old cell.

Although things were now much better, my depression was still there. I somehow didn't know how to beat it and the prison doctor decided to try out some drugs on me to see if they would help. They were very strong and I think they were meant to block me out. All I know is that they made matters worse. I would have all sorts of horrific hallucinations it was terrifying.

One night I was in such a state they took me into the medical wing and put me in what they call a stripped cell. This means that you have to sleep with no clothes on, obviously so you can't do yourself any harm. Well, the cell was so cold I wouldn't take my things off. But burly officers jumped me and tore off every shred of clothing. They also encouraged me not to cause problems with a few right handers and a boot in the stomach .
. .

Shortly after this violent incident a prison officer came to see me. He was not around to inquire after my health but to ask me to 'turn it all in' and not give evidence against my former mates. I reported this approach to the prison authorities and one day when I got back to my hospital cell I found that someone had put six live mice in my bed. I managed to kill two of them and took them to Chiswick next morning and handed them over to Chief Inspector Dave Dixon as proof of what had been going on at the Scrubs. He was horrified and I understand he wrapped them up and produced them at a top level meeting at Scotland Yard.

After a spell in the hospital wing, I was pronounced fit enough to return to my ordinary cell. This almost became bearable because of my visits to Chiswick. My girlfriend would bring me food, biscuits, chocolates and bottles of lemonade - which I used to drink and then fill up with spirits. I would take all of this back to the cell and get quite merry. I was even allowed a record player and I used to drive the other prisoners mad with my loud music. Each day, as I returned, the prison officers would search my carrier bags and find roast beef, lobster, Cokes, bars of chocolate and sugar. I knew they didn't approve but apparently I had been given clearance to have them in my cell. In prison you are not supposed to have chewing gum because you can stick it in locks and the screws can't open the doors. But I used to smuggle it in. Most evenings I would write letters to Susan, even though I saw her often, and then give them to her next morning. That, of course, should not have been allowed as every letter from a prisoner is supposed to be censored.

I know the trips to Chiswick were not only a day out for me, but also for the segregation unit officers who came along. Most of them were quite decent to me, and they must have had quite a tough time trying to figure out someone like me. I'd be hand-cuffed to one of them and taken in an unmarked car to the nick. Another car would follow in case of trouble.

But tensions were always there, even at Chiswick. And sometimes they would flare up into trouble for me. Like the day a prison officer who had come with me, Gordon Lunn, was searching my girlfriend's bag for anything that she shouldn't bring me. I told him that I thought a woman should be doing the searching and I yelled at him. We had quite a slanging match and when I got back to the Scrubs I was served what is called a Notice to Report for my behaviour. I was found guilty of verbally abusing the officer and given one day's confinement. It couldn't be called solitary, because I was already doing that. Gordon Lunn is a good officer and I think that was an occasion where we just got our lines crossed.

With a few personal belongings now being allowed in my cell, like photographs of my girlfriend and children, I began to resign myself a little more to life inside. I even got some paint from the prison authorities and decorated the walls. I was allowed papers to read and I would also spend hours doing the crosswords. But I never went out on exercise with the others in my block. After all, would you fancy having Graham Young and Ian Brady as walking companions?

My personal guard at Chiswick at this time was Detective Sergeant Peter Bowns, who is a good officer and did all he could to ease the mental pressures I was under. If I had a complaint or problem he would relay it to his senior. He really looked after me as a friend, not as a prisoner. He used to collect me from prison with Detective Sergeant Geoff Brown. We all got on extremely well and although this was a very serious business, there was lots of joke-cracking on both sides. I am sure they saw the funny side of having to protect a gangster whom once they hated. And I certainly thought it amazing that these former enemies of mine were now amongst my best friends.

Somehow the day at Chiswick would rush by, but the hours at the Scrubs went on for an eternity. I was living in two completely different worlds and at times it was mind blowing. At Chiswick I was an honoured guest, at the Scrubs I was just another prisoner. I hated the jail so much that one day I sent panic through the place by having a sitdown strike in the courtyard. It was in a cage with cameras silently watching me all the time. I had got so frustrated with everything I sat there and refused to move. Senior prison officials came out to try and get me to come in. But then it began to pour with rain, so I agreed. If any of them had tried to persuade me with force, there would have been hell to play.

Because I was such an awkward cuss, the prison officers began to get their own back on me. I would find my dinner being 'accidentally' dropped on the cell floor. The screw would pretend to trip over and the tray would go flying. Or I would discover that the main course had somehow got muddled up with the custard. I got so mad about all of this I went on a five-day hunger strike. I refused to eat anything until officers understood that I wasn't going to put up with this treatment.

Mike Tanner, senior officer at the prison, was very good to me and would come into my cell for chats. He did all he could to calm me down from my rages. I don't think people realise what it is like to be in solitary without television or recreation, without company. Here I was, a man trying to help protect society from evil men, and yet all society could offer me was the inhumanity of solitary confinement. Meanwhile murderers, rapists and people in that class were enjoying luxuries like television. I wasn't even allowed to go to church - if I had wanted to.

Drugs were continually pumped into me and the hallucinations were driving me up the wall. Each evening I would be given something that would knock me out until ten am next morning. I didn't mind being a guinea pig for society, but now I was being driven to the point of suicide. I'm not blaming the prison authorities, it's just that they haven't got the facilities to cope with someone like me. All they could do was give me drugs to keep me locked up. When I think of the agony I went through, I wonder if society wanted a witness or a cabbage. Punishing a man is one thing, but sentencing him to lingering mental agony is another. I know that several people in this segregation unit have actually committed suicide because of the strain.

The only good news I got during this awful time was that Susan was pregnant again. At weekends she would come and visit me and we would be allowed to meet in a room adjacent to the governor's office, and each time she came she was fatter. I used to pat her tummy and joke with her about the child – OUR CHILD. I was naturally determined this time nothing would go wrong, so I was always urging her to be careful. Sometimes the governor, Mr Honey, would come in and talk to us, and Susan's family when they came along. He was a very kind man who was always courteous. He even used to visit me in my cell and ask me if I had any problems he could help with. Mr Honey seemed to contrast strongly with the harsh surroundings of his own prison.

Then one day I was told that Susan had been rushed to hospital, and I got permission to visit her. I went first to Chiswick and then to the hospital. Just to show what great people my police guards were, they actually bought flowers and chocolates for me to take in, for I had no money on me at the time. The nurses must have wondered what had hit the place when this burly party came in. The prison officers had coats over their uniforms, but we all looked very conspicuous. I was un-handcuffed and put on trust that I wouldn't try and escape.

Apparently there were a few internal problems with Susan and in view of the last miscarriage it was thought she would be better off in hospital. We couldn't stay long, and I got very worried. On the way out Detective Sergeant Terry Wrefford bought me something to read to try and take my mind off the situation. Shortly afterwards I was allowed to go back to the hospital and again my guards bought the flowers and a card. 'You've just had an 8 lb son,' I was told by a delighted nurse. 'Both mother and baby are doing fine.' I was so excited. The officers shook my hand and congratulated me. When I got to Susan's bed she looked flushed but contented. I put my arms around her and held her close. When I saw our baby I was frightened to pick him up. He looked so fragile! The nurse told me not to be silly and handed him to me. He was so lovely to cuddle. Maybe things were at last looking up for me.

But my soaring spirits soon came crashing down. Next day I was summoned to the assistant governor's office at the Scrubs. 'O'Mahoney, you're leaving and going to a health resort,' he said with a twisted smile. My face lit up and I asked him where he meant. 'Brixton by the sea,' he said sarcastically. I couldn't believe it. 'You are putting me in the same prison as the men I am due to give evidence against. You must be joking. It's like putting a fly in a spider's web,' I protested. I was in a bad state when I returned to my cell and several of the officers tried to cheer me up. But I wouldn't be comforted. What a crazy decision, I thought.

14
Brixton

At ten o'clock every morning for more than six months in Brixton prison, two girls from Northern Ireland suffered the cruel torture of forced feeding. Their mouths were kept open with a wooden clamp, and a greased tube was pushed down their throats and into their stomachs. Then 24 ounces of a concentrated blend of skimmed milk, minerals and vitamins was poured down the tube.

These girls were the Price sisters, Marian and Dolours, from Belfast's Anderstown estate. Along with seven other people they had been convicted of the London bombings, including that one I've already mentioned at the Old Bailey. They, and their gang, were all given life terms.

Their 206-day hunger strike supposedly 'to the death' was a bid to force the British Government to return them to Ulster, where relatives could visit them more easily. More important to them, though, was the fact that in Northern Ireland they would be granted special category political prisoner's status, like the other terrorists held there. This would give them extra privileges. Marian and Dolours ended their protest after the then Home Secretary, Roy Jenkins, assured them that they would eventually be transferred to the country of their birth.

The Price sisters were moved for a time to Durham jail. Then, on March 18, 1975, they were taken to Armagh prison in Northern Ireland. They had got their wish.

So where do these girls fit into life at my new home - 'Brixton-by-the-Sea?' Well, after their move, I was put into their wing, part of a top security construction originally built to hold the Krays and I was given the run of their little block and I must be honest and say that at first I was surprised at the privileges they had been given. There was a television, rowing machines, bicycle exercisers, table tennis, a medicine ball, all the games you can imagine, a private bathroom and cooking facilities.

I had Dolour's cell – she was the eldest - and spent quite a bit of time during those first few days roaming around the wing. I suspected that she may have done some writing while there and been forced to hide it quickly when the sudden move to Durham came. One day I uncovered a secret cubbyhole and found some of her poems. They were fascinating, like one which was all about a 'Gelli Fish'. Gelignite obviously played quite a part in her life. I must say they made weird reading.

It wasn't long before word spread around the prison that the person who had replaced the Price sisters was me. The slags seemed determined to give me worse treatment than these sisters. Soon the insults came thick and fast. Most of the shouting came from the Bank of America team who were awaiting their trial and had been installed one floor down from me.

But, I was in for a nice surprise - Billy Williams then arrived to join me. He was given Marian Price's cell and we were delighted to be together. At least we could help each other through his nightmare, and share the never-ending abuse, instead of me taking the lot. When Billy was let into the wing he had a big grin on his face and said, 'Isn't this a riot, Mo? Have they all gone loopy putting us in here? It's like dangling a worm on the end of a fishing rod.'

We spent hours exchanging stories and comparing notes on the aggro we had gone through. Billy had also suffered greatly because of his squealing. He told me that he had had tremendous trouble from several prisoners while he was at Oxford because of his grassing and also because he too was having day-trip outings. An informer told him that several men had got hold of some strychnine and hypodermic needles. Their plan was to inject the poison through the top of a plastic bottle of orange juice. That way he'd never suspect anything was wrong when he drank it. As soon as he was warned, he stopped buying orange juice from the canteen. On another occasion, scalding water was thrown at him, but he ducked and it went 'over another geezer standing behind him. Then he was transferred to Gloucester jail. A prisoner tried to stab him with a screwdriver only days after he arrived. He was sent straight back to Oxford and subsequently to several other prisons for safety's sake.

It was great to have company again and we made full use of the facilities. We would play table tennis, then get on the exercise bikes and pedal like mad, and switch to the rowing machines. I'd say to Billy, 'Where are you going?' He'd laugh and say, 'I'm rowing to Spain,' and I'd tell him I was rowing to John O'Groats'. Then we'd hurl the huge medicine ball at each other. It was so heavy that it would nearly knock us off our feet.

After a keep-fit session we'd put our feet up and watch telly - all the afternoon programmes, especially the sport. We were always aware that we were being constantly observed by closed-circuit television cameras, so we used to have a little fun with the screw 'viewers' in mind. After a bath, we'd chase each other around in the nude and give them a quick flash.

We used to have all this fun to try and forget the barrage of threats and abuse that was being yelled at us by the canaries within shouting distance. One day one of them bawled up 'Give us a song, Mo.' I went to my window and shouted out, 'To all it may concern. When I get to the Bailey and get into that witness box I'll sing so loud that the echo of my voice will break every pane of glass in the building.' I could hear them responding with things like, 'You dirty slag,' so I concluded my 'broadcast' with, 'Goodnight, gentlemen. That is the end of the news, and its bad news for you lot.'

Sometimes that little wing - there were four cells as well as a recreation room and bathroom - got quite parky and at other times we had the added problem of hot water, or should I say, the lack of it. So Billy decided to take matters into his own hands and began searching for the water heater. We wanted a bath and the water was running cold. He found a big metal container with pipes going in and out of it and began messing with it. A prison officer came in and asked Billy what on earth he was doing. 'I'm trying to get the heater going for the bath,' he said. The screw smiled broadly and said, 'That's not a heater, you ninny, that's a sanitary towel disposal unit . . .' Billy's face dropped. 'Hell, I've had my hand in that,' he bleated. I nearly collapsed with laughter!

And we needed the laughs because the pressure on both of us was incredible. The other prisoners began shouting up to us that our food was being poisoned and we became so concerned that we wouldn't eat or drink anything unless screws sampled it first. We would wait for a few minutes to see if they keeled over before we'd tuck into the meal. You may think we were overdoing it, but then you don't realise how clever some of these villains are. They could easily bribe someone in the kitchen staff to slip some poison into a meal, and then you're a gonner.

The Bank of America lot would wait for about half an hour after our meals were served and one of them would shout up, 'Have you two gone yet?' We'd take great delight in telling them to 'F... off!'

We didn't stay in all the time and would go out on exercise together. But we were always on the alert for trouble. We would stick closely together and guards with dogs kept an eye on us. The area was cleared so we could be safe. I should have thought that the prison guards would have approved of what we had done, but many of them went out of their way to show their disapproval of us.

One boiling hot day we decided to sit on a wall and have a rest from the constant circling of the exercise yard. Suddenly we heard the voice of one of the screws, who said, 'Oi, grasses, get off the wall.' I said to Billy, 'He's talking to you.' He said, 'No, I think he's talking to you.' So I shouted back, 'Sorry, there's no grasses here.' Even as I spoke I could see behind this man, in another exercise area, fifteen other prisoners all sitting talking on a wall, so I didn't see why we should be victimised. He retorted, 'We're cancelling your exercises, grasses.' I just boiled over and hissed to Billy, 'He's had it now.' So we approached him and I could see his face turn white. I grabbed his Alsatian and said 'Look screw, I'll ram this animal up your arsehole. And if you ever call me or Billy a grass again, I'll smash your head in.'

Other officers intervened to cool the situation and we went back to our cells. Not surprisingly I was given a 'Notice of Report' and later had to go before the Governor to explain my action. I had Billy as a witness. I told the Governor the whole story and said, 'I was provoked. I didn't want to cause any trouble but this man pushed me too far.' He believed me and I was found not guilty.

The daily visits to Chiswick were stopped as soon as I arrived at Brixton, so Susan would come to see me when she was allowed. She would be taken into the D-wing chapel and I would meet her there. I became very worried about her condition because she was very frightened and cried a lot. It was not surprising because she needed armed protection and was not only scared for her own life, but also that of her children. I would sit there in the pews trying to comfort her.

Strangely enough my prison life was to come to an abrupt end through a sensational but unsuccessful bid I made at the Old Bailey, in the 'Mitchell Shooting' case, to clear the name of the Kray twins, who once ruled so much of London's underworld. I was allowed back to Chiswick. The Judge had ordered that I should be held there and stay until the court directed otherwise. That was great news to me and helped me make police history: more than 400 days in a police cell, something that had never been heard of before.

15

'O'Mahoney Is Innocent, OK? Ask George Davis'

I was sorry that I hadn't been given the chance to bid farewell to Epsom-born Billy, but I hoped that when he began giving his evidence at the Bailey, they would allow him to join me at Chiswick. I imagined the torture he must have been going through on his own from those baying hyenas at Brixton. It must have been a living hell for him. I heard he was soon transferred back to Oxford, but with a squealer like me or Billy, there is always the danger of something going wrong. For people like us, life in prison is quite terrifying. I nicknamed Billy the 'Doomsday Machine' because wherever he went people tried to kill him.

I knew this time I was to be at Chiswick for a long stay, so I 'phoned Susan and gave her a list of the things I needed to make my cells homely again, and transform them to their former glory. I ordered my colour television, three-bar electric fire, hair-dryer, clothes, and my stereo player. I had the two cells - one I looked upon as my television room and the other was where I dined and slept. I don't think I could have been more comfortable at a five-star London hotel. At my new home I was given a new role in life - baby sitter. I doubt if any villain had ever before been allowed to look after his own baby in a cell while his girl went shopping, but that's what happened to me at that super-modern police station. Susan would bring our son to me, then go out and do her shopping in Chiswick High Road, while I bounced our gurgling lad up and down upon my knees, talking to him in baby language and making him laugh. Sometimes I even changed his nappy in the cell. That was a job I never relished though - there wasn't any air conditioning in my cell, and the pong would linger for hours afterwards.

Susan usually brought an assortment of booze back from the shop with her and smuggled it in. I had managed to make myself a secret 'bar' behind a cupboard in the wall. There I would store champagne, whisky, gin and brandy. I must make it perfectly clear that none of the policemen ever knew about this drinks store, or gave me drinks. It was all brought in by Susan and my family. For hours on end I would be quite drunk, though, of course, never when I was given my baby-sitting duties to do. I nicknamed my cellblock Costa del Chiswick.

One man I felt sorry for at the nick was 'Old Harry', an ex-prison officer aged about 70 who worked as a cleaner. Almost every morning after I'd held my own private party with myself, or Susan, I would empty my rubbish into black plastic bags for the dustbin, and then clear them away. It's strange. I've always hated screws, but somehow 'Old Harry' was different. A real gem. He told me he had been in the prison service for 30 years, and even supplied me with all the cleaning material I needed to keep my cell shipshape.

When Harry needed a break he would come into my 'dining room' and sit down for a chat. I remember one day he told me that one of his most distasteful duties as a prison officer was to be present at hangings. 'It was a terrible experience, Mo,' he said. 'But that was the law of the land at the time and being there was part of my job. I couldn't duck out of it.'

Our discussions on capital punishment were both gruesome and fascinating. 'Just think, if I'd have been born in your era and carried on in the way I was going, you could have been present at my execution,' I told him. Make no mistake, I was on the verge of becoming a callous killer. As I mentioned before, I carried guns with me on most jobs and I would not have hesitated to use them if necessary.

'Would you have carried guns if you knew that you could have ended up dangling on the end of a rope, Mo?' asked 'Old Harry'. That really made me think. 'If you put it that way, Harry, I don't think I would have done,' I said. For like many gangsters today, I knew that if I killed I would probably get a life sentence, which usually works out at about 12 years. Then I would be free to kill again. Whereas if I knew that my misdeeds would result in a quick and awful death for me, then I would have definitely thought twice.

I know there is always the possibility that an innocent man could be hung, like Timothy Evans in the Christie case, but somehow the victim always seems to be forgotten in this argument. And what about his heartbroken family, who may never recover from the shock of the killing? Many MPs use this 'innocent man' argument, but they have no hesitation in sending thousands of 'innocent' soldiers, sailors and air-force men to their death at times of war and conflict.

Never having been in a death cell, I was interested to hear what Harry said about the last hours of a man convicted of murder. He said that the whole episode was quite harrowing for all concerned. You would play cards with the condemned man and try to take his mind off the horrible end he was due to face. He told me the death cell was next to the room in which the execution took place. When the final hour came, the prisoner's hands were bound behind his back, then a false cabinet door was slid back and he was marched in. Then his ankles were tied by a leather strap and a hood was put over his head. Over the hood and around the neck was slid the noose. The governor would nod at the executioner, who would pull a lever to open the trap door - and down would go the victim. His neck was broken immediately by the impact. He was left dangling for a few moments, and then taken down and checked by a doctor who would pronounce him dead.

'I'll tell you something, an execution sent ripples of fear throughout the whole prison,' said 'Old Harry'. 'I am sure it deterred many villains from carrying guns when they came out. It certainly terrified me from ever getting involved in violence.'

At this time all my family were given 24-hours-a-day police protection. That included Maureen and my two children, and Susan and our baby. Everywhere they went the guards went with them. There were male and female watchdogs, and they actually lived with them and protected them with their lives. Whenever Chief Inspector David Dixon came to see me, he did all he could to reassure me that all was well with my loved ones.

In a bid to take my mind off the dangers of my life, my three personal guards - Acting Detective Inspector Dennis Barnes, Detective Sergeant Harry Poole and Detective Sergeant Geoff Brown - would take me out as much as possible. Other guards quite regularly took me to the local swimming baths, where I'd join unsuspecting bathers in the pool. One of the guards would join me in the water, while the others would stay at the side of the pool, their fingers on the triggers of their guns in their pockets. After a swim we'd walk through nearby parks and sit on the grass. It was wonderful to breathe in fresh air and watch the passers-by. We looked like a group of lads out for the afternoon, but I expect the people out for a stroll would have been horrified to learn that I was once a dangerous criminal and was being guarded for my life by the Sweeney. One day they took me to Kew Gardens for a look around that beautiful botanical show-piece. I particularly enjoyed the hothouses with their tropical plants.

We also spent hours by the Thames at Chiswick Bridge. I'd wave to the pleasure boats from the tow path as they sailed by, and people on board would wave back. Often people out for a breath of air would come over and talk to us and we'd have some nice chats.

Back to my cell, I became something of an artist. Susan would bring me a canvas and paints and I would spend hours painting pictures, mainly landscapes. I would also construct model boats, including galleons, from special kits. I particularly enjoyed doing that, as I have always enjoyed making things with my hands.

I take great care with my appearance, and often Susan would style my hair for me. She would wash, cut it and then style it, using the hair dryer. No prisoner ever had such treatment!

She was a great help to me during this time, and would do all she could to cheer me up, especially after my wife had been to see me. Maureen and I would argue bitterly and it would break me up to see my lovely children caught up in all this insanity. Having a father locked up and having to live with armed detectives was bad enough, but the rows must have made it worse for them. The kids even had to move school and change their names during this time. I think they understood what was going on, but it was still very confusing for their young minds. Sometimes they would make cutting remarks to me, but I always felt these comments had been planted there by my wife, so they didn't hurt too much.

Sunday mornings were always a bit of a treat for me. I would be driven over to Brentford police station for my breakfast, as the Chiswick canteen was closed at weekends. Then we would to go to the newsagents and load up with all the Sunday papers. We would then go back to my cell and read them one by one. During the week I got some of the daily papers, but I enjoyed the Sundays the most because they seem to give more space to the sort of investigations I was interested in. It was one of these mornings that I first read that amazing *Sunday People* story which caused such a storm in court. I personally thought it was very good, though of course, I'm biased. When I read anything in the press about myself which I felt was untrue, I would get Susan to 'phone up the paper and protest. Sometimes they would rectify the error, sometimes they wouldn't.

Elvis Presley played quite a part in my stay at Chiswick ... not personally, of course, but through his records. My favourite album was 'Elvis Presley's 40 hits', which I constantly played. 'Jailhouse Rock' seemed particularly apt to my situation, but my favourite was 'My Boy' which made me think of my two sons - Maureen's and Susan's. For hour after hour, King Elvis and King Squealer were in tune together, for I would join in with the songs and sing them at the top of my voice. My cell block backed on to the main road, so passers-by heard my performances. I don't know what they thought! Elvis's death hurt me deeply, as I knew how much happiness he had brought me during those lonely hours. I know there has been a lot of scandal written about his personal life, but to me and millions of his fans, he was the greatest. Elton John records also came high in my cell Top 20. I would smile as I thought that if I'd kidnapped him as I planned, I'd have been having personal performances from him. As it was, I had to do with the records instead.

My holiday at Costa del Chiswick soon ended though, and I was back in business again when I was called to give evidence against thirteen of my former associates. Once more I was to make history, for this was to be the longest trial at the Old Bailey since it was opened in 1907. The cost of the 111-day trial, which began on June 4, 1974, was estimated at £400,000. The previous record in the present court was the 109-days Angry Brigade marathon in December 1972, which ended with prison sentences for the bomb-throwers.

On the first morning of the trial, I put on my best suit and looked out of the charge room window. A large escort of cars was waiting for me. I was handcuffed to one of my guards, in case I was ambushed and the attackers tried to drag me from the car. This meant they would have two people to deal with. The whole station was surrounded by armed police, because they had been told a man disguised as an officer might try and bluff his way in and shoot me in my cell. So they were taking no chances, and everyone coming into the station was thoroughly checked before being allowed to the front desk.

As the convoy sped into central London, we kept in radio contact with a helicopter charting our progress from aloft. We pulled up outside the judges' entrance and I was quickly bundled out of the car and into the building. I was taken into a lift and then to a room once used by Bertie Smalls. Each day I would make up a password for my guards to use before they would be allowed back into the room. They had to say something like doughnut or Pepsi Cola. I must say I had real butterflies on that first day of the marathon trial.

Then came the signal, and I was told, 'You're on.' I felt a bit like a pop star being hurried on-stage for my performance as I walked into court at double speed, with 12 armed policemen surrounding me. I could see the people in the passageway, who were kept to one side, stare in amazement at the number of guards I had. I remember looking through a door into the court and seeing the thirteen in the dock. Little did I realise that I would be in the witness box not for a few hours, or even a few days, but for more than THREE WEEKS. I was given a really tough grilling by defence counsel, but I believe I stood up well to it.

The thirteen - nine men and four women - faced charges alleging armed robbery, conspiracy to rob, receiving stolen money and conspiring to pervert justice. All denied the charges.

Mr Brian Leary, prosecuting, opened proceedings by telling the jury why I had decided to squeal. Under the headline 'Underworld put "frighteners" on robber's mistress, jury told,' the *Daily Telegraph* began its story in this way:

> Maurice O'Mahoney, a professional criminal, turned squealer when accomplices put the 'frighteners' on Miss Susan Norville, his mistress, to stop her talking to the police, an Old Bailey jury heard yesterday.
>
> Mr Brian Leary, prosecuting, said O'Mahoney was arrested soon after a successful £17,000 armed robbery of a Securicor van at Heston, Middlesex.
> Underworld warnings were also given to O'Mahoney's wife Maureen because she, like Miss Norville, knew of his activities.
>
> As a result of the pressures put on the two women, O'Mahoney decided to 'squeal.'

And it was because of my statements, he said, that the 13 faced these charges.

Mr Leary told the court that the men were professional robbers who plotted and carried out armed raids. He said I was one of them. Following my arrest the police interviewed Susan, he went on to say, and threats of violence were made to me and my wife and Susan in case I should squeal. He said I would be a prosecution witness and give evidence about the planning and execution of at least two daring and dangerous robberies. He said that I had admitted much crime and had been jailed at the Old Bailey for five years.

Opening the Crown's case, Mr Leary said that a bank messenger known as Paddy was plied with lager in a restaurant and encouraged to talk about £300,000 cash deliveries. Later, impressions of the bank keys - which he had left on a table - were made with cuttle-fish and soft soap. They were passed on to a gang, who in turn got a professional locksmith to make keys. But they were never used because the bank robbery never got beyond the planning stage. Those involved, he said, were arrested after a Securicor van had been held up near Heathrow and robbed of £17,000. He said it was noticed that Paddy frequently left the keys of the Allied Irish Bank at Hammersmith on his table at a nearby restaurant. The two proprietors encouraged him to talk about his job – and plied him with lager as he spoke of £300,000 deliveries. Two alleged gang members listened at another table and afterwards decided the bank would be a good target. It was arranged that the next time Paddy came into the restaurant and left the keys on the table, impressions would be taken of them. This, said Mr Leary, was done by one of the proprietors.

Police had been able to pinpoint a meeting held by the gang to plan robberies . . . because they had been watching the Princess Ann 'Mall' drama on television. The meeting was at a flat occupied by one of the accused men on March 20 or 21 in the previous year.

'They watched the screening of reports of that shooting in the Mall which we all remember - when the Royal Family was involved and a man called Ian Ball was eventually dealt with,' said Mr Leary. 'That is why the Crown say that the date can be accurately fixed.' At that meeting it was arranged to keep watch on the bank, he said.

However, once again the publication of a newspaper story caused problems at the trial. And there were applications to stop the case. They arose out of two stories published in the *Daily Telegraph* and the *Daily Mirror* on the same page as a report of the trial. It was a story about the annual report of Sir Robert Mark, the Metropolitan Police Commissioner. 'Sir Robert had said that major criminals were turning 'squealers' to help Scotland Yard. Judge Gillis QC, who rejected the application, recalled the jury and told them: 'It doesn't matter however eminent a person may be, who may have made some speech or published some report about a matter in connection with his duties which a jury may see, you alone the jury, are the judges of the facts.

'Part of the great heritage in this country is our determination always to ensure that an accused person receives a fair trial and the jury are the guardians of that heritage in the realm of evidence you are sovereign and supreme.'

Mr Brian Leary had begun his opening prosecution speech but not completed it when the applications for a retrial, based on the *Daily Telegraph* reports, were made by Mr Stuart Shields, QC, defending one of the accused and Mr Robert Flach defending another. The applications, opposed by the Crown, were made in the jury's absence.

During the trial it was alleged that I had once threatened that anyone who 'squealed' on me would have his head blown off. I made this threat, it was said, to a security guard who provided me with information about cash movements at premises where he worked. In a statement to police, he was alleged to have said: 'O'Mahoney said the police were after him for the job. He said whoever grassed on him would get his "head blown off".'

Quite regularly as I gave evidence, there were shouts from the public gallery and from the dock. On one occasion the judge got quite fed-up with the cat-calls and after one threat to me, he asked, 'Who said that?' There was a deathly silence in court, so I told him it was one of the accused. He told the man to stand up. 'Did you say that?' he asked. 'Yes, sir,' was the reply. 'Well, next time you say that you'll be sent downstairs.' I made great play about telling the truth in court on this occasion, and pointed out this was just a small example of the accuracy of my evidence.

My court ordeal was wearing. Often I was so tired during my three weeks in the witness box I would be allowed to sit down for a few minutes to recover.

At the end of a day in the court, I would be almost out on my feet. It was incredibly tiring both physically and mentally, but I somehow came through it. There were amusing moments too, though. One of the counsel asked me how much I charged to kill someone. I thought he was being sarcastic, so I said, 'It's like this blue eyes, how much are you worth?'

I was amazed to find out when I had finished giving evidence that I was followed by George du Buriatte. I thought that was quite ironic, because my former associates had accused me of being the grass in the first place, when in fact it was du Buriatte all along. Now they had the two of us to contend with.

Each night back at Chiswick I would need pills to get to sleep. My mind was in a whirl. In fact at first I nearly didn't even get into the witness box. Before I started giving evidence, I used to lie out on the roof at Chiswick in the beautiful sunshine, and sunbathe. I would have cold drinks there and stretch out in my swimming trunks. My binoculars were always at my side and each time a plane came over, I would try and identify it. Concorde was always the biggest thrill for me. Well, usually I put sun-tan lotion all over me, but this particular day I forgot and went to sleep in the blazing heat. When I woke up a couple of hours later I was in absolute agony. I was so badly burnt that a doctor was called and said I had sustained first-degree burns. I needed urgent treatment to get me fit enough to appear at the Bailey. And when I did I looked as if I just had a fortnight in the Canaries.

When I was told the result of the trial, at Chiswick, I promptly got drunk. I don't know if it was happiness or not, because I knew that many of the guilty people had a long, grinding stretch ahead of them. The *Daily Telegraph* headlined the result: 'Squealer helps convict 7 at longest trial'. One was jailed for a total of 15 years, two got 14 years, one was jailed for 12 years, another got six years. Two other members of the gang were each given two-year prison sentences, suspended for two years. Two of the accused were acquitted of conspiring to rob. During the trial, one of the women accused was found not guilty of conspiring to pervert justice, and was discharged.

As the judge announced one sentence, several women screamed at him from the public gallery and were led out shouting by the police. One screeched, 'Fourteen years for something he has not done. There is no justice in this country. I'm going to fight this all the way. You will have another George Davis case here.' One of the accused, as he was led away, stared at some members of the jury who had come along to hear the end of the 111-day trial and said: 'I hope you can live with your consciences. I am innocent and we will prove you wrong.'

Judge Gillis, QC, before passing sentence, told the men, 'It is obvious that these offences were planned with ruthless determination and the robberies were executed with callous indifference to the safety of others. Arms and ammunition and other weapons were carried on the occasion of both robberies and on one occasion shots were fired.

'The evidence has revealed the robberies were skilfully worked out and planned.

'The public are entitled to be protected for a substantial period from acts planned to rob honest people of their earnings and their savings. Each of you was capable of doing an honest day's work.'

The *Daily Telegraph*'s Old Bailey correspondent, C.A. Coughlin, commented: 'The men had been brought to justice because of information given to officers by Maurice O'Mahoney, the chief prosecution witness.'

Later two of the convicted men appealed. One, who received a two year suspended jail sentence, had it set aside and another who had a 14 year sentence also had his conviction quashed and his sentence set aside. He had served 18 months at the time. The main reason was that my testimony had not been supported by other, 'untainted' evidence.

At the appeal brought by nine others - seven men and two women - there was a big controversy over whether I was allowed sexual intercourse with Susan in the police station cell. An appeal court judge also asked why the Old Bailey trial had lasted 111 days, and cost £313,000 in legal fees. Lord Justice Lawton, sitting with Lord Justice Cumming-Bruce and Mr Justice Griffiths, made his remarks during the appeal hearing. All the accused were legally aided - at around £290,000 - and were a cost to the public as they were represented by four QCs and ten junior counsel.

Mr Michael Hill, the Crown Council, asked Lord Justice Lawton if he was 'observing that the trial took too long?' The judge replied: 'I am just wondering about the case, whether we might have to give some indication of how to deal with this type of case in the future.' Lawyers in the case, said Mr Hill, had done their best to make the trial 'manageable'. If it had been split up into separate trials, it would have taken even longer. The judge asked about me and my 'high life' with visits from Susan being allowed at Chiswick.

Finally the appeals were turned down.

Shortly after the trial I had another nightmare to contend with - and this related to the one and only George Davis, who was freed in May, 1976, after serving 14 months of a 20-year sentence for his alleged part in an armed robbery. Davis, in his thirties, from Bow in the East End, was jailed at the Old Bailey in March, 1975 following a raid on the London Electricity Board's offices in Ley Street, Ilford. Davis had always insisted he was innocent and the victim of a case of mistaken identity. An amazing campaign was launched to free him, with 'George Davis is innocent, OK,' slogans daubed all over East London. All sorts of crazy stunts were pulled to draw attention to his case, including the damage to the pitch at Headingley, which stopped a vital Test Match. Davis was finally freed by the then Home Secretary, Roy Jenkins. Many of Davis's supporters felt I could prove Davis was innocent, and one actually clambered onto a railway bridge over a busy East End main road and painted, 'George Davis is innocent, OK. Ask O'Mahoney.'

While Davis was still in prison, officers from A10 at Scotland Yard visited me at Chiswick - they are the people who investigate complaints against the police - to ask me if I had actually gone on the raid, in which a policeman was shot. I understand Davis was alleging he had been 'fitted up' by the police. Pictures had been taken of the raid and it was claimed that I was the masked man in the photograph pointing the gun. It had also been alleged by my enemies that I was the one who shot the copper. Apparently it was claimed I had done a deal with the police so I could not be charged with the job.

I told the A10 officers that I, and some of my associates, had been asked to go on the robbery, but had declined because we had more pressing villainy to do. So they said the best way I could clear my name was to take a blood test. An anorak, thought to have belonged to someone on the job, had been found abandoned in a toilet and none of the defendants' blood matched it. So they wanted to see if mine did. I willingly took the blood test and it didn't. I was in the clear. I actually met the wounded police officer at the Old Bailey while I was giving evidence on the Mitchell Shooting re-trial and I had a short chat with him. If he had felt I was the guilty man I'm sure there would have been a scene, but there wasn't. We got on very well.

16
Free At Last

The George Davis affair wasn't the only false allegation I had to deal with while I was at Chiswick. My enemies obviously couldn't hurt me physically at this time, so they resorted to making up lies about crimes I was supposed to have been on. Naturally the police had to follow up these allegations. One they interviewed me about was a job in Hill Street, Mayfair, close to the offices of the publisher of this book. An attack was made on a private house there, and a woman was tied up and robbed of jewels worth about £150,000. I had nothing to do with the job, though, naturally I knew all about it through the underworld grapevine. I was supposed to have tied up the victim, given her a kiss, then taken the safe key from around her neck and fled with all her jewellery. But once again the police believed what I said.

Another incident I was interviewed about concerned my own complaint to the police about a former detective who was serving time after being convicted of a serious crime. This slag approached me while I was in Wormwood Scrubs and tried to bribe me not to give evidence against my former associates. I told him to 'clear off' and reported him to the Yard. That sort of thing made me even more determined to give evidence. It wasn't the police who convinced me I should squeal, but my so-called friends. I did it of my own free will. The police never once did a deal with me or twisted my arm to carry on with my plan to help strike at the heart of the underworld. But their behaviour towards me certainly made me want to cooperate with them. They were marvellous.

While at Chiswick I had ample time to really get to know 'The Fuzz' - both the detectives and the uniformed men. From my passage door I was able to observe at close quarters the way they handled their customers. As my cells were near the charge room, I could see the suspects brought in and then hear the charges being laid before them. I would listen to the cross-examination, hear the villains make their excuses and threaten police with false claims, like alleging an officer had stolen their money from them and hadn't given proper receipts - that's an old ploy by crooks. I saw villains turn really nasty and attack officers, when they realised they had been outsmarted. Some of the struggles were really hair-raising, but the police always used only the minimum force that was necessary to overpower a violent prisoner, no more.

Some of the accused people would pressurise officers, saying that Sir Robert Mark, then the Metropolitan Police Commissioner, was their best pal, and when he got to hear of this, there would be hell to play. One drunk who tried this ploy was told by the sergeant dealing with him, 'Well, sir, if Sir Robert is your friend we'd better treat you as a VIP. Which suite would you like, the red or the blue?' The drunk thought for a moment and then replied, 'Well, I don't really mind as long as it's got a bar in it . . .' The sergeant smiled and said, 'It's got more than one bar in it, sir . . .'

One regular I had quite an affection for was Bess, an old 'soak' who always caused great hilarity when she was brought in after being found completely incapable through drink. One night she came in crying, but as soon as she got into the main body of the station, she suddenly leapt up on the station officer's table, lifted up her dress and revealed she had no knickers on. Not a pretty sight, I can tell you . . . I happened to be in the room at the time. Then she jumped to the floor and began dancing around like she was a ballerina. But when they tried to get her into a cell, the trouble really started. She fought, scratched, spat, and it took several officers to get her to her place of rest for the night.

One person brought in for questioning who really touched my heart was a young crook - a ten-year-old boy who was apparently doing 15 burglaries a week. A detective constable was desperately trying to help this lad and had already taken him home to meet his wife and children. He wanted him to feel part of a family. He couldn't have done more to help divert this lad from a life of crime. The DC knew that I had begun my terrible villainy after getting into trouble at an early age, so he asked me if I could try and talk the boy round. I was taken from my cell to see this tousle-haired youngster and I could have cried when I met him for I saw myself in him. He looked up at me with cheeky eyes as I walked in the room and said, 'Hey, mister, can I have a glass of orange juice to drink?' I got him a drink, and then we had a long chat. He told me he had been in various institutions and had run away from each of them. He said he had a drunken father who regularly beat up his mother in front of him and he couldn't stand it any more. So he had taken to roaming the streets with other boys who were a bad influence on him. 'My mum and dad don't love me, so why should I stay at home?' he asked. He said that he spent a lot of his time breaking into homes and factories. The poor kid didn't know what love and affection were, and was becoming as hard as I was as a youth. I felt all that I said was going in one ear and out of the other, and it made me feel so helpless. I knew the heartbreak path he was heading down, but he didn't seem to want to heed my warnings. Maybe he'd have to learn the hard way, like me.

The DC asked me what I thought of the boy. I told him that I felt the shocking home life he had obviously experienced had caused the villainy. 'He needs someone who can give him love and affection. I think he ought to be adopted by another family, if his parents will give their permission. That might just save him,' I said. He went back and asked the boy what he thought of the idea, and he said, 'Yes please. And I promise not to run away from them.'

I could see the detective was really choked with pleasure. He had done so much above the call of duty to help this lad, and now maybe, just maybe, here was a solution. I learned later that he had taken the boy with his own children fishing, boating, and even to football matches. I understand the lad is now with foster parents as a first move towards adoption, and is beginning to make good progress.

My routine at Chiswick had begun to fall into place, and I struck up a real friendship with my Flying Squad guards. They did shifts, and quite often the night duty boys would arrive with food cooked by their wives and share it with me. Sometimes they would have flasks of soup and loaves of bread and we would share that. Then we would play cards or chess or go up to the station recreation room and play snooker. I'll never forget one night one of them brought in a projector and we set up a screen and watched a colour film of the 1966 World Cup Final when we beat West Germany 4-2. There was a lot of cheering going on that night in the cells. I don't know what the other officers thought of us! I would often study the faces of these officers and they seemed really nice guys, so different from the underworld scum I had spent so much of my life with. Although their guns were always displayed prominently, I never once felt tempted to try and grab one and escape. After all, where would I go? These men were protecting me - with their lives.

I remember waking up one morning and hearing a rumpus outside my door. Thinking there was trouble, I jumped out of my bed, on which I had my own mattress from my flat, and peered through the spyhole. There I saw that Billy Williams was back. He was to give evidence in the bank raid trial in which PC Clements was shot. We both appeared in court and then Billy was put back in my cell block again. He was delighted to be back with me again and started off with a serious question. 'How's the beer situation, Mo?' he asked. I went to my secret 'cocktail cabinet' and said, 'I can do better than beer, how about some Moët?' His eyes popped as the cork hit the ceiling and I poured that lovely bubbly into a glass for him, and then one for myself. 'Here's to the two of us,' I said as we sipped the sparkling champers. The guard outside could hear our laughter and enquired if we were all right. 'Weee're fine,' I slurred.

These drinking sessions were quite amazing. One day we got through the astonishing total of six bottles of champagne and one of gin. But we always kept our behaviour within reason and although we laughed a lot, we never insulted any of our guards. Billy used to say, 'Cor f...' me, Mo, if the other lot could see me now, they'd all turn QE.' We'd take turns in drinking in each other's cell, though I kept all the booze safely hidden in my secret compartment. Soon Billy's wife and family were bringing in as much drink as Susan so we shared each other's. As we sipped our 'refreshments' we would play Scrabble or talk about our experiences in prison. He was quite a character and we really hit it off together.

When police wanted to enter, they would always knock first and we would quickly hide the booze and glasses before allowing them in. One senior officer who visited us, asked us if we were all right and we replied in unison, 'We couldn't be happier. . . hic.'

At tea time our guards would pop out and bring us back some decent food instead of the stuff served up by the canteen. I don't mean any disrespect to the catering staff at Chiswick, but the food there just wasn't my cup of tea, so to speak.

One day Billy said to me, 'What would you do, Mo, if they killed one of your family?' I thought for a moment, and then said, 'I would avenge that death.' We then agreed that if any member of either of our families was ever attacked or killed, we'd get the bastards who had done it. And we really meant that death pact.

We had a special party the day Billy's baby was born. It was a double celebration, because the child arrived on my birthday.

Although most of our time was spent together, we never went on exercise as a pair. I suppose the police figured two of us out together would be a good target for potential assassins, so we were always taken separately. My favourite place to visit was Richmond Park, where we would often kick a football around. One day one of the deer took exception to me and charged. Its dirty big antlers looked very dangerous but fortunately it pulled up at the last moment, stared at me, and then returned to the rest of the herd. Billy used to play football there, too, and came back most indignant one day because a park keeper had told him off for kicking the ball - apparently it was against the park by-laws.

At night our snooker tournaments against the guards used to be quite exciting, though a little one-sided to say the least. We played for about 5p a game, or the loser puts the money in the light meter for the next game. One night in our 'Robbers' versus 'Flying Squad' game we won seven games on the trot.

After snooker, Billy and I were often allowed on the police station roof to do some star spotting. Billy was interested in astronomy and he would point out various stars and galaxies to me. It was quite fascinating. Then we'd go back to our cells at about 3 am and have a 'nightcap' before turning in. If any criminal ever wanted to testify like I did and needed assurance about the way he would be treated by the police, I'd be happy to be a mediator and tell him of my experiences. I have no complaints at all.

I know some readers will disapprove of the VIP treatment we were given, but put yourself in the police's position. What would you have done? We were two very shrewd and dangerous men who were willing to help the public by informing on villains. Should we have been treated in the abysmal way we were in prison? Or like we were at Chiswick? All I can say is that the time I spent in jail almost broke my resolve to go through with my testimony. But my spells at Chiswick made me want to continue to help the police. So the right way to handle squealers was obviously the latter. I think the police were magnificent in the way they looked after us, especially as they had no rules to go by, as it was a unique situation for them.

Their behaviour towards us made us want to do all we could to ease their burden. One night I actually helped with emergency first aid when a badly injured soccer fan was brought into the station. He was a Scotsman who had been to Wembley for the England game. Afterwards he had been involved in a fight with some English fans which ended with him being thrown through a plate glass window. His pals, who were as drunk as him, had carried him to the station. I was just preparing to play cards with Billy when I heard the commotion and went out to see what was going on. The Scotsman's leg was pouring blood from a terrible wound caused by the jagged glass, so I volunteered to help. I had had St John's Ambulance training and passed the exams as a youngster, and it all came back to me. I had also worked in a hospital, as I've told you, and had seen this situation before. I realised he would need a tourniquet to stem the bleeding, so I went into the surgeon's room and got what I needed. Then I wrapped the bandage tightly around the wound, after extracting pieces of glass from the deep cut. When the doctor arrived he told me I had done a first-class job and Billy and I then set about mopping up the floor of the charge room where the man had been lying. 'I think you ought to become our honorary police surgeon,' said one of the officers afterwards.

Billy and I also became quite good photographers during our stay at Chiswick. We felt that no one would believe what had been going on there, so a camera was smuggled in without the knowledge of the police. Then we took pictures of each other. We felt that if there were any complaints about our behaviour later, this would prove the police were not aware of, or condoning, what we were up to.

Many nights Susan would join us in the cells for games of Ludo. Our behaviour in front of her was exemplary, and we rarely swore. You would never have realised we had been two of the most dangerous men in England if you had been there. You would have probably thought we were a couple of toffs. *

If we needed to ring any of our family, we would walk through to the fingerprint room, where the 'phone we could use was located. Everyone, from the cleaning ladies to the secretaries, knew us and would chat with us. Sometimes we'd have coffee with the secretaries and have quite a laugh with them. They were always very polite towards us and never made us feel like villains. If we had any problems we would talk them over with our guards - Dennis Barnes, Harry Poole and Geoff Brown. We always made it clear that it wasn't what happened to us that concerned us, but what might happen to our family. Any incidents would be a disaster as far as we were concerned.

Although we had lots of fun, I knew I was at Chiswick for one reason alone, and that was to continue to give evidence against my former accomplices. Clapping and cheering broke out in the public gallery at an Old Bailey court when men, who I alleged had committed a robbery six years before, were found not guilty by the jury. Naturally I felt quite sick about the decision, though for legal reasons I can say no more than that.

Another case I was involved in at the Old Bailey resulted in five of my former accomplices being jailed. The Common Sergeant of London, Judge Mervyn Griffith-Jones said that if Sir Carl Aarvold had known more about the robberies when sentencing me, I would probably be serving a longer term. Judge Griffith-Jones said he accepted that my behaviour was worse than those he was sentencing. However, he told one defendant: 'O'Mahoney did service to society by making a clean breast of everything and by giving the names of you and those who committed robberies with him.'

---

* Again for our American readers, Toff = Toffee Nosed (i.e upper class)

Three of the men were given 14 years each, one eight years, and the other seven years. The charges included a wages snatch, a house robbery, an attempted robbery at a warehouse, and the theft of watches from a jewellers.

After Billy had finished giving his evidence it was decided by the powers that be that he should be returned to prison, and he was taken to Reading. On the last night we spent together, he was terribly upset. We had a little drink and I tried to cheer him up. He packed all his kit and arranged for his television and personal belongings to be taken home. The next morning I could see he was well choked, knowing he was going back to a constant barrage of abuse again. I could have cried when he came to my cell door. I told him, 'See you pal,' and shook his hand. Our months together had been good fun and I knew how I would have felt if I was in his position. Terrible.

Life, however, continued at Chiswick for me. I was now playing golf with my guards, which was great fun, though I wasn't very good at it. They would get their own back on me for all those snooker thrashings I'd given them. The lads would always have their walkie-talkies switched on and would listen out in case we were needed back at the station. As well as the golf, I would go on nature walks through nearby woods with officers interested in the country. They would point out different species of plants and wild life. I even developed quite a professional car-wash for the Flying Squad officers who looked after me. Often I would go into the yard at Chiswick armed with cleaning implements and clean their unmarked cars. They looked gleaming after I had finished with them.

My stay at Chiswick was nearly brought to an abrupt end when a London evening newspaper came out with a front page story that highlighted my life of luxury at the station. The report also claimed that I went to football matches at Brentford, which was completely untrue. I told an officer who investigated this claim that I wasn't a football fan, and if I was, I would choose a better team than Fourth Division Brentford to watch!

With all the good food and drink I was getting, I needed lots of exercise, so I used to make Osterley Park a must. One day I had a race with a detective and ran so fast that I overbalanced and cut my hand to pieces on the gravel path, and then careered head first into a fence. When I got back to Chiswick I looked in quite a state. I was badly cut and had a bruised face.

Often I would take a loaf of bread to the park and feed all the geese and ducks. I loved to be surrounded by all those quacking birds.

Not long after Billy left, Christmas came round. I couldn't let this celebration pass me by, so I got Susan to buy me lots of decorations for my cells. I even had a Christmas tree. I put up some special winking coloured lights and then got red and blue bulbs for the ceiling lights and put balloons everywhere. It looked more like a night club than a police station cell. I got my children special presents and their eyes lit up when I gave them to them in my fairyland cell. I still see my children regularly but I am always closely guarded when I do. After all, I don't want what apparently happened to George Brett and his son to happen to me … They have never been found after disappearing from their Essex home.

Susan came in on Christmas Eve and 'saw-in' Christmas with me. We sat there drinking sherry and waiting for midnight to come. Then we wished each other - and our guards - a happy Christmas. The next morning Susan was there in time for a festive lunch and we set the table out with a turkey and champagne and wine. I had a candelabra on the table with three candles on it, so it was really romantic. It was the best Christmas I've ever had. Just the two of us dining together. As the day progressed, there was Christmas cheer all round. We watched television, played records and slowly danced in our cell to Elvis Presley and Elton john LPs, and I even had a glass of sherry with members of the Robbery Squad. We wished each other all the best. My cell was chock-a-block with food from my Susan's family. My dad even visited me and brought me some goodies, which pleasantly astonished me.

New Year was the next celebration for me to look forward to, and that was equally merry and boozy. At midnight a champagne cork hit the ceiling of my cell and Susan and I kissed. Then some of the policewomen came in and I kissed them, and then made uniformed officers kiss Susan. We all shook hands and wished each other well. As I went to bed in the early hours I realised that I had now been in a police cell for 14 months ... that's longer than anyone in British history. Usually it's three days, and then that's it. The person has to be charged or released.

My life took a lift when a governor at Wormwood Scrubs came to see me about the possibility of parole. He knew all about my situation, and when he saw my conditions at Chiswick, he was unhappy because he felt the cell was unsanitary. There was no proper ventilation and I had a toilet in the cell. It was like being sealed in a box, I told him. He said I must have a very strong will to have to put with the conditions. I smiled. Later I was introduced to a probation officer, whose name I can't reveal, and he was very kind to me and said that when I was released he would do all he could to help me.

Parole is considered when you have served one third of your sentence. Then your case is discussed to see whether you are suitable to have your freedom at an early date. Because of all the help I had given the police, I was considered eligible. But it was with mixed feelings that I received the news that my parole had been granted. Naturally I wanted to see the outside world again, but I knew that my life would now again be in great danger. When I was told the news I asked the chap who told me, 'What about my home leave?' H e said, 'What home leave?' I told him that before being released a prisoner was entitled to a weekend at home to get used to life outside. He said he would look into this and let me know. I asked if I could possibly be given leave from the 8th of March through to the 11th or 12th, as the 9th of March is my birthday. It was agreed, and I arranged a hotel room at Bournemouth for Susan and myself, and one for my security guards.

I couldn't believe it, but when I arrived under an assumed name, there were flowers for Susan at the front desk. I guessed my guards had thoughtfully provided them. What great guys they were. I was driven to Bournemouth in an unmarked police car. The whole holiday was a dream. I was very polite to guests and staff at the hotel. We would dress for dinner and have a few drinks in the bar before going in for a meal. Often guests would join us at the bar and we'd have some interesting conversations. I remember one particularly posh woman, a landowner's wife, telling us how she grew grapes and then made wine from them.

After a session on the beach, the guards challenged me to a round of golf, knowing that was my weakest game. When I teed off I sent my ball way off target and it smashed into the windscreen of a car. When I rescued the ball I found a courting couple adjusting their dress, as they say. Obviously my mis-shot had interrupted a passionate bit of the other. Then I hit a shot which was so bad that it finished up on the main London road. I nearly caused a pile-up because I wanted to drive off in the road. My guards yelled at me to just throw the ball to the side of the course. Then a ball from another player hit my arm and nearly paralysed me. It just wasn't my day! But except for that round of golf, I had four days of sheer heaven. I would smile as all those la-di-da guests talked to me. If they had known who I really was, I'm sure they'd have had instant heart attacks. And there would probably have been at least 100 vacancies . . .

I spent one more day at Chiswick before the big day – my release - arrived. I was really sad to be saying goodbye to all my friends there. I had spent the last evening packing up my things and trying to adjust my thinking to being a free man again. Well, not really free - for as long as I live, there will be the risk that an assassin's bullet or stiletto knife might claim me. On the morning of my release two 'governors' came to see me. They were Chief Superintendent John Swain, and Detective Chief Superintendent Jack Slipper. They assured me that I would be given 24-hour a day protection and told me not to worry about anything. They wished me good luck for the future and then at 8 o'clock in the morning I stepped outside Chiswick, with my guards. I was bundled into a car and taken to a secret hideout with Susan and our son.

The press quickly heard of my release and carried stories on it. One, the *Guardian*, read:

> A self-confessed, armed robber who has served a considerable part of his five-year sentence under armed guard at a London police station has been released on parole.
>
> This latest development in the unusual case of Mr Maurice O'Mahoney emerged yesterday as he was preparing to give evidence as the chief prosecution witness in the ninth trial in which he has been involved. His testimony was responsible for the conviction of more than a dozen of his former partners.
>
> Mr O'Mahoney, from Paddington, London, was sentenced at the Old Bailey in September 1974 for armed robbery and attempted burglary. He admitted to the police that he had been party to more than 100 crimes.
> Because of threats which had been made against him and his value to the police prosecutions, the Home Secretary authorised him to be held in police custody last May. Until his release on March 15th he was held at Chiswick police station.
>
> Dr Shirley Summerskill, Under-Secretary at the Home Office, said last month that Mr O'Mahoney would be kept in police custody for the duration of the trials he has still to give evidence in.

So King Squealer was on the outside, at last . . . but would life ever be the same after the experiences of the last two years? The answer is no . . . however long or short my life is.

17
A Bullet through the Post

I received a terrible welcome back into society - a bullet through the post. The .303 rifle bullet was posted to a relative with a chilling message for me: 'The next one won't come through the post, it will come through your head.' I carry it with me everywhere now as a graphic reminder to always be alert.

After the bullet came a wreath with a 'sympathy card' which read: 'In loving memory of Mo.' That was delivered to the front door of one of the family.

All these warnings from my former associates made me double careful to make sure they never had the chance to get at me. Then I heard that a £20,000 contract had been taken out on my life, and I awoke each day knowing that it could be my last. For a hired assassin could have found my secret hide-out and trained his sights on the front door. As soon as I walked outside, whoosh … I would lie in a crumpled heap on the floor. Every day I still live with knowledge that this can happen.

But what should I do? Should I become a recluse and never go out? To ward off my enemies the Yard had allotted me a fine bunch of armed guards who took care of me, Susan, and our baby. These 'life preservers', who were with us for 24 hours every day, were a mixture of men and women. They worked two 12-hour shifts – the night shift would have to stay up all night in our home, their guns at the ready, while Susan and I slept soundly in our bed.

I told them right at the beginning that I wanted to try and live some sort of normal life. 'I've been caged up for long enough and now I want to go out as much as possible,' I said. This was obviously quite a headache for them and, as we walked through parks and down busy streets, they would keep looking over their shoulders, in case of attack. But even with their dedicated protection, I was nearly assassinated in a pub. My moment of horror came while I was drinking with my guards and I went into the loo. They watched the door as I entered and didn't think twice when a moment later a man followed me in. Little did they realise the drama that was soon going on in that toilet. I was in full flow at the urinal when this man, a former associate who had recognised me in the bar, pulled a gun. I froze as he aimed it at me, and said, 'I'm going to blow your head off, Mo.' I knew he was a highly dangerous man and realised it would be foolhardy to try and make a desperate grab for the gun. So I kept my cool, although my heart was beating quite a bit faster than usual. 'If you pull that trigger you'll never get away with it. The minute you get out of that door you'll be shot dead by my armed guards,' I told him. He obviously didn't realise that the guys I had been supping with were, in fact, armed police, and that made him hesitate. Then I told him I had made a decision not to give any more evidence against villains.

All the time the gun was trained on me and I could see he was beginning to waver and think that maybe shooting me wasn't, after all, the greatest idea in the world. Then he asked me if I'd do a deal with him. 'Give me five minutes to get out of here, Mo,' he said, 'and I won't shoot you.' 'As far as I'm concerned I never saw you,' I said. I knew from the first he meant business and I was hoping and praying that if he did pull the trigger I wouldn't die instantly. So I could grab it from him and at least take him with me to that great exercise yard in the sky. But he decided discretion was the better part of valour, put his gun back into his pocket and sauntered out. Then, as he reached the door, he made a dash for it.

'Are you alright Mo?' asked one of the guards as I came out looking a bit pale. 'I'm fine,' I said trying to appear composed. 'Now what are you having to drink?' I could have waited a moment and then tipped off my guards about the incident, but I knew they would have been after him at breakneck speed and there could have been a shoot-out which might have cost innocent lives. So I said nothing at all, and thought long and hard about how close I had been to death.

That wasn't my only close shave. Susan and I sometimes went for a day out at the seaside with our faithful bodyguards. It was always a lovely experience - until one day I spied two of my arch enemies just a short way in front of me. I stopped in my tracks, then put my arm on one of the officers and said, 'Quick, this is it.' He started to go for his gun as he too recognised the men. But then the not so daring duo turned on their heels and ran as fast as their legs would take them. I told him, 'I wonder what's wrong with them?' He chuckled, wiped the perspiration from his brow, and commented, 'I think they must have diarrhoea.'

Another time I stared death in the face made my protectors howl with laughter. I had a little inflatable rubber boat which I used on the Thames near Chiswick Bridge. I would pump it up and then row up and down the river, with the boys keeping a watchful eye on me from the top of the bridge. As I was blissfully rowing by one day, Dennis, one of them shouted down, 'Don't look now Mo, but I think you're in trouble.' I looked around and saw this huge boat bearing down upon me. I rowed about 100 strokes a second to get out of the way but I still couldn't go fast and the monster wave hit me and sent me flying into the murky waters of old Father Thames. The inflatable boat was by now upside-down and I was spitting polluted water. I looked up at my guards, expecting one of them would dive in and rescue me from a watery grave, and found instead that they were holding their sides with laughter. 'That's the funniest thing I've seen for years, Mo,' shouted Dennis as he hopped about. I shook my fist at him and managed to swim to the rubber boat, turn it over and clamber aboard.

Burl got my own back on one of those guards sometime later when I first met writer Dan Wooding, who has worked with me on this book. I told him to meet me on board a floating hostelry on the Thames Embankment. 'Be at the bar of the ship holding a copy of the *Sunday People* under your arm, so I can recognise you,' I told him over the 'phone. I arrived with my guard and when we got there Dan was standing there all embarrassed with the paper stuck under his arm. We had a meal to discuss the project and then he left to return to his office. My guard and I went to get into his unmarked Flying Squad car, but he found, to my great amusement, that it was not there. It had been towed away by the police! We had to flag down a passing Panda car to go to the nearest nick and get it back. I nearly died laughing.

You may wonder what security precautions I take these days to stay alive. Well, I constantly change my appearance – sometimes times I'm bearded, other times clean shaven - and I never keep the same car too long in case the number gets known. Every meeting I have with journalists and people I don't know is arranged through a system of last-minute 'phone calls. And I always pick the spot. When I'm in a pub or a restaurant I'm always on the alert.

All the time we have been working on this book I have told Dan Wooding only at the last moment where we are to meet. Even then I have always arrived a little late and thoroughly checked the area around the venue before going in. I always look for a place to make a quick escape if anyone there recognises me. I have formed a real friendship with Dan, but even now I haven't given him my 'phone number or the address of my secret hideout.

On one occasion while driving to meet Dan, I nearly caused the death of Chancellor Dennis Healey in The Strand. I was rushing along and Healey opened his car door outwards into the street - he was going to a dinner at the Savoy - and I swerved at the last minute and missed him by inches. Judging by the high taxes in this country, I am sure some people would have been happy if I'd not reacted so fast . . .

Talking of politics, my guards and I would spend endless hours discussing that thorny subject. I think they were surprised to learn that a working-class man like me was an ardent supporter of Mrs Thatcher and her Tory policies. We never actually argued but I would forcibly tell them that I believed she was the only person capable of leading this country back to greatness again. India and Israel have both had women Prime Ministers, so why shouldn't we?' I would ask.

Another topic I would become heated about was unions. 'They're the Mafia of Britain,' I would shout. 'They now have as much power here as the American Mafia have across the Atlantic.'

Our sessions became like debating societies and for me it was quite mind-broadening. I realised how intelligent and well-informed my guards were, and I think they enjoyed these discussions as much as I did. Of course it wasn't all debates, we also had time for lots of fun and jokes.

One topic that regularly came up, however, was whether policemen should have guns. After all, they knew that I once carried firearms. Although they were usually armed when they looked after me, they were unanimous in saying that they would be against carrying firearms all the time. Only on special occasions, like when they were watching over King Squealer, they said. I agreed entirely with their views. I think if we in Britain ever got to the deplorable state they have in America, we might as well give up as a nation. We are still the only country in the world that has an unarmed police force. And that is certainly something to be proud of. If they were armed, I can imagine what might happen. Let's say a 13-year old kid grabs an old woman's purse and runs off. A policeman who witnesses the theft takes out his gun and shouts, 'Stop, or I'll shoot.' And if the youngster keeps running the policeman will fire - and possibly kill him. That sort of thing seems to happen regularly in America and I think it would be terrible if it was repeated here. I can also see violent criminals being tempted to ambush police officers on the beat to grab their guns to use on armed jobs. This would be an easy operation and many coppers and passers-by could be killed if it happened, especially if the officer put up a fight and discharged his firearm. I know from first-hand experience that if an armed policeman had got involved in a raid that I was on, many innocent people might have died in the shoot-out.

Sir Robert Mark, London's controversial police overlord, was also frequently discussed. All the officers I knew had a great respect for him. They knew he had been brought into the Yard to flush out corruption, and he did his job with a ruthless determination. He must certainly rank as one of the best commissioners that the capital has ever seen. I know it was a terrible blow to many officers when Sir Robert quit. Now we have 'The Hammer', David McNee from Glasgow. I believe he has got off to a good start by asking people to help the police because the force is understaffed and cannot put a bobby on every corner. With good co-operation from the public, the police can continue in the effective way they operated under Sir Robert, and continue to 'hammer' London's underworld.

Quite often in our chats the subject of A10 would be raised, and I know that many coppers resent the activities of this Yard branch that probes allegations by the public - usually criminals and their families - against serving officers. I have been interviewed several times on various matters by these A10 people, who are known by their colleagues as the 'Rubber Heel Mob'. One session was over allegations by certain criminals against members of the Robbery Squad. I told the A10 men that top East End villains had tried to frame some officers. These crooks had set up statements and tape recordings alleging corruption. I told detectives of the plot but they could not crush it as there was insufficient evidence. It was part of a careful campaign against the Robbery Squad, whose success rate was worrying the underworld. Squealers like myself, Smalls and Billy Williams were doing immeasurable damage to big-time criminals and so a plan was hatched by top crooks to undermine the Robbery Squad. The detectives were really putting themselves around and getting some good arrests so the crooks decided to take action. I was later approached by someone, not a criminal, and asked whether I would help 'nail' certain squad officers. I made a statement about this to A10 at the same time I helped them clear the detective who had been framed by Moisher. The series of statements and tape-recordings about these Robbery Squad officers was rigged by two East London criminals. One is a burglar and the other an armed robber.

You may wonder why I have this affection for the Robbery and Flying Squads. Well, over the period we got to know each other, they never once double-crossed me. During the time I was regularly guarded, while at Chiswick and later, I had in all about 90 officers working with me. None of them ever stuck me up to be killed. Yet villains would have paid them at least £20,000 just to reveal where I would be at a particular time. A hit man could have done the rest. The cops didn't do it because they are decent men, honest citizens who are just trying to fight crime in a period when so many people are anti-police because of their few bent colleagues. I hope the people of Britain don't judge the whole police force by a few bad apples. Most are good men, doing their duty for a pittance.

I know many of my guards must have hated having to protect a man like me, who had been so vicious and violent. Yet we quickly formed friendships. One officer would actually take me on nature rambles in the countryside, and we'd spend hours tramping through woods in and around London, learning about the various plants and animals. It was a new world for a person like me used only to the rotting inner areas of London. In return Susan, a great cook, would titillate their taste buds with exotic meals at our hideout.

I was beginning to get really fit with all this exercise and lose some of the weight I had put on during my amazing stay at Chiswick. It was lovely to feel free again . . . well, as free as I'll ever be. One of my real delights was to return to Osterley Park to feed the ducks and geese there. I always left home with a loaf of bread for them. One day, however, I got a shock when I was sitting on the grass eating my packed lunch from Susan with my police friends. A cheeky grey squirrel suddenly appeared from nowhere, made a grab for a sandwich and dashed off clasping it. Once again my guards roared with laughter.

As we drove around London we would be cracking jokes and generally making the best of a difficult situation. One day we were in for a right royal surprise at a set of traffic lights at Talgarth Road, Hammersmith. For who should pull up beside us in his Aston Martin but Prince Charles, with his personal guard sitting alongside. My police friends were horrified when I pretended to begin to shout to the heir to the throne. Prince Charles smiled at me and appeared to say, 'It's a nice day.' Before I could reply the traffic lights changed to green and he shot away, and my friends heaved a sigh of relief. 'I wondered what on earth you were going to say to him,' said one. 'I was convinced you'd say the wrong thing and we'd all finish up in solitary for the rest of our lives,' another gasped. I told them that all I was going to tell the prince was that we had something in common - we'd both served his mum.

Although I didn't have favourite guards, Dennis was an officer that I had high regard for. My estimation of him went up even more when I found out from another officer about the time Dennis faced a desperate gunman in my home area of Paddington. The villain pointed a sawn-off shotgun at Dennis and as he approached him to try and take it from him, the man pulled the trigger. Fortunately the gun failed to go off and Dennis jumped on him and hurled him to the ground. Then he grabbed the weapon and arrested the gunman, who was later convicted. Dennis earned the Queen's Commendation for that brave action.

One day my officers decided to give me a history lesson, so they drove me to the Tower of

London. It was at the time of that shocking IRA explosion there in which a little New Zealand boy lost a leg, so security was tough. Every person was being searched. When we got to the entrance a beefeater asked if we had any weapons to declare. 'Only a gun,' said the policeman – and the beefeater nearly collapsed. With that my guard opened his coat to reveal a holster with a pistol in it. Then he produced his warrant card to show he was a policeman, and we were waved in. When we got to the room where the priceless Crown Jewels are kept, one of the officers said, 'Whatever you do, Mo, don't break the glass, because it could prove rather embarrassing for us.' I smiled, knowing they were only joking. At least I thought they were.

With this friendly relationship between myself and the police, I know it came as quite a shock to them when I decided that I was not going to testify any more. I was summoned to give evidence at the Old Bailey at the trial of more former associates, but I refused. This might come as a surprise to many of you, but the reason was that I didn't want a mockery made of British justice. For I was told by the gunman in that pub toilet that a main witness in a forthcoming trial I was due to testify in had been bought off and later heard that other witnesses in other trials had also been interfered with. I knew too that there was the distinct possibility of juries being rigged, which would mean that my testimony and that of honest police officers would be held up to contempt. It took a lot of heart searching on my part to decide to call a halt to my activities. There was no question of me having no more information to tell the world. With my evidence, scores of villains would have appeared in the dock and some could have gone down. But knowing what I did about the way the judicial system was being out-manoeuvred by these desperate men, I knew that justice would not be done. So I decided that was it. King Squealer would sing no more - in the witness box.

Soon after I made my decision, my 24-hour protection ceased and there was some bad feeling on my side because officers told me that I ought to go out now and get a job. Money from a special police fund was also stopped. Well, how can I get out and get a job? Whatever job I do I could be recognised and gunned down. I've now learned to live life on my own, but at the time I was upset, to say the least. I told a *Guardian* reporter, 'I've risked my life giving the police information. Now they've dropped me flat – the canary that fell from his cage.' I added: 'I'm running scared and in fear of my life every second of the day. The police have dropped me in it, without warning. I'm in a terrible state, and could go around the corner and cry.

'They've fed me all this bullshit about helping society, got all they could out of me, then shit on me. They've told me to go out and get a decent job. The only trade I know is how to break into banks ... I just don't think that it's justice that someone in my position should be deserted - left to die.'

I missed the constant companionship of the officers, though many of them kept in daily telephone touch, and still do.

Although I am no longer a Crown witness I still have a hotline to the Yard, which will bring me or my family immediate help. I have a regular number to ring there and if I miss my 'check in' call an immediate alert is put out. The police know the names of all the villains who are after me, and if anything happens to me or my 'loved ones', they will all be turned over until the truth is discovered. But even the police know that one day I might be found shot through the head. I lived by the gun and have to be prepared to die by it.

I know that an informant who knows my movements might be tempted to put me up for a large price to be shot. But anyone who does had better watch out, because the gunmen would have no hesitation in ending his life too -- because he would be the vital link in the chain. Desperate men will take desperate action to kill me and they will wipe out anyone who knows about it.

As I am in hiding, I have many hours each day to think about my unique case and my treatment. Something that made me think deeply was a suggestion by a London detective of a new deal for the Supergrass. Detective Superintendent Bob Robinson, of the City Road station, has spent 20 years dealing with informers and recently spent three months on a course which included the Supergrass cases. His charter for such a person includes:

- A reward to encourage him in the form of special remission.
- Official backing for the police trying to help him change his identity for life.
- A special security wing in prison for Supergrasses.

He says, 'I have no doubt about it, the 1970s have become known in both legal and criminal circles as the Age of the Supergrass.'

Detective Superintendent Robinson studied the cases of Smalls, myself, Billy Williams, James Trusty and Charles Lowe and the police and Director of Public prosecution's attitude towards each of us. He believed that people like us should have a golden deal to wipe the slate clean if we inform. 'Police are under a considerable handicap in that they are unable to offer any incentive to him. The whole matter has now become a hit or miss affair, with so much in the Supergrass's unwritten message getting to the judge.

'The sentence, if imprisonment is imposed, counts for so much in the Supergrass's future attitude to his giving Queen's evidence or not.'

Mr Robinson has the good sense to realise that a Supergrass has great problems in coping with imprisonment in an ordinary prison. Often the only safe place is in the punishment block.

He added: 'Collectively, however, it could be another matter if the Home Office could find a secure wing in which to incarcerate these people in a satisfactorily placed prison, with specially trained prison staff sympathetic to the police problems I feel the police would get the best out of them.

"This is a violent age, with many people prepared to kill for money. Revenge is sweet, but if society needs and accepts Supergrass then society must make every effort to ensure that he does not become the sweetness of the criminal's society revenge.'

Mr Robinson believes that Supergrass is only a short-term solution to the fight against crime. He says, 'In recent years the credibility of police evidence has reached an all-time low. This is proved beyond doubt by the number of jury acquittals, especially in cases where there is a direct contradiction of evidence between police and criminal.

'The present-day detective has come to accept that a jury is more liable to accept the evidence of one admitted criminal accomplice than that of ten experienced police officers.

'He therefore not only looks but hopes for the Supergrass to put the final icing on the prosecution case.'

I find Mr Robinson's ideas most interesting, though I must say that I totally disagree with giving criminals 'golden deals'. It's up to a jury and then a judge to sentence a criminal and not a policeman. I believe it is morally wrong for officers to do deals with villains. I did no deal, but the judge recognised what I had done and took that into account when he sentenced me. That should happen with every Supergrass. He must be prepared to face up to his punishment, however long or short that is. In my case I got five years, plus LIFE on the run.

I do believe, however, that the police should be given the Crown's backing in giving Supergrasses a new identity. That is absolutely vital. That, at least, gives people like myself some chance of remaining alive. We need new papers to 'prove' our new identity. I have got these, but this should always be the case. That isn't doing a deal, but it is something that is very important, in starting a new life.

I can understand the reasoning behind suggesting a squealer's wing in a prison, 'but after my experience in Brixton and Wormwood Scrubs. I don't believe that jail is the place to keep squealers. Nor do I think informers should be kept for long periods in police cells. It's bad for health reasons. So what can be done? Well, I think the Home Office should immediately build a special squealers' house. It should be purpose-built. Somewhere in the country, for dealing with this type of person. Its first requirement, of course, must be that it is secure and free from the possibility of attack from hit men. It should be operated by serving or retired police officers rather than men from the prison service, because only the police understand our mentality. To the screw we are all just another prisoner. Having police there means squealers can build up relationships with the men with whom they are co-operating. If the man taking the statements is also a friend, that helps relieve a lot of the tension. Recreation is also vital to keep the squealer sane during this traumatic time, so there should be a concealed yard and lots of indoor activities like table tennis. Each grass should have his own private room - you note I don't say cell - and be allowed to furnish it how he likes within reason. Naturally radio, television, and a record player should be allowed. I believe that a judge should be empowered to sentence a squealer to an establishment like this. For if you lock up people like me in solitary, we are not going to be able to mentally stand up to days in the witness box. If this squealer centre is not made a priority by the Home Office, I believe that very soon the age of the Supergrass will be over. No one will want to risk being killed in prison by former accomplices, or the hell of solitary that I had to endure for months on end. It would be better to serve a full sentence in safety than a shorter one with the daily risk of death or insanity.

I now live each day as it comes. I expect you wonder if I have any regrets in doing what I did? Well, the truthful reply is that I don't know. It's too early to say. All I know is, I take full responsibility for whatever I have done as a crook and later as a squealer. I have stood up and taken my punishment like a man. My big wish is that when my time comes, I will also die like one. The thought of terrible and violent death is with me all the time. Susan knows all about this fear - she lives with it herself.

If I had to do it all again I'd still do what I did for the law. The British police have taught me a hell of a lot and now I am on their side all the way. And I hope that by my actions I have at least saved some lives. Though whether I've saved my own is highly questionable . . .

AFTERTHOUGHT

by Maurice O'Mahoney Jr., the son of 'Mo'

It may seem rather strange, but I am fortunate that my father turned into a Supergrass, as I would not be here today if he had not done so. You see, I am the result of one of the conjugal visits to Chiswick Police Station by my mother. I am not sure if too many people can say they started out in life in a police station.

I am told that after I was born, my father used to baby sit me in the cells, although I don't remember any of this. He told me later that he had many bottles of wines and spirits hidden in the cells and that 'there is probably a stash still there that hasn't been discovered by the police'.

As I grew up, I had no idea about what was going on with my father, but there were odd things that would occur that now made sense to me. Like the police lady who used to be with us lots of the time. Her name was Jane, and I called Aunty Jane and, sometimes, she would take us all to Brighton for a few days, as she knew that my dad loved this seaside town and we would eat lots of Candy Floss and ice cream.

However, in my childhood, I never quite understood why there were often police around us, but I now do as I realize they were there to protect us.

There were times when my father would drive my mother and I to police stations, or Scotland Yard, and we would park outside and then wait for hours for him to come out. As I got older. I began to wonder why some people called him 'Mo,' while others called him 'Dave', but now I understand that the police were giving him a new name and persona.

Dad was very security aware and would always be armed and he would always be looking around before he went anywhere. When driving, he would go round a roundabout three or four times, or when sitting at traffic lights on green, he would then pull away as they turned red. He would never sit with his back to a door, even with his own family, and they never knew anything about where we lived or anything like that. If we visited family members, he would take me aside and drum it into me that I must not tell them anything about my current second name or anything that would reveal anything to anyone that could cause us problems. I know my older sister found this hard to deal with, not really knowing her dad.

I was about ten years old when I first saw the original version of this book. It was in a drawer in our home and, as I read through it, I knew right then that he was, in fact, 'King Squealer'. though I never told him so. We later moved out of London for our safety, and it was when I was fourteen that he sat me down at his bar -- it was a nice Italian wood and marble bar which I still have it to this day -- and explained to me about his life and how he grew up and the things he had done. He told me how it was important for me to be aware that one day somebody might try and kill him, or try to harm us, for what he had done. So all the things in the past, like the going round and round roundabouts, constantly looking over his shoulder, and having the police being with us for so much of the time -- all now made sense to me.

He did a great job at protecting us and was very clever and cunning and you couldn't ever get one over on him. He was a great chess player, and one told me, 'Son, life was like a game of chess, except, in my case, people are the pieces, and I am a master manipulator with a brain like a computer.'

At times, he could be quite overpowering and he suffered from terrible nightmares and night terrors in his later years. When they happened, he would jump up from his bed and start pulling the curtains down or knocking things over. I think he must have had a lot of stress and pressure in his life.

After his release from prison, and after the initial book came out, my dad tried to go straight and worked on and off as an electrician, He started to hang around a wine bar in south London which I believe was off bounds to serving police officers. There he met a man whom I later discovered my father would help in the laundering of some of the proceeds from a large robbery. With the profits be bought and sold jewels and gold, and even made a trip to New York.

Around this time, he managed to get an inside man in a security company and pulled off a £250,000 security van robbery. I'm not sure what it would be worth in today's money -- quite a bit, I should think – and he let me and my older brother count it out. When we got to £100,000 and gave up. He later told me it was supposed to be his 'retirement', but the inside man didn't throw out all the money so he had decided to keep his share, so with this money, plus £40,000 pounds from my grandfather who was quite wealthy, he set up home in Reading, Berkshire, where he led a lavish lifestyle for a while in a mock Tudor house in an area where a lot of footballers would live nearby.

Towards the end of the 1980s, dad lost a lot of money in the housing market and it was then that he decided to move to the north east of England and not long after we moved there. He was really sad as he then learned the news that his mother had died and shortly after this, he was arrested for allegedly taking part in an armed robbery in west London. He was acquitted of the robbery in which shots were fired -- all by the Flying Squad from a moving car -- and my dad told me that he had been set up by them and were trying to kill him because he was already talking of writing a new book about police corruption going back to the 1960s.

I would like to say a few words about growing up around my dad. It could be quite strange moving all the time, and having different names, new schools, new friends, and not being allowed to have people around. I've only had one friend, who has been there all the way, and he knows who he is, but when you're young you don't know any better and think it is normal, but on the other hand, dad was a real good dad for me; the best and fearless.

He would take me out to meet rock stars like Rick Wakeman and all sorts of famous people. He was a joker and a real character that we will not see the likes of again. When my nan died, he had heard there may be a revenge attack on him, so we went to all the pubs in Paddington, and he told the customers, 'Can I have everyone's attention please, I'm Maurice O'Mahoney. If anybody has a problem with me, here I am.' Nobody did, as he had a 44 magnum in his coat.

Near the end of his life, there was an armed robbery committed near to our house and then, a couple of days later, the police came knocking on the door, and one of them said, 'We have received a phone call from someone purporting to be you, saying you could help us with our inquiries.

My dad looked quizzically at the officers, and said, 'I've no idea what you are talking about. Why would I ring you up about a robbery?' As they went away, he then said to me 'Something is going on here', and he was correct, as the next day, the police turned up in force, and they began wrecking our home. We found out later that it was someone making up a story to try and get him into trouble.

But that wasn't the end of his troubles, as we then discovered that a friend of my mother had 'grassed' on him and went and told the police where we would be at a certain time. When my dad saw the police waiting outside our house, he rushed me to his car and sped off. But then saw that they had blocked off the road, so he quickly put the car in reverse, but then there was a transit van blocking the way and soon the car was surrounded by armed police and they fired a stun grenade under it. The explosion sounded like a bomb going off, and sent billows of smoke all over the place. I could not see a thing, and we are both arrested for robbery and taken to a local police station.

As you can imagine, I was by now very sacred, but my father had a different view on the situation. As the sergeant was charging us, my dad couldn't stop laughing and when the officer asked him why he was chuckling, he said, 'It's because the officer who arrested us wants to make a name for himself!' However, at the time, I don't think the Sergeant knew anything about my father's background.

Then, my dad said to me, 'Don't worry son. We will be back home by tea time.'

The sergeant told him, 'No way. I'll bet you ten pounds that you aren't.'

'You're on,' my dad told him.

We were then locked up in separate cells to each other, and my dad then began telling me jokes and making me laugh. It was his way of trying to calm this stressful situation. After a short time, my father was put on an identity parade and was not picked out and so, as he predicted, we were both back home by teatime.

The police sergeant never did pay up when he lost the bet, but I didn't really care as it was so weird to be in a situation like that with your dad. It was most interesting for me to see some his highs, and lows, his funny and sad times, and you never knew what would happen next with him.

In the conversation, during which we had been drinking a few bottles of wine, he began sharing with me about the old times and said that he had enjoyed a great life and met all types of people and lived life his way.

'If I go tomorrow, I would have no complaints', he told me. He died shortly afterwards, on the 27th September, 2003, at the age of 54, from a massive heart attack in a small village in Northumberland.

I miss him dearly. He was my mentor, best friend -- and my dad!

Mo and Mo Jnr out on the town on holiday in Florida.

ABOUT THE CO-AUTHOR, DAN WOODING

Dan Wooding's career must rate as one of the most unusual in journalism. For he has gone from being a correspondent for the National Enquirer and a staffer on two of Britain's raciest tabloids, to an undercover reporter and campaigner for persecuted Christians in the restricted countries of the world.

Educated at Queensbridge School, Moseley, Birmingham, England, Wooding, 72, began his journalistic career in 1968 in London, England, with The Christian, Britain's oldest evangelical newspaper, rising to become its chief reporter. His first-ever interview for the paper, then owned by Billy Graham, was with Coretta Scott King at St. Paul's Cathedral where she was due to speak at a memorial service for her late husband, Dr. Martin Luther King Jr.

When The Christian closed, he then moved to the Middlesex County Times in Ealing, London, where he wrote some of the earliest stories on the Monty Python team, who made most of their programs in Ealing. After five years with this local paper, when he also became a correspondent for all of Britain's national newspapers, including The Times, he was given a staff job as a senior reporter with the Sunday People in London, which at that time had the second highest circulation of any newspaper in Europe. Specializing in crime, religion and show business, he interviewed people like Ronnie Kray, Britain's

most infamous gangster, Johnny Mathis, Burt Lancaster, David Soul, as well as Paul McCartney and Ringo Starr from The Beatles. He also interviewed Mother Teresa in Calcutta. Wooding was also a London-based correspondent for the National Enquirer, America's largest circulation tabloid and later worked as a senior reporter with London's Sunday Mirror.

After a spiritual renewal in his life, Wooding left this form of journalism and has specialized in eyewitness reporting of persecuted Christians around the world. He has filed stories from Albania, Burma, China, Cuba, El Salvador, Ethiopia, Grenada, Lebanon, North Korea, Romania, Uganda and Vietnam, to name some of the hot spots. (He was one of the first-ever Christian journalists to be invited to report from North Korea and he spent a week there filing stories for the UPI Radio Network in Washington, DC.)

His articles on Christians being persecuted for their faith are published worldwide and his weekly commentary was carried for ten years on the UPI Radio Network. Besides his reporting activities, he has also assisted in taking Bibles behind the then Iron Curtain to Russia and Romania, and also to Cuba.

Wooding has worked as a writer and broadcaster with Billy Graham in Moscow, Russia; Essen, Germany and in San Juan, Puerto Rico. He wrote the cover story on Billy Graham, his wife Ruth, and son Franklin, for the March/April 1996 issue of the Saturday Evening Post.

Wooding is the founder and international director of ASSIST (Aid to Special Saints in Strategic Times) based in Lake Forest, California, and is the president of ASSIST News Service (www.assistnews.net), a daily news service that sends stories to 2,600 media outlets around the world.

While still in London, Dan was an interviewer for BBC Radio 1. In the United States, he has been the co-host of the TV show, "The Hollywood Connection," as well as a regular guest on the "700 Club." He is now a host of "His Channel Live," a one-hour live Internet talk show that that goes out to 192 countries. It can be seen at www.hischannel.com .

Dan also hosts a weekly radio show called "Front Page Radio" which is carried each Sunday on the KWVE Radio Network (www.kwve.com) in Southern California and Nevada and on many Calvary Chapel stations in in the US and also on Calvary Chapel Radio in the UK, UCB UK, and Lighthouse Radio in Belize.

Wooding is also a regular guest on "In the Market with Janet Parshall" on the Moody Radio Network, to talk about the latest stories featured on his news service.

Dan Wooding is a member of the National Union of Journalists and the International Press Association, and, since moving with his family to the United States in 1982, Wooding has received numerous awards for his writing.

In 1984, he was awarded the Bronze Halo award from the Southern California Motion Picture Council for his stories on the "Suffering Church." The Evangelical Press Association in the USA awarded him first prize in their 1984 "Higher Goals" contest for his eyewitness reporting from war-torn Lebanon. In February 1987, he received a Silver Angel from the Hollywood-based Religion in Media organization for eyewitness reporting from Albania.

The Friends of the Library of the University of California, Irvine, has honored him with awards for 8 of the 45 books he has written. One was Blind Faith, which he co-authored with his 93-year-old mother, tells the moving story of her work as a pioneer Braille Missionary amongst the blind people of Nigeria.

Queen Elizabeth has subsequently honored the book. The Christian Film & TV Commission based in Hollywood, California, gave Dan Wooding a special award for his journalism at their annual media breakfast in Beverly Hills, California, in March, 2002.

In February of this year, Wooding as given the "Passion for the Persecuted" award by Open Doors USA at the National Religious Broadcasters Convention at the Gaylord Opryland Resort on Monday, Feb. 20, in Nashville for his work in publicizing the plight of persecuted Christians around the world.

Then in November, 2012, the British Pakistani Christian Association in London presented Dan with a special award for his services as a journalist and broadcaster in reporting on the terrible situation for Christians in Pakistan for many years now.

Wooding's autobiography, From Tabloid to Truth (www.FromTabloidToTruth.com) was released on February 13, 2004, and carries a foreword by Brother Andrew – "God's Smuggler" – with whom Dan worked as a writer for seven years, and endorsed by Rick Warren, author of the best-selling book, The Purpose Driven Life. In his message, he said, "Dan Wooding has lived one of the most amazing and exciting lives you could ever imagine. This is a book you won't put down once you pick it up."

One of his latest books, Red Dagger, is a fast-moving story based mainly in Gaza and Israel, but also in Ireland and the United Kingdom. Veteran American entertainer, Pat Boone, said of the book, "Red Dagger is a gripping novel about terror, betrayal and redemption. Much of it is set in Gaza, but also features a Northern Ireland terrorist and an American journalist who, after moving to London, finds himself spending too much time in a bar called 'The Stab in the Back' with other drunken hacks. The conclusion of the book has a most dramatic twist that held my attention right to the very end. I enthusiastically endorse Red Dagger, which is written by one of the world's most traveled journalists."

In 2012, two of Dan's books were re-released in the UK – Caped Crusader – Rick Wakeman in the 1970s – with a foreword by Sir Elton John, -- and Terry Dene: Britain's First Rock and Roll Rebel, with a foreword by one of Britain's most well-known rock and roll singers, Marty Wilde, the father of Kim Wilde. A third – King Squealer, with a foreword by Rick Wakeman, is due for re-release sometime in 2013 early in the New Year.

Wooding was born in Nigeria of missionary parents. He has toured Southeast Asia and other parts of the world as a speaker. He has been married to Norma for 50 years and they have two sons, Andrew and Peter, both living in the UK. Andrew is the author of eight books and Peter is the UK correspondent for CBN and owns his own media production company.

Some books by Dan Wooding

Junkies are People Too
Stresspoint
I Thought Terry Dene Was Dead
Exit the Devil (with Trevor Dearing)
Train of Terror (with Mini Loman)
Rick Wakeman, the Caped Crusader
Farewell Leicester Square (with Henry Hollis)
Uganda Holocaust (with Ray Barnett)
Miracles in Sin City (with Howard Cooper)
God's Smuggler to China (with Brother David and Sarah Bruce)
Prophets of Revolution (with Peter Asael Gonzales)
Brother Andrew
Guerrilla for Christ (with Salu Daka Ndebele)
Lord, Let Me Give You a Million Dollar (with Duane Logsdon)
Million Dollar Promise (with Duane Logsdon)
Twenty-Six Lead Soldiers
Secret Missions: Stories of Faith in Action (with Brother Andrew)
To Catch the Wind (with Eddie Cairns)
Singing In The Dark (with Barry Taylor)
Lost for Words (with Stuart Mill)
Let There Be Light (with Roger Oakland)
Rock Priest (with David Pierce)
He Intends Victory
Only Believe (with Hannu Haukka)
A Light To India (with Lillian Doerksen)
Blind Faith (with Anne Wooding)
Never Say Never
From Tabloid to Truth
God's Ambassadors in Japan
Red Dagger
Caped Crusader – Rick Wakeman in the 1970s
Terry Dene: Britain's First Rock & Roll Rebel
Films
Featured in Hollywood on Fire documentary

Lightning Source UK Ltd.
Milton Keynes UK
UKHW021107251022
411064UK00007B/1156